Houghton
Mifflin
Harcourt

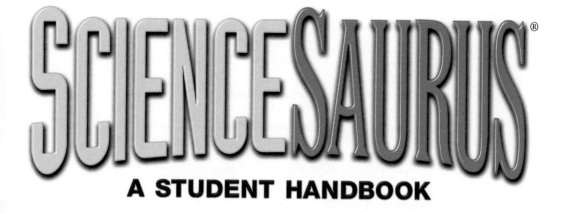

# SCIENCESAURUS®

## A STUDENT HANDBOOK

**NEW EDITION**

# Acknowledgments

## Reviewers

**Deb Barnes**
Junction City, KS

**Kalpana Guttman**
Newton, MA

**Charles Harmon**
Los Angeles, CA

**Jodie Harnden**
Pendleton, OR

**Dr. Kenn Heydrick**
Pflugerville, TX

**Marilyn LeRud**
Tucson, AZ

**Thomas Medcalf**
West Palm Beach, FL

**Susan Paganelli**
Solon, OH

**Maxine Rosenberg**
Newton, MA

**Dr. Kenneth Russell Roy**
Glastonbury, CT

**Dwight Sieggreen**
Northville, MI

**Nadine A. Solomon**
Arlington, MA

**Richard Sturgeon**
Glastonbury, CT

**Tom Vaughn**
Arlington, MA

**Lynn J. Young**
Houston, TX

Photo and Illustration credits start on page 514.

*sci*LINKS® is a registered trademark of the National Science Teachers Association. The *sci*LINKS® service includes copyrighted materials and is owned and provided by the National Science Teachers Association. All rights reserved.

All registered trademarks are shown strictly for illustrative purposes and are the property of their respective owners.

Printed in the U.S.A.

ISBN 978-0-544-05876-7 (hardcover)

ISBN 978-0-544-05843-9 (softcover)

26   1083   21 20 19 18 17

4500643804     ABCDEFG

# Table of Contents

## Earth Science — 156

## Physical Science — 240

## Natural Resources and the Environment — 318

## Science, Technology, and Engineering — 354

## Almanac — 370

## Yellow Pages — 411

# How This Book Is Organized

*ScienceSaurus* is a resource book. That means you're not expected to read it all the way through from cover to cover. Instead, think of *ScienceSaurus* as a kind of "mini-encyclopedia." Keep it handy for times when you want to find out more about a science topic or when you need help with definitions or explanations.

Here's what you'll find in *ScienceSaurus*.

## Sections and Subsections

*ScienceSaurus* has eight major sections. Each section is divided into subsections. The sections and subsections are listed in the Table of Contents on pages iii–v.

You'll also find subsections listed on the first page of each section.

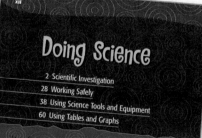

The first page of each subsection has its own table of contents. It lists all the topics in that subsection and their page numbers.

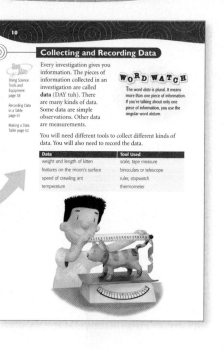

### Collecting and Recording Data

Every investigation gives you information. The pieces of information collected in an investigation are called **data** (DAY tuh). There are many kinds of data. Some data are simple observations. Other data are measurements.

**See Also**
Using Science Tools and Equipment page 58

Recording Data in a Table page 61

Making a Data Table page 62

**WORD WATCH**
The word *data* is plural. It means more than one piece of information. If you're talking about only one piece of information, you use the singular word *datum*.

You will need different tools to collect different kinds of data. You will also need to record the data.

| Data | Tool Used |
|---|---|
| weight and length of kitten | scale, tape measure |
| features on the moon's surface | binoculars or telescope |
| speed of crawling ant | ruler, stopwatch |
| temperature | thermometer |

Why did the dinosaurs disappear? A question like this sparks a scientist's curiosity. Many questions that scientists ask begin with *What, How, When, Where,* or *Why.* After they ask a question, scientists gather information. Then they come up with a possible answer to the question.

What happened to the dinosaurs? Maybe little pebbles on a sandy beach in Florida are clues to the answer. Scientists found and analyzed the pebbles. They discovered that the pebbles were tektites. A tektite is a glassy pebble that is made when something big from outer space hits Earth.

**Tektite**

## Almanac

The Almanac section includes information about things that will help you as you study science. Check out the Almanac's subsections and topics. You'll want to refer to them often.

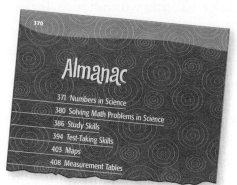

**396**

### Concept Maps

A concept is an idea. A concept map is a way to show what you understand about ideas. Making a concept map can help you see how ideas are connected to each other.

**Making a Concept Map**

1. List words that describe the concept.
2. From the list, choose the one word that best describes the main concept. Put that word at the top. Circle it.
3. Choose words that help support the main concept. Write those below the main concept. Circle them.
4. Draw lines to connect the main concept to the ones below it. Near the lines, write how the concepts are related.
5. Continue until you've used all your words.

Concept maps can show what you still need to learn. This map made a student wonder if all three kinds of rocks were made of minerals. He looked it up before the test.

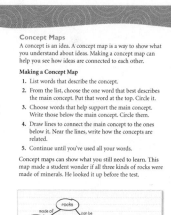

## Yellow Pages

This section of *ScienceSaurus* has three subsections: **History of Science, Science Word Parts,** and a **Glossary of Science Terms.**

**History of Science** includes a time line showing important science events from 1450 until today. It also includes short biographies of some famous scientists and inventors.

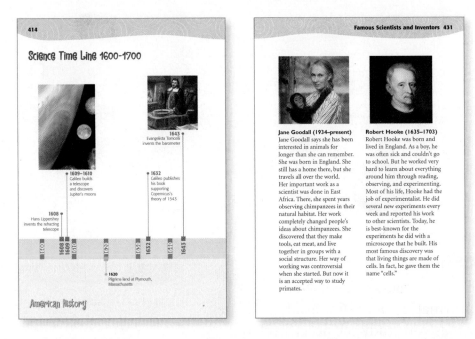

414

Science Time Line 1600-1700

1643
Evangelista Torricelli invents the barometer

1609–1610
Galileo builds a telescope and discovers Jupiter's moons

1632
Galileo publishes his book supporting Copernicus's theory of 1543

1608
Hans Lippershey invents the refracting telescope

1620
Pilgrims land at Plymouth, Massachusetts

American History

Famous Scientists and Inventors 431

**Jane Goodall (1934–present)**
Jane Goodall says she has been interested in animals for longer than she can remember. She was born in England. She still has a home there, but she travels all over the world. Her important work as a scientist was done in East Africa. There, she spent years observing chimpanzees in their natural habitat. Her work completely changed people's ideas about chimpanzees. She discovered that they make tools, eat meat, and live together in groups with a social structure. Her way of working was controversial when she started. But now it is an accepted way to study primates.

**Robert Hooke (1635–1703)**
Robert Hooke was born and lived in England. As a boy, he was often sick and couldn't go to school. But he worked very hard to learn about everything around him through reading, observing, and experimenting. Most of his life, Hooke had the job of experimentalist. He did several new experiments every week and reported his work to other scientists. Today, he is best-known for the experiments he did with a microscope that he built. His most famous discovery was that living things are made of cells. In fact, he gave them the name "cells."

**Science Word Parts** lists prefixes, suffixes, and word roots that will help you figure out the meaning of science terms that are new to you. The **Glossary of Science Terms** gives definitions of all the important science terms used in this book and many other terms that you'll see in science books.

## Inside Back Cover

Here you'll find several handy tables that list metric units of measurement. Another table will help you change units back and forth between the metric system used in science and the English system we use every day.

## On the Pages

Here's an example of what you'll see on *ScienceSaurus* pages. This page is from the Physical Science section.

**Pronunciations** are given for words that can be hard to pronounce or words that might not be familiar to you.

**See Also** notes tell you where you can find information about related topics.

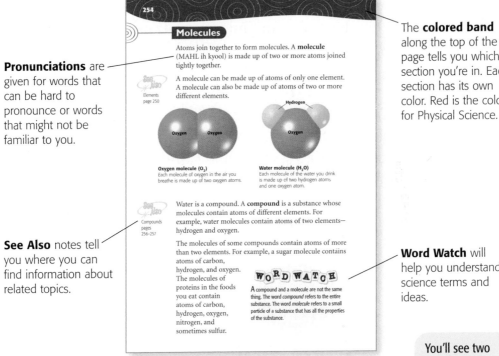

> **254**
>
> ### Molecules
>
> Atoms join together to form molecules. A **molecule** (MAHL ih kyool) is made up of two or more atoms joined tightly together.
>
> *See Also* Elements page 250
>
> A molecule can be made up of atoms of only one element. A molecule can also be made up of atoms of two or more different elements.
>
> **Oxygen molecule (O₂)**
> Each molecule of oxygen in the air you breathe is made up of two oxygen atoms.
>
> **Water molecule (H₂O)**
> Each molecule of the water you drink is made up of two hydrogen atoms and one oxygen atom.
>
> *See Also* Compounds pages 256–257
>
> Water is a compound. A **compound** is a substance whose molecules contain atoms of different elements. For example, water molecules contain atoms of two elements—hydrogen and oxygen.
>
> The molecules of some compounds contain atoms of more than two elements. For example, a sugar molecule contains atoms of carbon, hydrogen, and oxygen. The molecules of proteins in the foods you eat contain atoms of carbon, hydrogen, oxygen, nitrogen, and sometimes sulfur.
>
> **WORD WATCH**
>
> A compound and a molecule are not the same thing. The word *compound* refers to the entire substance. The word *molecule* refers to a small particle of a substance that has all the properties of the substance.

The **colored band** along the top of the page tells you which section you're in. Each section has its own color. Red is the color for Physical Science.

**Word Watch** will help you understand science terms and ideas.

You'll see two other features in the book, too.

**Science Alert!** gives important information to help you work safely, do science investigations correctly, and understand science ideas.

### Science Alert!

Always pay attention to what's going on around you. If something is happening that you think is dangerous, tell the adult in charge.

**Did You Know?** tells interesting facts about the science topics discussed on the pages.

### Did You Know?

You can't see the water vapor in your breath when you exhale. But if you're outside on a cold day, your breath makes a "cloud" in the air. The cloud is made of tiny droplets of water. The cold air made the water vapor in your breath change to liquid water.

# How to Use This Book

There are three ways to find information about a topic in *ScienceSaurus*.

## 1 Look in the Table of Contents

If you're looking for a main topic, such as *energy*, look in the Table of Contents on pages iii–v. There you'll find the titles of the book's sections and subsections. Those titles identify main topics. But if you're looking for a detailed topic, such as *fossil fuels*, you won't find it in the Table of Contents. You'll need to look in the index or the glossary.

## 2 Look in the Index

All the main topics and detailed topics are listed in the index. We listed any words we thought you might use when you're looking for a certain topic. For example, suppose you want to find information about *fossil fuels* as sources of energy. You'll find **Fossil fuels** listed by itself and *from fossil fuels* listed under **Energy.**

## 3 Look in the Glossary of Science Terms

Use the glossary like a dictionary. Whenever you come across a science word you don't know, look in the glossary to find its meaning. For many words, you'll see a number at the end of the definition. That's the number of the *ScienceSaurus* page where the term is defined.

**fossil fuel:** a fuel that formed from the decayed remains of ancient plants and animals (322)

# How to Use sciLINKS

You might want to know more about a topic you find in *ScienceSaurus*. *Sci*LINKS can help by connecting you with sites on the Internet.

You'll see *sci*LINKS items on many pages throughout this book. Here's what each item includes.

*sci*LINKS icon

SC*LINKS*
NSTA

Keyword: Weather
www.scilinks.org
Code: GSS45080

The topic covered in this link

The URL (Web address) for the *sci*LINKS Web site

The code to type in at the *sci*LINKS Web site

Here's how to use *sci*LINKS.

1. Go to the *sci*LINKS Web site by typing the URL www.scilinks.org.

2. Log in. (If you don't know how to do this, ask your teacher.)

3. Type the code for the *sci*LINKS keyword you want. You'll get a list of Web sites for that topic.

4. Choose a site to visit and click on "Go to site" or on the site's URL. *Sci*LINKS will take you to the site.

5. When you're finished with that site, close the window. You'll see the list of sites again. You can choose another site to visit.

*Sci*LINKS was developed and is maintained by the National Science Teachers Association (NSTA). The links have been checked by science teachers and scientists to make sure they are good for students your age and the information is up to date.

# Doing Science

It's a CLUE, Watson—but what does it MEAN?

Nature is full of riddles, puzzles, and mysteries. Is there water on Mars? Where do frogs go when winter comes? How did the Grand Canyon form? Why did the dinosaurs die out? Looking for answers to questions like these is what scientists do. They collect clues to nature's mysteries. Then they try to figure out what the clues mean.

Well, Sherlock,
I think it means
"LET'S GET OUT OF HERE!"

# Scientific Investigation

Why did the dinosaurs disappear? A question like this sparks a scientist's curiosity. Many questions that scientists ask begin with *What, How, When, Where,* or *Why.* After they ask a question, scientists gather information. Then they come up with a possible answer to the question.

What happened to the dinosaurs? Maybe little pebbles on a sandy beach in Florida are clues to the answer. Scientists found and analyzed the pebbles. They discovered that the pebbles were tektites. A tektite is a glassy pebble that is made when something big from outer space hits Earth.

**Tektite**

Scientists tested the tektites from the Florida beach.
They discovered that the tektites were 65 million years
old. Scientists already knew that the dinosaurs disappeared
65 million years ago. The tektites from Florida were formed
at the same time the dinosaurs disappeared!

The tektites gave scientists an idea about why the dinosaurs
disappeared. A huge rock from space crashed into Earth
about 65 million years ago. The crash threw great clouds of
dust into the air. The dust blocked sunlight, so plants died.
Plant-eating dinosaurs did not have enough food to eat, so
they died. Then meat-eating dinosaurs that ate plant-eating
dinosaurs didn't have food, so they died, too.

When you ask a scientific question, you can use the same steps as a scientist to search for an answer. The search is called a scientific investigation. This table shows all the different steps in a scientific investigation.

**Steps in a Scientific Investigation**

| Step | What It Is |
|------|-----------|
| Asking a question | asking *What, How, When, Where,* or *Why* |
| Making a hypothesis | making a smart guess about the answer to the question |
| Planning the investigation | deciding how to gather evidence to answer the question |
| Collecting and recording data | gathering and recording information to test the hypothesis |
| Organizing data | making graphs and tables to better understand the information that has been gathered |
| Explaining results | figuring out what the information means |
| Thinking of new questions | using the information that you gathered to identify new questions |
| Sharing results | sharing your information with other investigators |

An **experiment** (ik SPER uh ment) is a scientific investigation that tests a hypothesis (hy PAHTH ih sis).

Keyword: Scientific Method
www.scilinks.org
Code: GSS45005

Not all questions are scientific questions.

This is not a scientific question because "big" and "small" mean different things to different people.

This is a scientific question because you can measure the depth of the puddle.

Different kinds of scientific questions require different kinds of investigations.

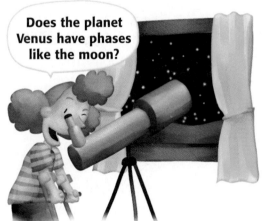

To find the answer to this question, you would need a thermometer, some water, a heatproof container, and a source of heat. You also need to wear safety goggles. The investigation might take only 5 minutes.

To answer this question, you would need a telescope and a notebook or calendar for recording your observations. You would need to observe Venus for several months.

## Making a Hypothesis

Once you have decided on a question you want to answer, you need to come up with a hypothesis. A **hypothesis** (hy PAHTH ih sis) is an idea that can be tested by an experiment or an observation. Here's an example of how you might come up with a hypothesis.

You know that the trees in your neighborhood sprout new leaves every spring. You ask yourself, "What makes trees sprout leaves in the spring?" Based on your experience, you think of two changes that occur in the spring. Days become longer in the spring, and temperatures become warmer. You decide to investigate "days become longer." Then you write a hypothesis that you can test.

**Variable 1:** Days grow longer.

**Variable 2:** Temperatures grow warmer.

**Hypothesis:** Trees sprout leaves in the spring when they get at least 12 hours of daylight.

See Also

Controlling Variables page 8

Your hypothesis is testable. You could shine light on different indoor trees for different amounts of time and see which tree sprouted leaves first.

For many science activities you do in school, you will not need to make a hypothesis. That's all right. Not every scientific investigation involves a hypothesis or even an experiment.

# Planning the Investigation

Before you go on an outing, you plan what you will need and what you will do. That way, your outing will go smoothly. Different outings require different equipment and supplies.

Careful planning makes an investigation run smoothly.

The same is true for a science investigation. Different science investigations require different tools and equipment. Different investigations also have different steps. What you will do in an investigation depends on what question you are trying to answer.

For example, should you do your investigation indoors or outdoors? If you are studying changes in the population of robins in your neighborhood, you will work outdoors. If you want to find out what causes a bottle of cold soda to suddenly fizz when you twist off its cap, you will probably work indoors.

Before you begin your investigation, list the steps you will follow. Important steps are listed here. You might want to add more steps, too.

1. Learn as much as you can about the topic of your investigation. Also learn about similar investigations that other people have done.

2. Decide what equipment you will need for your investigation and where you can get it.

3. Ask your teacher for help or advice.

4. Find out whether there is anything dangerous in your investigation. Find out how you can do the investigation safely.

## Controlling Variables

Suppose you want to perform an experiment to test this hypothesis.

> **Hypothesis:** Trees sprout leaves in the spring when they get at least 12 hours of daylight.

Many things, or factors, might make one tree sprout leaves sooner or later than another tree. The amount of water that the trees receive might make a difference. Changes in temperature might make a difference, too. These factors are called variables. A **variable** (VAYR ee uh bul) is any factor that can change in an experiment.

Imagine that in your experiment, you give your trees different amounts of water *and* you expose them to different amounts of light *and* you keep them at different temperatures. Suppose that Tree A sprouted leaves before Tree B. How can you tell which variable made Tree A sprout leaves first? You can't tell because you don't know which variable caused the earlier sprouting.

In every experiment, you have to keep all the variables the same except the one you are testing.

In this experiment, all the variables except light are controlled. Both trees get the same amount of water. Both trees are kept at the same temperature. Only the amount of light hitting the trees is different. What caused Tree A to sprout leaves earlier than Tree B? More light!

**Tree A:** 12 hours of light each day

**Tree B:** 10 hours of light each day

## Collecting Materials

Many investigations require materials. The materials might be special tools, such as a microscope, or just paper and pencil. You will need to collect different kinds of materials for different investigations. You will also need to know where you can get the materials.

What would you need to investigate the structure of a leaf?

To investigate the structure of a leaf, you will need a magnifier. If you want to record your observations in a drawing, you will also need paper and colored pencils, markers, or crayons.

How many breaths do you take in one minute?

To find out how many breaths you take in a minute, you will need a stopwatch or a watch with a second hand. You will also need paper and a pencil to record the count.

How much does an apple weigh?

8 oz.

8.0 oz

To measure the weight of an apple, you will need an apple and a small scale. You will also need paper and a pencil to record the measurements.

To make the job of collecting materials easier, make a list like this one.

### Structure of a Leaf

| Material | Where I can get it |
|---|---|
| magnifier | teacher |
| drawing paper | school or art supply store |
| colored pencils | home |

# Collecting and Recording Data

Every investigation gives you information. The pieces of information collected in an investigation are called **data** (DAY tuh). There are many kinds of data. Some data are simple observations. Other data are measurements.

**WORD WATCH**

The word *data* is plural. It means more than one piece of information. If you're talking about only one piece of information, you use the singular word *datum*.

You will need different tools to collect different kinds of data. You will also need to record the data.

| Data | Tool Used |
|---|---|
| weight and length of kitten | scale, tape measure |
| features on the moon's surface | binoculars or telescope |
| speed of crawling ant | ruler, stopwatch |
| temperature | thermometer |

## Making Scientific Observations

Scientists are trained observers. What is a scientific observation? It's an observation that anyone can make and the result will always be the same. What's an unscientific observation? It's an observation that not everyone would agree on.

> The tree has a trunk, branches, and leaves. The trunk is 40 centimeters wide.

> The tree's leaves have a funny shape. The trunk is wide.

These are scientific observations. Everyone who looks at the tree can see that it has a trunk, branches, and leaves. Everyone who measures the trunk would get the same result.

These are not scientific observations because "a funny shape" and "wide" mean different things to different people.

Many tools can be used to collect data that everyone agrees on. What's your normal body temperature? A thermometer can tell you. What's the structure of a strand of your hair? Look through a magnifier or a microscope, and you will find the answer. What's the weight of a brick? A scale will give you the answer. Could you just say a brick was heavy? Yes, but that would not be a scientific observation. The word "heavy" means different things to different people.

**Unscientific**          **Scientific**

## Repeating Trials

Suppose you want to find the normal heart rate of your friend Roxanne. **Heart rate** is the number of times a heart beats in one minute.

You can feel heartbeats if you hold your fingers on the side of your neck or the inside of your wrist. The beats you feel are called your pulse.

You take Roxanne's pulse and count 92 beats in one minute. But you can't say for sure that this is her normal heart rate. Maybe you counted wrong or read your watch incorrectly.

How can you be sure of Roxanne's normal heart rate? You can do more trials. A **trial** (TRY ul) is a repeat of a test or an observation. The more trials you do, the more you can trust the data that you collect.

Suppose you decide to do six trials. You record the data in a table like this one.

The six trials tell you that Roxanne's normal heart rate falls in a range between 89 and 93 beats per minute.

You can also find Roxanne's average heart rate. First, add the heart rates you found in each trial.

Roxanne's Heart Rate

| Trial | Heart Rate (beats per minute) |
|---|---|
| 1 | 92 |
| 2 | 89 |
| 3 | 92 |
| 4 | 90 |
| 5 | 93 |
| 6 | 90 |

$$92 + 89 + 92 + 90 + 93 + 90 = 546$$

Then divide by the number of trials.

$$546 \div 6 = 91$$

Roxanne's average heart rate was 91. An average of the trials gives you a more accurate idea of Roxanne's heart rate than the results of any single trial.

## Keeping Records

Scientists keep careful records of their investigations. So should you. This page shows what a careful record should look like.

See Also

Making a Data Table page 62

Always write your name and the date at the top of each page. If you need more than one page, also number the pages.

Serina Blanford                                    February 15, 2004

Write the idea that you want to test.

**Hypothesis:** The temperature goes up in the morning, is highest at noon, and then goes down in the afternoon.

List the materials and tools you used.

**Materials:** outdoor thermometer, paper, pencil

**Procedure**

1. Put a thermometer outside a window.
2. Read and record the temperature every hour for 4 hours.

In this section, describe all the steps in your investigation. List the steps in the order you did them.

**Data**

| Time | Temperature |
|------|-------------|
| 11:00 A.M. | 22°F |
| 12:00 noon | 25°F |
| 1:00 P.M. | 27°F |
| 2:00 P.M. | 28°F |
| 3:00 P.M. | 26°F |

Record all data right away. Also make sure you record data accurately, even if you think the data are wrong or if other students have collected different data.

**What the Data Mean:** The data do not support my hypothesis. The temperature keeps going up after 12:00 noon. It doesn't start to go down until later in the afternoon.

Record the units for all measurements. Don't record just the numbers.

Write your ideas about what the data mean and whether they support your hypothesis.

## Science Alert!

Never cross out and change data so that your results come out the way you think they should. Remember, you are trying to answer a question. Don't decide on the answer before you finish the investigation!

## Keeping a Science Journal

A science journal (JUR nul) is a kind of science diary. It's a place to record what you have done in science over a long period of time. It's also a place to jot down notes about what you would like to do in the future. You can also write down day-to-day observations that you are curious about. These observations might lead you to ask yourself questions about nature that you would like to answer.

Your journal might be made up of a collection of loose-leaf pages from different investigations. These pages might be three-hole punched so you can keep them in a binder. Your teacher will tell you how to put together a science journal and what should go in it.

If you are curious about an event in nature, make a note in your science journal.

## Looking at Data

After you collect data, you need to look at them and ask yourself, "What do the data tell me?"

For example, a weather forecaster might collect data about a hurricane. The data might include where the hurricane is, how fast it is moving, and in which direction it is moving. A weather forecaster can use these data to predict where and when the hurricane might hit land.

### How Good Are These Data?

When you collect data, you must be sure they are accurate. "Accurate" means "correct." Damaged tools can give you inaccurate data. For example, a damaged tape measure may not measure length accurately. Here are some tips for getting accurate data.

See Also

Controlling Variables page 8

Collecting and Recording Data pages 10–13

**Tools:** Tools that don't work well can produce bad data.

**Variables:** If you are performing an experiment, make sure you are changing only one variable, such as light.

**Record:** Record your data right away. If you wait until later, you might forget what you observed.

**Double-Check:** Double-check all your measurements.

**Trials:** Repeat the investigation.

See Also

Line Graphs
pages 70–73

## Looking for Patterns in Data

Once you have collected data, you can look for patterns that will give you new information. For example, humans usually get taller as they grow from a child to an adult. Look at the graph below. It shows the average heights of girls from birth until age 18.

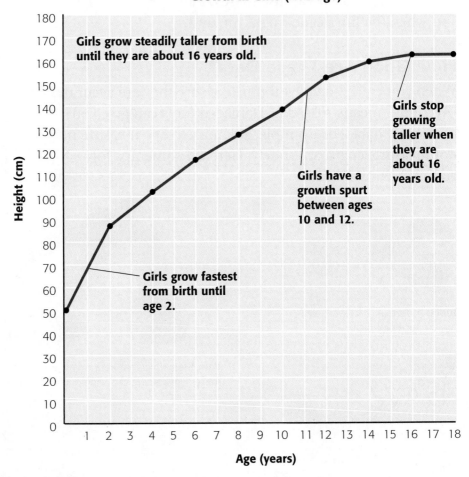

**Growth in Girls (Average)**

Girls grow steadily taller from birth until they are about 16 years old.

Girls stop growing taller when they are about 16 years old.

Girls have a growth spurt between ages 10 and 12.

Girls grow fastest from birth until age 2.

Height (cm)

Age (years)

See Also

Moon Phases
pages 222–223

You can find patterns in other kinds of data, too. For example, as days pass, the lighted part of the moon changes shape in the same pattern every month. Scientists used this repeating pattern of data to figure out how the moon moves in space.

## Comparing Your Data With Your Hypothesis

Data are often collected to test a hypothesis. A hypothesis could be a simple statement like this.

*Fruit grows from flowers.*

Suppose you perform an investigation to test this hypothesis. You examine flowers on an apple tree every two weeks. You make drawings to record your observations. The observations are your data.

See Also

Making a Hypothesis page 6

Looking at Data pages 15–16

At the end of your investigation, you study your data. You ask yourself, "Do the data support my hypothesis?" Your drawings show that an apple formed where a flower once bloomed. The data that you collected support your hypothesis.

If your data do not support your hypothesis, check for errors in your experiment. If you do not find any errors, your hypothesis was incorrect.

If your drawings showed that apples do not grow from flowers, the data you collected would not support your hypothesis. This result might lead you to perform another investigation to find out where apples come from.

## Explaining Results

Making a Data
Table page 62

Making a
Bar Graph
pages 68–69

Making a
Line Graph
pages 71–73

What do you do after you gather and record data? First, you organize the data. For example, you might organize the data in a table or a graph. If you made drawings to collect data, you might line up the drawings to show when things happened. Then you examine the organized data so you can figure out what your results mean.

### Drawing Conclusions

A **conclusion** (kun KLOO zhun) tells what an investigation showed you. The conclusion must be based on your observations and the data that you collected. A conclusion might be a simple statement like this one.

> Before you decide on a conclusion, you should ask yourself, "Are there any other explanations for these results?" Sometimes, the same data can lead to different conclusions. Then you would need to do more investigations to test the other explanations.

*Apples grow from the flowers
on an apple tree.*

**Making Inferences** An **inference** (IN fur uns) is an explanation that you figure out without actually observing something yourself. For example, suppose you wake up in the morning and see puddles in the street. You figure out that it rained during the night. You didn't observe rain falling, but your explanation makes sense.

An inference is not the same as a conclusion. A conclusion is based on your own observations. An inference is something you figure out based on your past experience. For example, there could be another explanation for the puddles on the ground. Maybe someone hosed down the street while you were sleeping!

## Making Predictions

The observations you make and the data you collect in an investigation might lead you to make a prediction. A **prediction** (prih DIK shun) is an idea about what will happen in the future.

Here's an example of a prediction. Imagine that it is the last week of school before summer vacation. You get up before dawn and check your clock just as the sun rises. The time is 5:20 A.M. On Tuesday, you discover that the sun rises at 5:19 A.M. On Wednesday, the sun rises at 5:18 A.M. You go to school and tell the class, "I predict that the sun will rise at 5:15 A.M. on Saturday."

The word *predict* has two parts. The *pre* part means "before." The *dict* part comes from a Latin word that means "say." Put the two parts together and you have "say before."

| Sunday | Monday | Tuesday | Wednesday | Thursday | Friday | Saturday |
|---|---|---|---|---|---|---|
|  | sunrise 5:20 A.M. | sunrise 5:19 A.M. | sunrise 5:18 A.M. |  |  | Prediction: sunrise 5:15 A.M. |
| 15 | 16 | 17 | 18 | 19 | 20 | 21 |

Your prediction is based on observations you made and data you collected for three days in a row. You noticed a pattern. The sun rose one minute earlier each day. Saturday is three days after Wednesday. So the sun should rise three minutes earlier on Saturday than on Wednesday. You do some simple arithmetic: 5:18 A.M. minus 3 minutes equals 5:15 A.M.

Looking for Patterns in Data page 16

## Thinking of New Questions

Scientists perform experiments to answer questions. The results of one experiment can lead a scientist to think of new questions. For example, a long time ago, no one knew what caused the diseases that people caught from other people. Then a scientist made this hypothesis.

*Diseases are caused by germs.*

The scientist performed experiments to test this hypothesis. Sure enough, he found evidence to support the hypothesis. These results led other scientists to think of a new question.

*How are germs carried from one person to another?*

This question led to more questions that could be tested.

Do insects carry germs from one person to another?

Does polluted water carry germs from one person to another?

Does air carry germs from one person to another?

Over time, scientists discovered that different germs are carried in different ways. For example, the disease called malaria (muh LAYR ee uh) is caused by a germ that is carried by mosquitoes.

Sometimes, an experiment would only show scientists how a germ was *not* carried. Then the scientists would ask themselves, "If the germ is not carried this way, which way *is* it carried?" The scientists would do more experiments to find out.

## Sharing Results

One person's discoveries can lead to new discoveries by other people. But this can only happen if people share their results.

When a scientist shares the results of an experiment, other scientists can check the results by repeating the experiment. If many people get the same results, everyone can be pretty sure the results are correct.

You can share the results of your science investigations by doing these things.

- You can give an oral report.
- You can hand out a written report.
- You can post your report on a computer.

In your report, write the question or hypothesis you were testing. Describe the steps you followed in your investigation. Give the data you collected. Include any tables or graphs you made. Explain your results and give your conclusion.

# Writing About Your Scientific Investigation

The best way to share your work is to write a report that describes what you did and what you found out. Writing a report can be helpful to you, too. It may help you find errors in your work. It may also lead you to ask new questions. These questions might spark new investigations.

Here is one good way to set up a written report.

**Title of the investigation**

**Date of the report**

**Students' names**

**Your hypothesis**

**The tools and supplies you used to collect and record data**

**What you did**

**The information you collected**

**What you found out about your hypothesis**

**Ideas for follow-up investigations**

## What Do Squirrels Eat?
October 15, 2004
by Sam Tinker and Marcy Wu

**Hypothesis:** Squirrels eat only plants and plant products.

**Materials:** binoculars, notebook, pencil

**Procedure:**
1. We sat in Marcy's backyard. She watched squirrels through the binoculars.
2. When she saw a squirrel eating something, she told Sam what the food was.
3. Sam wrote down what Marcy saw the squirrels eat.

**Data:** We observed that the squirrels ate acorns, maple seeds, and some flower buds. We did not observe the squirrels eating insects or other animals.

**Conclusion:** Our hypothesis was supported. Squirrels eat only plants and plant products.

**New questions:** We would like to find out which foods squirrels eat the most.

# Sample Investigations

## Phases of the Moon
### by Serena and Dustin

See Also

Moon Phases
pages 222–223

**Questions:** What is the order of the moon's main phases? How far apart do they occur? How long before they repeat?

**Materials:** astronomy book, large calendar, drawing pencils

**Procedure:** We looked for the moon twice a week. Using an astronomy book, we identified the four main phases of the moon. They are first quarter, full moon, last quarter, and new moon. A new moon is invisible because its bright side faces away from Earth. We started our investigation on November 1, 2003. On that day the moon was in its first quarter phase. We observed the moon until the next first quarter phase. On a calendar, we drew pictures of each phase on the date it appeared. On some nights, we didn't see the moon because the sky was cloudy. On November 23rd, the sky was clear but we didn't see the moon because it was a new moon.

**Data:** This calendar page shows what we observed.

**Explanation of Results:** Our observations show that the phases of the moon happen in a repeated pattern.

**Conclusions:** The four main phases of the moon occur in this order:

| November 2003 | | | | | | |
|---|---|---|---|---|---|---|
| Sun. | Mon. | Tues. | Wed. | Thurs. | Fri | Sat. |
|  |  |  |  |  |  | 1 |
| 2 | 3 | 4 | 5 | 6 | 7 | 8 |
| 9 | 10 | 11 | 12 | 13 | 14 | 15 |
| 16 | 17 | 18 | 19 | 20 | 21 | 22 |
| 23 / 30 | 24 | 25 | 26 | 27 | 28 | 29 |

full moon, last quarter, new moon, first quarter, and full moon again. The time between any two phases is 7 or 8 days. The phases repeat about every 29 days.

**New Questions:** We would like to investigate the cause of the moon's phases.

# Does Activity Change Your Heart Rate?

by Tanika, Chu, Gloria, and Richard

**Hypothesis:** The more active you are, the faster your heart beats.

**Materials:** watch with second hand, graph paper, pencil

**Procedure:** We took Tanika's pulse while she was sitting. We then took it while she was standing. Then we took Tanika's pulse right after she walked slowly down a hallway. Then we took her pulse right after she walked quickly down the hallway.

**Data:** We organized the data in a table.

Making a Data
Table page 62

Making a
Bar Graph
pages 68–69

| Activity | Heart Rate (beats per minute) |
|---|---|
| Sitting | 82 |
| Standing | 86 |
| Walking slowly | 93 |
| Walking quickly | 98 |

We used the data to make a graph. The slowest heart rate was 82, so we labeled the vertical axis starting at 80.

**Explanation of Results:** Tanika's heart rate was faster when she was more active.

**Conclusion:** The data support our hypotheses. The more active you are, the faster your heart beats.

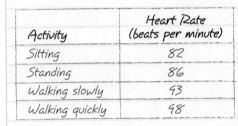

Tanika's Pulse

**New Questions:** We would like to find out if breathing rate changes in the same way that heart rate does.

## How Different Materials Absorb Sound
### by Derek

**Question:** What materials absorb sound best?

**Materials:** CD player, music CD, bubble wrap, newspapers, aluminum foil, bathtowels, tape

**Procedure:** I set the volume dial to number 6 for all trials. I put a music CD in the player. For each test, I wrapped the player in one of the materials. In one test, I didn't wrap the player at all. All materials were about 2 cm thick around the player. I taped the materials in place. I left a little opening to turn on the player. In each test, I played the same song from the beginning. I then rated the sound as soft, medium, or loud.

**Data:** I recorded my results in this table.

| Trial | Material | Rating |
|-------|----------|--------|
| 1 | none | loud |
| 2 | bubble wrap | medium |
| 3 | aluminum foil | loud |
| 4 | bathtowels | soft |
| 5 | newspaper | medium |

**Explanation of Results:** Aluminum foil and air are not good absorbers of sound. Paper and bubble wrap are better absorbers of sound. A fluffy material like bathtowels absorbs sound best.

**Conclusion:** In this investigation, towels absorbed sound best.

**New Questions:** I would like to find out if other materials, such as wood, rubber, and sand, absorb sound better than towels.

Students just like you have worked on their own science projects and investigations. Here are some project and investigation ideas that you can do in class or just for fun!

### Food Chains from the Sea

Do you like salmon, shrimp, or scallops? Choose your favorite fish or seafood, and predict what that animal eats. Then do some research to find out if you're correct. Make a food chain that includes that seafood and ends with you. Display your food chain on a bulletin board to share with the class.

### Asteroid Impact

Asteroids are chunks of rock that orbit the sun. What do you think happens when they hit a planet or a moon? Design an investigation to find out. You might drop pebbles into a tray of cornstarch and then compare the surface to the surface of the moon. Write a report, or create a display, describing what you found out.

### Long-Distance Listening

How far can sound travel to reach your ears? Choose an object, such as an alarm clock, that makes a sound with a constant intensity. Design an investigation to find out how far away from the object you can hear its sound. Make a prediction of that distance. Then gather the materials, and carry out your investigation. Write a report with your findings.

### Earthworm Behavior

Design an experiment to see how earthworms react to changes in their environment. What do they do when they're uncovered? How do they respond to the light and heat of a flashlight? What do they do when it rains? Make a project display showing your findings. Be sure to return the worms to a garden.

### Weather and the Seasons

How does weather in your area change from season to season? Design an investigation in which you use various weather instruments to measure weather over the course of a year. Record data regularly. Use your data to compare measurements such as average daily temperature, wind speed and direction, and amount of precipitation among the different seasons. Then draw graphs that show how weather in your area changes over the year and display them on a three-sided project display.

### Solar Energy

What is solar energy? How can you measure it? Can you build a device that uses solar energy for power? Design one or more investigations that will help you find out more about solar energy. Then gather the materials you need, and carry out your investigations.

# Working Safely

Investigating the mysteries of nature can be exciting. But some investigations can be dangerous if you're not careful. Here are some tips to keep you safe when you do science investigations.

**Tips for Safe Science Investigations**

- **Always** wait for your teacher's permission to begin an investigation.
- **Follow** all directions you are given.
- **Ask** for help from an adult if you don't understand any directions.
- **Never** fool around during an investigation.
- **Only** use equipment the way it is supposed to be used.
- **Keep** your work area neat and clean.
- **Always** wear appropriate safety equipment such as goggles.
- **Know** what to do in case of an emergency or accident.
- **Never** taste any substance you are using in a science investigation unless your teacher tells you to.

## Safe Behavior

Even safe equipment must be handled carefully to keep you safe. For example, a ruler is a safe piece of equipment. But a ruler has a sharp edge. If you play with it, you could cut yourself or someone else, or you could break the ruler. Only use a piece of equipment the way it should be used.

### Follow Instructions

The best way to stay safe is to follow instructions exactly as you get them. The instructions might be written on a handout or in a book. Your teacher might write instructions on the board or tell them to the class out loud. If your teacher writes the instructions or tells them to the class, write them down. If you are not sure you have written them down correctly, check with your teacher.

Always stop work right away when your teacher tells you to.

Some instructions, such as safety rules, might be for all investigations that you do. Other instructions might be for just one kind of investigation. You may get instructions all at once or at different times. No matter what the instructions are and how you get them, you must follow them *completely*.

Always follow steps in the order they are given to you. Don't skip steps or do them out of order. The last instruction might be to clean up. Always follow that instruction.

## Science Alert!

Always pay attention to what's going on around you. If something is happening that you think is dangerous, tell the adult in charge.

## Working in Groups

Some investigations have many jobs. Because of this, many investigations are done by groups. Each member of the group has a different job.

You and all the other members of your group need to work together. The whole group should plan the investigation. Everyone in the group should decide on the hypothesis or the question you will investigate. And everyone should discuss the results and agree on a conclusion.

## Washing Your Hands

Why do you wash your hands before you eat or after you go to the bathroom? You wash to stay healthy. You should do the same if you are handling things like chemicals, household cleaners, pond water, or soil in a science investigation.

Dry your hands completely with a paper towel. Then throw the towel into the wastebasket.

Rinse all the soap and dirt off.

Wash your hands thoroughly with soap and water in your classroom sink or school washroom. Rub for as long as it takes you to count to 10 slowly. Make sure you rub all over your hands.

# Handle With Care!

If you want to build a house, you have to know how to use many different tools and how to take good care of them. The same is true when you do science investigations.

Science tools are a very important part of an investigation. They include measuring tools, such as a balance, a thermometer, and a meter stick. Tools for making observations include magnifiers and microscopes. You will also work with containers such as beakers and test tubes.

*See Also*

Measuring Tools
pages 38–50

Using Magnifiers
and Microscopes
pages 51–53

Equipment for
Cooling and
Heating
pages 54–55

Working With
Substances
pages 56–57

Here are some important safety rules when you work with science tools and materials.

- Handle tools with respect. Don't do anything that might damage them.

- Keep tools in good working order. Make sure tools are clean before you use them. Clean them after you use them.

- When you are finished using a tool, put it back where it came from. That way, you or another student will be able to find it again.

- Do not waste materials. You might run out before you are finished.

- Do not use another student's materials unless you have permission.

Keyword: Safety in the Science Classroom
www.scilinks.org
Code: GSS45010

# A Safe Work Area

If you watch a cook preparing a meal on TV, what do you see? The work area is neat and organized. Ingredients are prepared in advance and are placed so they can be found easily. Breakable objects are away from the edges of countertops. Knives are placed or stored to avoid accidental cuts. Tools are laid out neatly. Nothing unnecessary is cluttering up the work area.

You should organize your science work area in the same way. This will make your investigation go smoothly. It will also reduce the chances of you or a classmate being injured.

Clean the desktop or tabletop where you will work *before* you put anything on it. Clear away everything except what you will use for your investigation.

Organize your tools and materials neatly.

Make sure there are no strings or cords dangling from your work area. Make sure strings or cords do not cross areas where people might walk.

Hang up jackets, hats, and other outerwear.

When you stand up, push in your chair so you or someone else won't stumble against it.

Clean the desktop or tabletop again when you have finished the investigation.

Keep part of your workspace free for the notebook you will record in. Don't place anything near the notebook that is easy to knock over.

Clear the floor near and under your desk or worktable.

## Dressing for Safety

Soccer players, inline skaters, and bike riders dress for safety. You should dress safely too when you do a science investigation. You probably won't need to wear shin guards, elbow pads, or a helmet! But there are other safety rules you should follow. Here are a few.

### How to Dress Safely for Science

- Don't wear loose or baggy clothing.
- Roll up loose sleeves.
- If you have long hair, tie it back.
- Don't wear open-toed shoes or sandals.
- Store jackets and hats away from your work area.
- Leave dangly jewelry at home, or remove it and put it away before you begin.
- If you have any cuts on your hands, cover them before you start the investigation.
- Wear lab gloves and a lab apron if needed. Avoid latex gloves. You might be allergic to latex.
- Always wear safety goggles when you are working with liquids that might splash or with other materials that might get in your eyes. Make sure your safety goggles are clean before you put them on. Dirty goggles could give you an eye infection.

Safety goggles protect your eyes.

# Working Safely Outdoors

Working outdoors has some special safety hazards. Here's how to avoid them.

- If you have asthma, an allergy, or another condition that might flare up, tell your teacher before the field trip.

- Do not touch plants or animals unless your teacher or adult supervisor says it's okay. Never put any part of a wild plant in your mouth. Wash your hands after handling animals and plants.

- Know what poison ivy, poison oak, and poison sumac look like. Do not touch these plants!

- Wear socks and sturdy shoes or sneakers, not sandals.

- Wear long pants and long sleeves. Cover as much skin as you can.

- Apply a sunscreen to all uncovered skin. Wear a hat to shade your eyes and face.

- Spray exposed skin with insect repellent. Wash off the repellent as soon as you return indoors. (*Caution:* Do not use insect repellent if your skin is sensitive to it.)

- Never drink water from a pond, a stream, a lake, or any other place outdoors.

- Know the boundaries of your work area and stay inside them.

- Always stay in sight of your teacher or adult supervisor.

- Work with a partner or team. Stay together at all times.

- After your field trip, look for ticks on your clothes and skin. Be especially careful to check your shoes, socks, and pant legs. If you find a tick, tell your teacher right away, and let your teacher remove it.

Poison ivy

Poison oak

Poison sumac

Tick

Ticks are very small, about the size of this dot. ●

## In Case of Emergency

Although you try to avoid accidents, they happen. When they do, they may cause an emergency. You must act quickly in case of an emergency. What you do when an emergency happens can keep you or someone else from being badly hurt.

First, you have to recognize an emergency when it happens.

### Science Alert!

Anything that seriously threatens the life or health of a person is an emergency.

### KINDS OF ACCIDENTS That Cause an Emergency

- A serious fall or collision
- An object stuck in a person's eye, ear, nose, or throat
- A bad burn
- A deep cut
- A chemical splashing on someone's skin or in someone's eyes
- A person having trouble breathing for any reason
- A person having a seizure or becoming unconscious
- Someone falling through the ice into a pond
- Someone at risk of drowning
- An electric shock
- Swallowing a poisonous substance
- A fire in your school or home
- Someone choking

## BE PREPARED for an Emergency

- Know ahead of time how to deal with certain emergencies. For example, know where the emergency exits are in your school.
- Know the best way to call for help from your classroom. Find out if there's an intercom in the room or nearby.
- If your school or classroom has emergency equipment, know where to find it.

Emergency equipment in your school includes fire extinguishers. Your science classroom also might have eyewash, a fire blanket, and a special shower.

## HOW TO ACT in an Emergency

- Stay calm.
- Immediately tell your teacher or adult supervisor if an emergency happens.
- Follow all directions that your teacher gives you.
- Stay out of the way unless someone tells you to help.

# Using Science Tools and Equipment

## Measuring Tools

Measuring tools allow you to collect accurate data. Measurements are more accurate than the guesses or estimates you would make if you used just your senses.

Metric Units and Equivalents page 408

English Units and Equivalents page 409

No matter what you measure, you will use one of two measuring systems. They are the metric system and the English system. The metric system is used in all scientific investigations. Either the metric system or the English system can be used to make everyday measurements.

In the United States, people use the English system for everyday measurements. Most other countries use the metric system for everyday measurements.

This table shows some measurement units in the two systems. In each row of this table, the metric unit and the English unit are not the same measurement. For example, one meter does not equal one foot. One liter does not equal one quart.

Changing Units
page 410

**Measuring Systems**

| What Is Measured | Metric Unit (symbol) | English Unit (symbol) |
| --- | --- | --- |
| length | meter (m) | foot (ft) |
| mass | gram (g) | no unit for mass |
| weight | newton (N) | pound (lb) |
| volume | liter (L) | quart (qt) |
| time | second (s) | second (s) |
| temperature | degrees Celsius (°C) | degrees Fahrenheit (°F) |

These measurement units mean the same thing to everyone everywhere. For example, suppose you feed two hamsters different kinds of food. You want to find out whether one food makes hamsters grow larger. After two weeks, you use a balance to find the mass of each hamster. **Mass** is the amount of matter in an object.

Measuring Mass
and Weight
page 46

Using a Two-Pan
Balance page 47

You find that one hamster has a mass of 250 g. The other hamster has a mass of 300 g. If you tell your classmates about your investigation, they will know exactly what the measurements mean. And if your classmates measured the mass of each hamster, they would get the same results. Measurements can be repeated.

## Estimating

When you don't need an exact measurement, you can estimate. For example, imagine that you have $10 to buy materials to make a model volcano. You go to an art supply store to buy the materials. As you walk down the aisles, you put things in your shopping basket. How do you know if the total reaches $10? You can find out by rounding the prices and adding in your head.

$3.85

Rounds to $4.00

$1.05

Rounds to $1.00

$1.89

Rounds to $2.00

$2.00 + $1.00 + $4.00 = $7.00

### Useful Everyday Estimates

| Length/Distance | |
|---|---|
| thickness of a dime | 1 millimeter |
| width of a large paper clip | 1 centimeter |
| width of a nickel | 2 centimeters |
| width and length of notebook paper | 22 cm wide, 28 cm long |
| length of a football field | 90 meters |
| **Volume** | |
| 10 drops of water | 1 milliliter |
| tablespoon full of water | 15 milliliters |
| **Mass** | |
| dollar bill | 1 gram |
| nickel | 5 grams |
| stick of butter | 100 grams |
| small car | 1,000 kilograms |

Suppose you need to cut a piece of string about 30 cm long for a science investigation. And suppose you know that notebook paper is about 28 centimeters long. You can cut the string just a little bit longer than the notebook paper. This table gives some other handy estimates you can use.

# Choosing the Right Measuring Tool

You have to use the right tools to make different measurements. Here are some tools and the units they measure.

Take good care of measuring tools. Broken or damaged tools won't give you correct measurements.

Use a thermometer to measure temperature. In science, the units for measuring temperature are degrees Celsius (°C).

Measure mass with a balance. **Mass** is the amount of matter in an object. Units of mass include milligrams (mg), grams (g), and kilograms (kg).

Use a graduated cylinder to measure the volume of liquids. This graduated cylinder has marks for every 10 milliliters (mL).

Measure length or distance with a metric ruler, a meter stick, or a tape measure. These tools have lines that show millimeters (mm), centimeters (cm), and meters (m). Use the longer tools to measure longer things.

See Also

Measuring Length and Distance pages 42–43

Measuring the Volume of Liquids pages 44–45

Measuring Mass and Weight pages 46–48

Measuring Temperature page 49

Measuring Time page 50

## Measuring Length and Distance

How long is a carpenter ant? How far is it from your house to the mailbox on the corner? You can answer these questions and others like them by measuring length and distance. This table shows the units for measuring length and distance in the metric system.

Metric Units
and Equivalents
page 408

| Unit Name (symbol) | Example |
| --- | --- |
| millimeter (mm) | A dime is about 1 mm thick. |
| centimeter (cm) | A nickel is about 2 cm wide. |
| meter (m) | The rim of a basketball basket is about 3 m above the floor. |
| kilometer (km) | The driving distance from New York to San Francisco is about 4,700 km. |

10 mm = 1 cm          100 cm = 1 m          1,000 m = 1 km

In the United States, people use English units to measure length and distance. These units are the inch (in.), foot (ft), yard (yd), and mile (mi).

12 in. = 1 ft                    3 ft = 1 yd                    1,760 yd = 1 mi

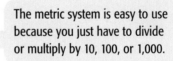

The metric system is easy to use because you just have to divide or multiply by 10, 100, or 1,000.

Here are some ways to measure lengths and distances.

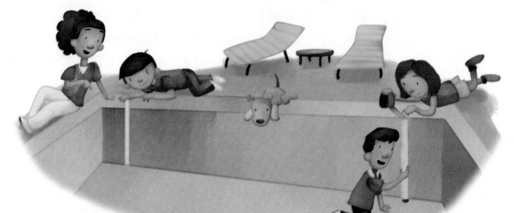

You can find the depth
of the deep end of a swimming
pool with a tape measure. You can find
the depth of the shallow end with a meter stick.

How much paper will you
need to wrap the box? To find
out, you can use a metric ruler
to measure the length, width,
and height of the box.

A ruler, meter stick, or tape measure might be damaged or
worn down at the zero end. You can still use it to measure
things. Just start away from the damaged end.

Suppose you want to measure
the length of a twig. Put the
ruler's mark for 1 cm at one
end of the twig. Read the mark
at the other end of the twig. It
is 5 cm. Subtract 1 cm from 5
cm. The twig is 4 cm long.

## Measuring the Volume of Liquids

Suppose you want to find out how much water bean plants need. You want to give Plant A just a little water. You want to give Plant B more water. And you want to give Plant C the most water. How should you measure the water?

You need to measure the volume of the water. **Volume** (VAHL yoom) is the amount of space that something takes up. This table shows the units for measuring the volume of liquids in the metric system.

Metric Units
and Equivalents
page 408

| Unit Name (symbol) | Example |
| --- | --- |
| milliliter (mL) | A teaspoon holds about 5 mL of liquid. |
| liter (L) | A medium-size soda bottle holds 1 L. |
| kiloliter (kL) | 1 kL of gasoline could fill the gas tanks of about 20 small cars. |

$$1,000 \text{ mL} = 1 \text{ L} \qquad\qquad 1,000 \text{ L} = 1 \text{ kL}$$

In the United States, people use English units to measure the volume of liquids. These units are the fluid ounce (fl oz), cup (c), pint (pt), quart (qt), and gallon (gal).

$$8 \text{ fl oz} = 1 \text{ c} \qquad 2 \text{ c} = 1 \text{ pt} \qquad 2 \text{ pt} = 1 \text{ qt} \qquad 4 \text{ qt} = 1 \text{ gal}$$

**Measuring Cups and Spoons**  Measuring cups and measuring spoons are used to measure liquids and powdered solids. Measuring cups and spoons come in different sizes. Some are marked with metric units. Others are marked with English units. Some are marked with both metric and English units.

**Beakers and Graduated Cylinders**
Scientists use beakers and graduated cylinders to measure liquids. The word *graduated* means that the containers have marks on them. The marks show units such as milliliters.

**Beakers**        **Graduated cylinders**

**Reading Volume**  Here's how to read the volume in a measuring cup, a beaker, or a graduated cylinder.

Choose the right size beaker or graduated cylinder for the job. Use smaller beakers or graduated cylinders to measure small amounts of liquid. Use larger ones to measure larger amounts.

Don't read here.

Read here.

**Science Alert!**

Glassware can break. Handle it carefully!

Mass page 244

Mass and
Weight
page 271

## Measuring Mass and Weight

**Mass** is the amount of matter in an object. **Weight** is a measure of the pull of gravity on an object.

The metric system uses units of mass to describe how much "stuff" is in an object. The English system uses units of weight to describe the same thing. This table shows the metric units for measuring mass.

| Unit Name (symbol) | Example |
|---|---|
| milligram (mg) | One drop of water has a mass of about 60 mg. |
| gram (g) | A dollar bill has a mass of about 1 g. |
| kilogram (kg) | A liter bottle of soda has a mass of 1 kg. |

See Also

Metric Units
and Equivalents
page 408

1,000 mg = 1 g          1,000 g = 1 kg

The English units for measuring weight are the ounce and pound.

16 oz = 1 lb

**Using a Spring Scale** You can use a spring scale to find the mass of an object. The object pulls down on a spring. The spring moves a marker. The marker points to the object's mass.

Each line on the spring scale shows 10 g. The marker is two lines above 100. The mass of the marbles is 120 g.

Keyword: Mass / Weight
www.scilinks.org
Code: GSS45015

### Using a Two-Pan Balance

1. Put the balance on a level surface.

2. The empty pans should be exactly even with each other, and the pointer should line up with the 0 mark. If it doesn't, turn the zero adjustment screw until the pointer stops at 0.

Known masses

Pans

**50 g + 20 g + 5 g = 75 g**
The mass of this rock is 75 g.

3. Put the object you want to measure on one pan.

4. Put known masses on the other pan until the pointer lines up with 0 again. (*Known masses* are the small metal things that you use to balance the scale.)

5. Add up the numbers that are marked on the masses you put on the pan. The total tells the mass of the object.

## Science Alert!

Be sure to *add the numbers* that are marked on the masses. Don't count the masses.

How could you measure 5 g of salt?

1. Make sure the balance is on a level surface.

2. "Zero" the balance as in step 2 above.

3. Put an empty cup on one pan.

4. Put known masses on the other pan until the pointer lines up with 0 again.

5. Add a 5 g known mass to the other masses on the pan.

6. Add salt little by little to the cup.

7. When the pointer lines up with 0, you have 5 g of salt.

### Using a Triple-Beam Balance
A triple-beam balance is used to measure mass. It has three beams with sliding masses called *riders*.

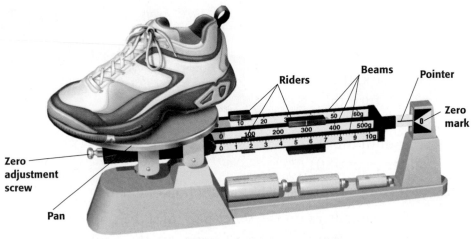

**Riders** · **Beams** · **Pointer** · **Zero mark** · **Zero adjustment screw** · **Pan**

300 g + 10 g + 1.8 g = 311.8 g

The mass of the sneaker is 311.8 g.

Here's how to use a triple-beam balance to measure mass.

1. Make sure the balance is on a level surface.

2. Move the riders all the way to the left so they all read 0.

3. The pointer should aim at 0. If it doesn't, turn the zero adjustment screw until the pointer stops at 0.

4. Put the object on the pan. The pointer will move up.

5. Move the largest rider to the right until the pointer is below the 0 mark. Then move the rider back one notch. The pointer will rise above the 0 mark.

6. Do the same thing with the medium-size rider.

7. Now move the smallest rider to the right until the pointer dips just below the 0 mark. Move the rider back a little. Then move it back and forth a tiny bit at a time until the pointer is on the 0 mark.

8. Add the measurements shown on all three riders.

## Measuring Temperature

What should you wear when you go out today? A light sweater? A heavy jacket? You look at the thermometer outside your window. It reads 20°F. Now where did you put that heavy jacket?

A thermometer measures temperature. Thermometers come in many shapes and sizes.

In the United States, people measure temperature in degrees Fahrenheit (°F). Scientists measure temperature in degrees Celsius (°C). People in most other countries measure temperature in degrees Celsius, too.

How do you read a thermometer that has a liquid column? Look at the top of the liquid column. Then look at the mark on the thermometer that the top of the column reaches. Read the value for that mark.

C°

60°
55°
50°
45°
40°
35°
30°
25°
20°
15°
10°
5°
0°
−5°
−10°
−15°
−20°
−25°

**20°C + 2°C = 22°C**

The numbers on this thermometer are 5°C apart. There are four lines between numbers. Each line stands for 1°C. In this picture, the liquid reaches two lines above 20°C. That means the temperature is 22°C.

## Science Alert!

Do not use a thermometer that has silver-colored liquid in it. The liquid is mercury, which is a poison. Give the thermometer to your teacher.

Keyword: Temperature Scales
www.scilinks.org
Code: GSS45020

## Measuring Time

In some of your investigations, you will need to measure time. Time is measured in seconds, minutes, hours, and days. For each kind of measurement, you will use a different tool or a different part of the same tool. Here are some examples.

How long does it take a toy car to roll from the top of a ramp to the bottom? The car will make this trip in seconds and fractions of a second. You will need a stopwatch to measure the time.

How long will it take a mouse to run through a maze? The mouse may take a number of minutes plus some seconds. You will need to read both the minute hand and the second hand on a watch or clock. Or you could use a digital watch.

How long will the sun be in the sky today from sunrise to sunset? You will need to measure hours and minutes. A watch or clock would be right for this investigation.

How long will it take a seed to sprout after you plant it? The answer will be a number of days. Your measuring tool should be a calendar.

# Using Magnifiers and Microscopes

When you look at a color picture in a book, you see pink, orange, green, purple, and all the other colors of the objects. But if you look at the picture through a magnifier, you can see the red, blue, yellow, and black dots that make up all those other colors.

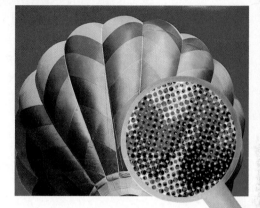

Magnifiers and microscopes are tools that let you see things you cannot see with just your eyes alone.

## Magnifiers

Do you want to get a better look at the parts of a flower? Use a magnifier. It's the right tool for this job.

### How to Focus a Magnifier

Hold the magnifier between your eye and the object. Move the magnifier slowly back and forth between the object and your eye until you see the object clearly.

### Science Alert!

Never use a magnifier to look at the sun.

# Microscopes

Some objects you will investigate are too small to see with a magnifier. You will need to use a microscope.

**Parts of a Microscope** A microscope is made of many parts that work together to help you see very small objects.

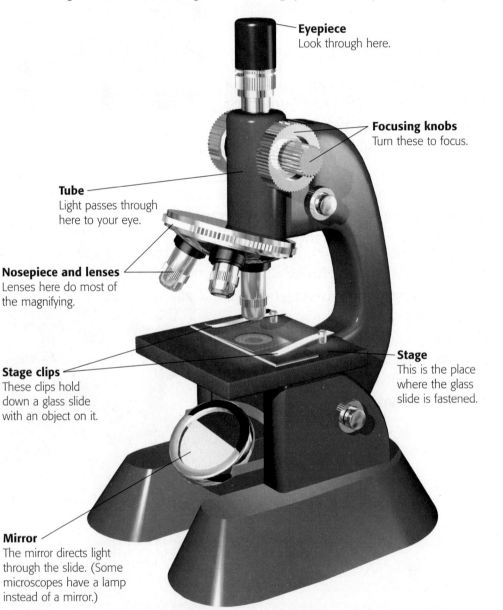

**Eyepiece**
Look through here.

**Focusing knobs**
Turn these to focus.

**Tube**
Light passes through here to your eye.

**Nosepiece and lenses**
Lenses here do most of the magnifying.

**Stage**
This is the place where the glass slide is fastened.

**Stage clips**
These clips hold down a glass slide with an object on it.

**Mirror**
The mirror directs light through the slide. (Some microscopes have a lamp instead of a mirror.)

**How to Focus a Microscope** Here is what you do to see an object clearly through a microscope.

1. Make sure there is already an object on the slide that you will be examining.

2. Put the slide on the stage.

3. Center the slide's object over the opening in the stage.

4. Hold the slide down with the clips.

**Steps 2–4**

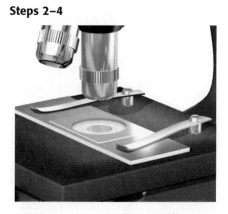

5. Turn the focus knob away from you to lower the tube. As you do this, look at the microscope from the side. *Make sure the lens does not touch the slide!* If it does, the slide and the lens could be damaged.

**Step 5**

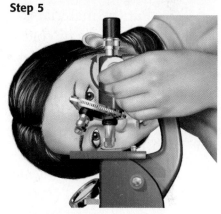

6. Next, look through the eyepiece. (*Caution:* Be careful you don't poke your eye with the eyepiece!) Turn the focus knob toward you *very slowly* to raise the tube.

7. Keep raising the tube until the object on the slide looks very clear to you.

**Step 6**

SCi
LINKS
NSTA

Keyword: Microscopes
www.scilinks.org
Code: GSS45025

# Equipment for Cooling and Heating

In some investigations, you will need to control the temperature of materials. You might want to keep the materials at room temperature. You might want to cool them. Or you might want to warm them. Here is how you can safely cool and heat materials.

## Water Baths

To cool a material, you can put it in a refrigerator or freezer. Or you can put it in a cold water bath or ice bath. An ice bath is made of ice, water, and sometimes salt.

Put the material you want to cool in a small container. Put the ice or cold water in a large container. Then put the small container into the large container.

You can do the same thing to warm a material. Just use warm water in the large container instead of cold water or ice water.

Make sure the ice water or warm water in the large container is up to the level of the material in the small container.

## Science Alert!

Never put a glass container that is hot into ice water or very cold water. The glass might break!

# Hot Plates

A hot plate heats water slowly and safely. Most of the time, your teacher will be the one who uses a hot plate. But if you are asked to use one, here's how to do it safely.

**Safety goggles**
Always wear safety goggles and a lab apron when you or anyone else is using a hot plate.

**Heat-resistant container**
Always use a container made of metal or heat-resistant glass. Never heat a container if you are not sure if it is heat-resistant. Never heat an empty container.

If anything spills on the hot plate, ask an adult to unplug it and clean up the spill. Don't do it yourself.

**Platform**
This is the part of the hot plate that gets hot. *Never touch it!*

**Heat-resistant mitts**
Avoid burns by wearing mitts to move hot containers.

**On-off indicator**
When this light is on, the hot plate is on.

**Control knob**
Turn this knob to raise or lower the heat.

**Three-prong plug**
Make sure the hot plate has a three-prong plug. Do not plug in or unplug the hot plate. Your teacher will do that for you.

## Science Alert!

**NEVER** heat a closed container. It might blow up and seriously injure you or a classmate.

## Working With Substances

You'll work with lots of substances in science. When you do an investigation, you must act responsibly. That means you must know how to handle the materials you use. Take only the amount you need for the investigation. Clean up when you are finished. Know how to dispose of different kinds of substances. The table on the next page tells you how to work with substances safely.

### Labeling Containers

Many substances you might use in an investigation look alike. For example, salt, sugar, baking soda, and cornstarch are all white powders. Before you choose a substance, read the label on the container. It will tell you which is which.

Always label an empty container before you put something in it. Make sure to label all containers that you will store after your investigation is finished. Never use a substance from an unlabeled container.

## Working With Substances

| How to Handle | How to Clean Up |
|---|---|
| **Outdoor Materials (examples: sand, soil, rocks, minerals)** | |
| • Look out for sharp edges. <br>• Do not get sand or soil near your eyes or mouth or in cuts. <br>• Work on newspaper or another disposable surface. | • Sweep up any spilled materials. <br>• Wrap the newspaper around the materials. <br>• Throw the materials in the trash. <br>• **Never** pour sand, soil, or water that contains them into a sink drain. |
| **Household Materials (examples: baking soda, vinegar, salt, food coloring, borax)** | |
| • Follow instructions for using materials. <br>• Do not mix materials unless your teacher tells you to. <br>• Do not inhale powders. <br>• Do not taste any substances. <br>• Avoid spills. | • Do not return unused liquids or solids to their original containers. <br>• Sweep up solids and throw them in the trash. Do not create dust when sweeping. <br>• Most liquids can be poured into a sink drain. If you're not sure, ask your teacher. |
| **Art Supplies (examples: plaster of Paris, papier mâché, modeling clay, glue)** | |
| • Work on newspaper or another disposable surface. <br>• Clean up spills right away. <br>• Do not inhale powders. | • Sweep up spilled solids. <br>• Wash soiled surfaces with soap and water. <br>• Throw unused plaster of Paris and papier mâché in the trash. <br>• **Never** pour art materials or water containing them into a sink drain. |
| **Special Science Materials** | |
| • **Iron filings:** Wear safety goggles. <br>• **Indicator paper:** Use one strip of paper at a time. Make sure your fingers are clean and dry when you handle it. | • **Iron filings:** Sweep up the filings. Dispose of them as your teacher tells you to. <br>• **Indicator paper:** Throw used indicator paper in the trash. |

# Science Alert!

Do not taste or smell any substance without your
teacher's permission. Do not play with any substance.
Wear goggles when your teacher tells you to.

Keyword: Safety in
the Science Classroom
www.scilinks.org
Code: GSS45010

# Working With Living Things

In some science investigations, you will observe living animals and plants. You must respect the living things you investigate. Here are some rules to follow.

- Be responsible for keeping living things safe and healthy. They can't care for themselves.
- If you need to catch butterflies or other flying insects, learn how to use a net so you do not harm them.
- Wear gloves when you are using water from wild places. The water might be polluted.
- Wash your hands with soap and water before and after you handle plants or animals.

## Plants in the Classroom

When you examine plants, follow these rules.

- Follow all directions that your teacher gives you.
- **Never** put plant parts in your mouth.
- Keep plant parts away from your eyes, nose, and ears.

When you care for plants indoors, follow these rules.

- Choose a place in the room where the plants won't be disturbed.
- Make sure the plants are not near a source of heat or air conditioning.
- Make sure the plants get enough light and water to grow well.
- Find somebody to take care of the plants during school vacations.

- If you grow plants in a terrarium, make sure they have enough space and fertile soil.

## Animals in the Classroom

Follow these rules when you work with any animals.

- Animals must be cared for correctly, even during school vacations.
- Observe animals quietly. Don't tap on their containers.
- Don't handle animals that might bite or scratch you. If you do get injured, tell your teacher right away.
- If you are allergic to any animals, do not handle them.
- Wash your hands before and after you handle animals.

**Small Mammals** These animals include mice, rats, gerbils, hamsters, guinea pigs, and rabbits. **Never** keep wild mammals in the classroom. Handle small mammals gently. They need fresh food and water every day. They need clean bedding and something like wood or cardboard to chew on. Gerbils and hamsters also need an exercise wheel.

**Fish** Keep fish in a good-size aquarium, not a small bowl. Find out what temperature they need, and keep the water at that temperature. You might need a heater, filter, and bubbler. Don't overfeed fish. Keep the water clean.

**Invertebrates** These animals include earthworms, snails,  insects, and other very small animals. Observe the conditions where the animal normally lives. Then copy those conditions in the classroom.

**Reptiles and Amphibians** These animals include snakes, turtles, lizards, frogs, toads, and salamanders. Many of these are available in pet stores. Each kind of animal needs its own special environment. If you catch a wild reptile or amphibian, put it back where you found it after a few hours. Do not try to keep it in school. *Wash your hands after you handle these animals!* Some carry germs that can make you very sick.

# Using Tables and Graphs

You gather data in an investigation. You and others will have a hard time making sense of the information unless you organize it. When data are organized in a table or a graph, you can understand their meaning more easily.

## Data Tables

A data table can be organized in any way that lets you compare data easily.

How would you show the five highest mountains in the United States? This data table lists the mountains from highest to lowest. The table makes it easy to compare the heights of the mountains.

The five highest mountains in the U.S. are all in Alaska. This is Mt. McKinley.

| Mountain | Height |
|----------|--------|
| McKinley | 6,194 m |
| St. Elias | 5,489 m |
| Foraker | 5,304 m |
| Bona | 5,029 m |
| Blackburn | 4,996 m |

*Source: Time Almanac*

## Reading a Data Table

A data table is made of columns and rows. To find information, you read down columns and across rows. This table shows information about July temperatures and rainfall in six United States cities.

**Average July Temperature and Rainfall in U.S. Cities**

| City | Temperature (°F) | Rainfall (inches) |
|------|------------------|-------------------|
| Austin, TX | 85 | 2.2 |
| Boise, ID | 75 | 0.2 |
| Chicago, IL | 76 | 3.4 |
| Miami, FL | 82 | 6.8 |
| New York, NY | 77 | 3.7 |
| San Francisco, CA | 63 | 0.0 |

*Source: Climates of the World, U.S. Department of Commerce*

Suppose you want to find Chicago's average temperature or average rainfall in July. Find Chicago in the first column. Then read across the row. The second column tells the average temperature. The third column tells the average rainfall.

Here's how you would find the city with the highest average rainfall in July. Read down the rainfall column to find the highest number. It is 6.8. Then read backwards across the row to the city column. The city is Miami.

## Recording Data in a Table

For some investigations, you will get a table for recording data. Here are some tips about how to fill in a data table.

- Be sure to record data in the correct column and row.
- Record the correct units for your data.
- Record each piece of data as soon as you collect it.
- Write neatly and clearly.

## Making a Data Table

This student collected data on air temperature and time. But he will have a hard time making sense of the data because they are not organized.

1:00 P.M. 65°F

60°F 9:00 A.M.

11:00 A.M. 63°F

58°F 8:00 A.M.

2:00 P.M. 66°F

12:00 noon 65°F

3:00 P.M. 64°F

10:00 A.M. 62°F

The best time to make a data table is *before* you collect the data. The student's partner did that. Here's what her data table looks like.

### Hourly Temperature, May 10, 2004

| Time | Temperature (°F) |
|------|------------------|
| 8:00 A.M. | 58 |
| 9:00 A.M. | 60 |
| 10:00 A.M. | 62 |
| 11:00 A.M. | 63 |
| 12:00 noon | 65 |
| 1:00 P.M. | 65 |
| 2:00 P.M. | 66 |
| 3:00 P.M. | 64 |

To set up a data table, first figure out how many kinds of data you need to record. These students needed to record two kinds of data—time and temperature. Set up as many vertical columns as you need to record each kind of data.

Next, figure out how many times you will make a measurement. These students measured temperature eight times, so they needed eight rows. They also needed a row for the labels at the top of the columns. That's a total of nine rows. Write the labels in the first row. Remember to give your table a title, too. Then you're ready to start recording data.

## Tally Charts

In some investigations, you will count how many times you see something or how many times something happens. A tally chart is an easy way to keep track of your count. A tally chart always has only three columns.

See Also
Making a Data Table page 62

Suppose you want to keep track of the different kinds of birds you see during one week.

Give your tally chart a title.

### Bird Sightings May 9–15, 2004

| Bird | Tally | Number of Birds |
|------|-------|-----------------|
| Robin | 卌 卌 ‖ | 12 |
| Crow | 卌 卌 ‖‖ | 14 |
| Chickadee | 卌 ‖ | 7 |
| Mourning dove | ‖ | 2 |
| Blue jay | 卌 | 5 |
| House sparrow | 卌 卌 ‖ | 12 |
| Cardinal | ‖‖ | 4 |

**3.** At the end of your observations, add up the tally marks for each kind of bird. Write the number in the third column.

A tally chart is really helpful when you're counting things that are happening quickly. By just making a tally mark each time, you don't have to keep track of numbers while you are observing.

**1.** In the first column, write the names of the kinds of birds you will count.

**2.** Every time you see one of those birds, make a tally mark in the second column. Instead of every fifth tally mark, draw a line through four marks. This will make it easy for you to count the marks by fives.

# Circle Graphs

A circle graph shows parts of a whole. The parts always add up to 100 percent. You can easily tell which part is biggest, which is next biggest, and so on, down to the smallest part. The sizes of the parts tell you.

The circle graph on this page tells about Earth's atmosphere. The atmosphere is made up of many gases. All the gases together make up 100 percent of the atmosphere. The graph shows how much of the atmosphere is made up of each gas.

The **atmosphere** (AT muh sfeer) is the air above Earth's surface.

The gas that makes up most of Earth's atmosphere is nitrogen. Oxygen is second. All the other gases add up to only 1 percent.

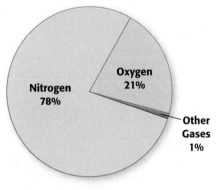

*Did You Know?*

The atmosphere of Mars is much different from Earth's atmosphere. Mars's atmosphere is 95 percent carbon dioxide gas, about 3 percent nitrogen, and less than 1 percent oxygen.

## Line Plots

A line plot lets you see how data are grouped. Suppose one night, you and your friends count meteors, or "shooting stars." You record each person's final count in a table.

How many meteors did most of you count? What was the largest number of meteors that anyone counted? What was the smallest number that anyone counted? You can easily show the answers to these questions by making a line plot.

| Name | Number of Meteors |
|------|-------------------|
| Josh | 6 |
| Edwinta | 4 |
| Carmen | 8 |
| Darryl | 5 |
| Ivan | 6 |
| Maria | 1 |
| Hideki | 6 |
| Sarah | 4 |
| Sally | 5 |

**1.** Draw a number line that includes all the numbers in the second column of the data table.

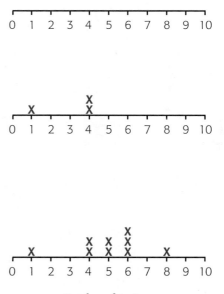

**2.** Draw an X for each friend's meteor count. For example, one friend saw one meteor. Draw an X above the number 1 on the line. Two friends saw four meteors. Draw two Xs above the number 4 on the line.

**3.** When you have finished drawing all the Xs, write a title for your line plot.

**Number of meteors**

# Bar Graphs

A **bar graph** shows the same kind of data for different things. Bar graphs are used to compare numbers. The numbers are shown by the lengths of the bars.

## Reading a Bar Graph

What is the tallest mountain on each of Earth's seven continents? How do the heights of those mountains compare? This bar graph tells you.

The title tells you what the graph is showing.

The up-and-down line at the left side of the graph is called the **vertical axis**. It has numbers next to it, from 0 to 10,000. The numbers tell you heights. The label for this axis tells you that the heights are in units of meters. Each mountain's height falls between two numbers. You have to estimate the mountain's height as close as you can.

The side-to-side line at the bottom of the graph is called the **horizontal axis**. The label for this axis tells you what is being measured. Each bar is labeled with the name of a different mountain.

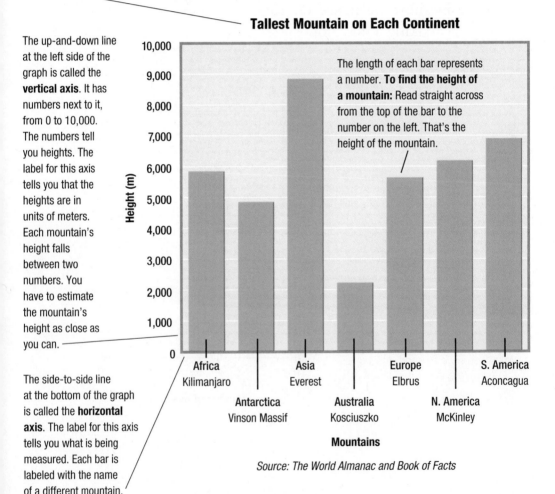

**Tallest Mountain on Each Continent**

The length of each bar represents a number. **To find the height of a mountain:** Read straight across from the top of the bar to the number on the left. That's the height of the mountain.

Africa — Kilimanjaro
Antarctica — Vinson Massif
Asia — Everest
Australia — Kosciuszko
Europe — Elbrus
N. America — McKinley
S. America — Aconcagua

**Mountains**

*Source: The World Almanac and Book of Facts*

Some bar graphs have horizontal bars. The things that are being measured are named on the vertical axis. Numbers are labeled on the horizontal axis. To find the length of an animal on this graph, read *down* from the end of the bar to the numbers at the bottom.

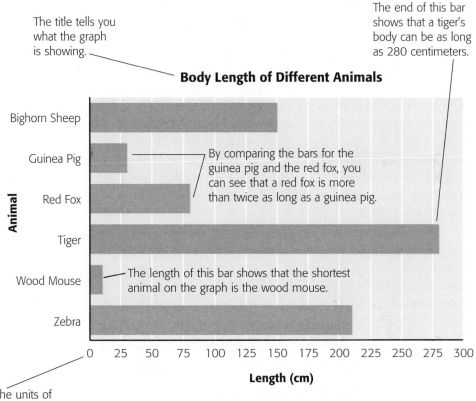

The title tells you what the graph is showing.

The end of this bar shows that a tiger's body can be as long as 280 centimeters.

**Body Length of Different Animals**

By comparing the bars for the guinea pig and the red fox, you can see that a red fox is more than twice as long as a guinea pig.

The length of this bar shows that the shortest animal on the graph is the wood mouse.

The units of length in this graph are centimeters.

*Source: The Simon & Schuster Encyclopedia of Animals*

*Did You Know?*

This graph gives the length of a wild guinea pig. Wild guinea pigs are bigger than the kind of guinea pigs that are sold as pets.

Keyword: Presenting Scientific Data
www.scilinks.org
Code: GSS45030

## Making a Bar Graph

Suppose you're going to give a science report on the amount of protein in different foods. You list the foods and their protein content in a data table like this one.

**Protein in Foods**

| Food | Protein (grams) |
|------|-----------------|
| American cheese (1 slice) | 7.1 |
| Banana (raw, large) | 2.4 |
| Beef (1 serving) | 24.7 |
| Broccoli (1 cup cooked) | 5.0 |
| Cabbage (1 cup cooked) | 2.4 |
| Egg (medium) | 6.1 |
| White rice (1 cup cooked) | 4.2 |

Source: Home Facts, World Book

To make a bar graph of the data in this table, follow these steps. As you read each step, look at the finished graph on the next page.

1. On a sheet of graph paper, draw the two axes. The **vertical axis** is the line at the left side of the graph. The **horizontal axis** is the line at the bottom of the graph.

2. In this graph, the vertical axis will show amounts of protein. The horizontal axis will name the foods. Label each axis to tell what it will show.

3. Choose the units that you will use for the vertical axis. The table lists protein in units of grams. The units you use for the graph also should be grams.

4. The vertical axis should start with 0 at the bottom. Decide what number will be at the top. The highest amount of protein listed in the table is 24.7 grams. So the top number on the vertical axis should be a little more than 24.7.

5. Decide what the value for each line on the vertical axis will be. Choose values that make sense for your data and are easy to read. Try multiples of 2, 5, and 10. Then write the numbers next to the vertical axis. This graph uses multiples of 2.

6. On the horizontal axis, write the names of the foods. Write each name where the food's bar will be. Leave space between the names so the bars won't touch each other.

7. Draw a bar to show the protein in each food. For example, 1 cup of cooked broccoli has 5.0 grams of protein. The top of the broccoli bar should line up with 5.0 on the vertical axis.

8. For each food, mark the top of the bar first. Then draw the lines for the sides of the bar. Draw the lines down to the horizontal axis.

9. You can shade in the bars or color them if you want to.

10. Don't forget to give your graph a title.

**Step 7**

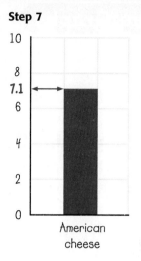

A slice of American cheese has 7.1 g of protein. The vertical axis doesn't have 7 labeled on it. But you know that 7 is halfway between 6 and 8. Mark the top of the American cheese bar so it is a little bit more than halfway between 6 and 8 on the vertical axis. You'll have to estimate like this for all the foods listed in the table.

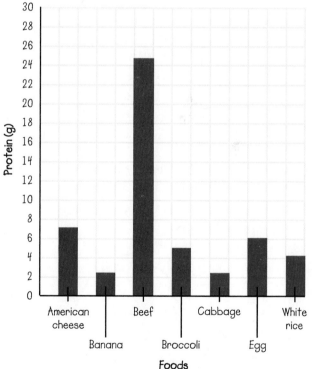

## Line Graphs

A **line graph** shows how data changed as time passed. The shape of the line tells you whether something increased, decreased, or stayed the same.

### Reading a Line Graph

How did the population of wolves in Wilderness Park change over time? You can see the changes if you read the numbers in this table. But with a line graph, you can see the pattern of changes at a glance.

The numbers on the vertical axis tell you how many wolves lived in Wilderness Park. The horizontal axis tells you the years. Each dot on the graph represents a number. **To find the number of wolves in any year:** Read straight across from the dot to the number on the left. That's the number of wolves in the park that year.

**Wolf Population in Wilderness Park**

| Year | Number of Wolves |
|------|------------------|
| 1998 | 90 |
| 1999 | 100 |
| 2000 | 110 |
| 2001 | 120 |
| 2002 | 125 |
| 2003 | 125 |
| 2004 | 105 |

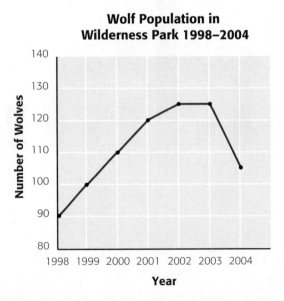

**Wolf Population in Wilderness Park 1998–2004**

The shape of the line shows these patterns.

- The wolf population increased from 1998 to 2002.
- The population stayed the same from 2002 to 2003.
- The population decreased from 2003 to 2004.

## Making a Line Graph

Suppose you measure the depth of snow that is falling in your neighborhood. You do this every 30 minutes until the snow stops. You organize your data in a table like this one.

When did the snow fall the fastest? To find the answer, you make a line graph of your data in a table. Follow the steps on the next two pages.

**Snowfall on My Street
December 20**

| Time | Snow Depth (cm) |
|---|---|
| 9:00 A.M. | 0 |
| 9:30 A.M. | 0.5 |
| 10:00 A.M. | 1.5 |
| 10:30 A.M. | 2.5 |
| 11:00 A.M. | 4.5 |
| 11:30 A.M. | 5.5 |
| 12:00 noon | 6.5 |
| 12:30 P.M. | 7.0 |
| 1:00 P.M. | 7.0 |

Keyword: Presenting Scientific Data
www.scilinks.org
Code: GSS45030

**Step 1**

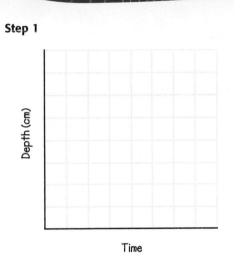

Time

**Steps 2 and 3**

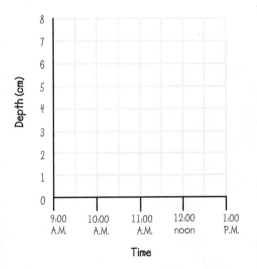

Time

1. On a sheet of graph paper, draw the two axes. The side-to-side line at the bottom of the graph is called the **horizontal axis.** The up-and-down line at the left side of the graph is called the **vertical axis.** The label for each axis tells what is shown on that axis. Time is usually shown on the horizontal axis. The quantity you are measuring, such as the depth of snow, is usually shown on the vertical axis. The label tells the units you are using for the measurements.

2. Decide what the value for each line on the vertical axis will be. Choose a range of values that will cover all the measurements you made. The vertical axis should start with 0 at the bottom. The deepest snow you measured was 7.0 cm. So the top number on the vertical axis should be a little more than 7.0 cm. In this graph, the lines on the vertical axis represent depths every 1.0 cm.

3. On the horizontal axis, write the times that you made the measurements. The times start at 9:00 A.M. and end at 1:00 P.M. On this graph, the lines on the horizontal axis are 30 minutes apart. To save space, only the full hours are labeled.

**Step 4**

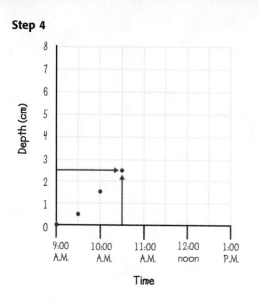

**Step 5**

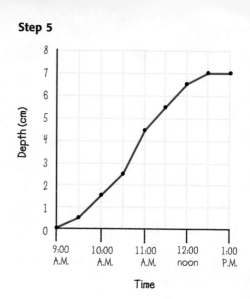

4. Locate and mark the dots on the graph. For each dot, read up from the time on the horizontal axis and left to right across from the depth on the vertical axis.

5. Draw a line to connect the dots.

6. Give your graph a title. The title should tell what the graph shows.

Your finished graph will look like this.

The steepest part of the graph's line is between 10:30 A.M. and 11:00 A.M. That's when the snow fell the fastest.

**Step 6**

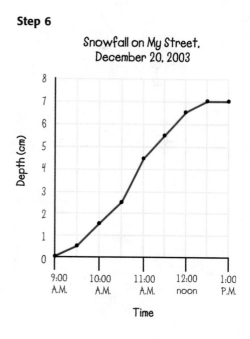

Snowfall on My Street, December 20, 2003

# Life Science

How are a butterfly, an elephant, and a cactus plant alike? This isn't a riddle, and the answer is easy. All three are living things. The study of plants, animals, and all other living things is called **life science.** Another word for life science is *biology.*

Sorry, DUDE—we can't let you be in the band.

WHAT?! But it's a *ROCK* band!

# Characteristics of Living Things

**A sponge made in a factory**

It's not always easy to tell the difference between a living thing and a nonliving thing. For example, the colored sponges sold in grocery stores were made in factories. Natural sponges are the remains of simple animals that used to be alive.

**A natural sponge**

A living thing is called an **organism** (OR guh niz um). All organisms share the same basic characteristics. Nonliving things do not have those characteristics.

## Organisms' Basic Needs

All organisms have basic needs. They need water and other nutrients. A **nutrient** (NOO tree unt) is a substance that an organism needs in order to survive and grow. Most organisms need oxygen and sunlight, too. Organisms also need space, shelter, and the right range of temperature.

## Adaptations

You take in oxygen by breathing air into your lungs. Fish take in oxygen through their gills. Lungs and gills are structures. A **structure** (STRUK chur) is a body part that does a certain "job" for an organism. The "job" that a structure does is called its **function** (FUNGK shun).

Structures that help organisms survive in their surroundings are called **adaptations** (ad ap TAY shunz). Lungs are an adaptation for living on land. Gills are an adaptation for living in water.

A behavior can be an adaptation, too. For example, some desert animals hide under rocks during the day to escape the sun's heat.

**WORD WATCH**

A **behavior** (bih HAYV yur) is something an organism does.

## Getting and Using Energy

All organisms carry out basic life processes. Life processes include moving, growing, and making more organisms of the same kind. All life processes require energy. Different kinds of organisms get energy in different ways.

See Also

Cell Respiration
pages 78–79

Photosynthesis
pages 80–81

Animals get energy from nutrients in the food they eat.

Plants get energy from sunlight. They use the energy to make their own food.

Mushrooms absorb nutrients from their surroundings. They get energy from these nutrients.

Keyword: Behaviors and Adaptations
www.scilinks.org
Code: GSS45035

## Cell Respiration

Animals take in food and oxygen. Their bodies break the food down into nutrients. Nutrients and oxygen travel to every cell in the body. The nutrients are used to make new cells, repair damaged cells, and create other materials that the animal's body needs.

One important nutrient is a kind of sugar called glucose (GLOO kohs). Inside each body cell, glucose is combined with oxygen. This releases energy. The process of releasing energy from nutrients is called **cell respiration** (res puh RAY shun).

Cell respiration also produces wastes that the cell gets rid of. The wastes are water and carbon dioxide.

This diagram shows what happens during cell respiration.

See Also

Cells page 99

Animal Cell
pages 100–101

The Oxygen and
Carbon Dioxide
Cycle page 132

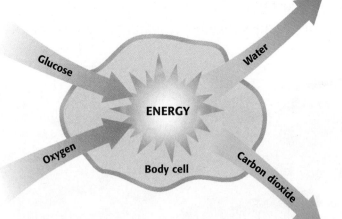

Glucose

Water

**ENERGY**

Oxygen

Body cell

Carbon dioxide

### Getting Oxygen for Cell Respiration

Many land animals get oxygen by breathing air into their lungs, like you do. But not all animals get oxygen this way. Different animals have different structures for getting oxygen.

Adaptations page 77

Fish and many other water animals have gills. Water passes through the gills. The water has oxygen in it. The gills remove oxygen from the water.

Earthworms take in oxygen through their skin. The skin is so thin that oxygen can pass right through it.

Grasshoppers and some other insects have small holes on the sides of their bodies. Oxygen passes through these holes and spreads out inside the insect's body.

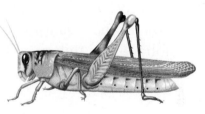

Adult frogs have lungs that remove oxygen from the air around them. Frogs also take in some oxygen through their skin. Before tadpoles develop into frogs, they have gills for getting oxygen from the water around them.

Frog Life Cycle page 85

Cell Respiration
pages 78–79

Cells page 99

Plant Cell
pages 102–103

The Oxygen and
Carbon Dioxide
Cycle page 132

Producers
page 133

## Photosynthesis

Like animals, plants carry out cell respiration to get energy from food. But unlike animals, plants make their own food.

Inside each leaf cell are tiny green structures called **chloroplasts** (KLOR uh plasts). The green color comes from a substance called **chlorophyll** (KLOR uh fil). Chlorophyll captures the energy in sunlight.

> Photosynthesis also produces oxygen. The plant uses some of the oxygen for cell respiration. It gets rid of the "extra" oxygen as waste.

The plant's roots take in water from the soil. Water travels to the plant's leaves. The leaves take in carbon dioxide from the air. The chloroplasts use the sun's energy captured by chlorophyll to combine water and carbon dioxide. This produces a kind of sugar called **glucose** (GLOO kohs). Glucose is the plant's food.

The process of using the energy in sunlight to produce food for the organism is called **photosynthesis** (foh toh SIN thih sis). This diagram shows what happens in photosynthesis.

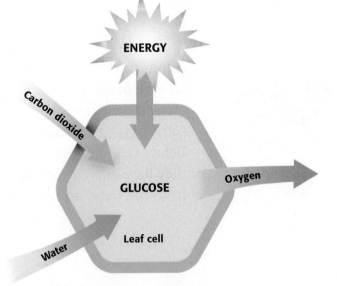

ENERGY

Carbon dioxide

GLUCOSE

Oxygen

Leaf cell

Water

**Moving Materials Inside the Plant** Leaves need water to carry out photosynthesis. Water moves from the plant's roots up the stem to the leaves. During photosynthesis, the leaves make food for the plant. Food moves from the leaves to all parts of the plant. How do these movements happen?

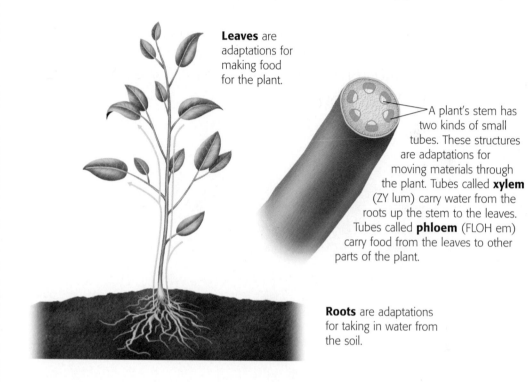

**Leaves** are adaptations for making food for the plant.

A plant's stem has two kinds of small tubes. These structures are adaptations for moving materials through the plant. Tubes called **xylem** (ZY lum) carry water from the roots up the stem to the leaves. Tubes called **phloem** (FLOH em) carry food from the leaves to other parts of the plant.

**Roots** are adaptations for taking in water from the soil.

During the growing season, plants make a lot of food. They use the food to carry out their life processes. Sometimes they make more food than they need right away. They store the extra food in their roots and stems.

*Did You Know?*

Potatoes are underground stems that store food. Carrots, beets, and radishes are roots that store food.

# Reproduction

See Also

Animal Life
Cycles
pages 84–85

Plant Life Cycles
pages 86–87

Mammals
page 151

Birds page 152

Reptiles
page 153

Amphibians
page 154

Fish page 155

Every kind of organism makes more organisms of the same kind. Making more organisms of the same kind is called **reproduction** (ree pruh DUHK shuhn). The new organisms are called **offspring.**

Some animals give birth to live offspring. Dogs, horses, elephants, human beings, and most other mammals reproduce this way. Some fish and some snakes give birth to live offspring, too.

Some animals hatch from eggs.

Birds lay eggs with hard shells.

Turtles, alligators, and many other reptiles lay eggs with soft, leathery shells.

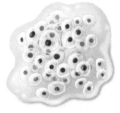

Frogs, toads, and other amphibians lay jellylike eggs that do not have shells.

Many one-celled organisms reproduce by dividing in half.

Many kinds of plants grow from seeds. Sometimes the seeds are hidden inside a shell, a pod, a fruit, or other structure.

**Offspring Look Like Their Parents** Offspring inherit certain traits from their parents. An **inherited trait** is a characteristic that is passed from parents to offspring. For example, a baby elephant inherits the traits of four sturdy legs, two big floppy ears, and a long trunk from its parents.

# Growth and Development

There are two ways that organisms change as they develop into adults. They grow larger, or they change form.

**Growing Larger** Some organisms start out small and grow larger.

You started out small. Maybe you weighed 7 or 8 pounds. You might have been about 20 inches long.

Today you weigh much more and are much taller. You grew larger. And you will keep growing larger until you are an adult.

Plants start out small and grow larger, too. Some plants never stop growing until they die.

**Changing Form** Other organisms start out in one form and change to another form.

A moth starts out as a caterpillar.

The caterpillar changes into an adult moth.

See Also

Butterfly Life Cycle page 84

Frog Life Cycle page 85

## Science Alert!

Some things that grow larger are not alive. Have you ever seen ice crystals grow on a window in winter? Crystals grow, but they are not alive.

## Animal Life Cycles

Growth and
Development
page 83

Animals go through different stages during their lives. They are born, they grow, they develop into adults, and they reproduce. **Reproduce** means making more animals of the same kind. The stages of growth and development that an animal goes through in its life are called its **life cycle.**

Different kinds of animals have different life cycles. Many kinds of animals look very much like their parents when they are born. Other kinds of animals start out in one form and change to another form as they develop.

See Also

Animals With
an Exoskeleton
page 148

**Butterfly Life Cycle**  Butterflies and some other insects change form at each stage of their life cycle. The changes in form are called **metamorphosis** (met uh MOR fuh sis). During metamorphosis, a butterfly goes through four stages.

**1. Egg**  A female butterfly lays hundreds of eggs.

**2. Larva**  A small wormlike caterpillar hatches from each egg. The caterpillar eats leaves and grows larger.

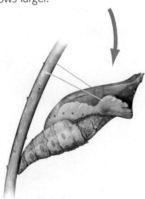

**4. Adult**  A butterfly breaks out of the case. It doesn't look anything like the caterpillar.

**3. Pupa**  A hard case forms around the caterpillar. Inside the case, the caterpillar changes shape and develops new body parts.

**Frog Life Cycle** Frogs, toads, and salamanders are amphibians. An **amphibian** (am FIB ee un) is an animal that typically lives in water when it is young and lives on land when it is an adult.

Like butterflies, frogs go through metamorphosis during their life cycle. But unlike butterflies, frogs don't change form all at once. Instead, they change form slowly as they develop. And a developing frog isn't hidden inside a hard case. You can see the changes as they happen.

See Also

Adaptations
page 77

Amphibians
page 154

**1. Egg** A female frog lays hundreds of eggs.

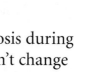

**6. Adult frog** The young frog grows larger until it is a full-size adult.

**2. Tadpole with gills** A tiny tadpole hatches from each egg. The tadpole has a tail for swimming. It also has gills for taking oxygen out of the water. A tail and gills are adaptations for living in water.

**5. Young frog** The young frog has four legs and no tail.

**3. Tadpole with hind legs** The tadpole grows hind legs. Inside its body, lungs start to develop. Legs and lungs are adaptations for living on land.

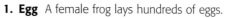

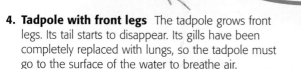

**4. Tadpole with front legs** The tadpole grows front legs. Its tail starts to disappear. Its gills have been completely replaced with lungs, so the tadpole must go to the surface of the water to breathe air.

**See Also**

Photosynthesis
pages 80–81

Reproduction
page 82

## Plant Life Cycles

Different kinds of plants have different life cycles. Some plants, such as apple trees, produce flowers as part of their life cycle. Other plants, such as pine trees, produce cones.

Flowers and cones contain seeds. A **seed** contains the beginnings of a young plant and a supply of food for the plant. This diagram shows the life cycle of a plant that reproduces with seeds.

**3.** The roots grow deeper, and the stem grows taller. The young plant develops leaves. Now the plant can start making its own food.

**2.** The root grows longer and starts to branch out. A stem sprouts from the top of the seed and pushes above the soil. The stem is an adaptation for carrying water from the roots to the leaves that will develop later.

**1.** The seed sends out a root that grows down into the soil. The root is an adaptation for taking in water from the soil.

Mosses and ferns do not grow from seeds. They grow from spores. **Spores** are structures that produce new plants.

**Flowering Plants** Flowers come in many different shapes, sizes, and colors, but they all have the same function. They help plants reproduce. Flowers are the parts of a plant where seeds are made. And seeds produce new plants.

**Stamens** are the male parts of a flower.

Stamens produce a powdery material called **pollen.** Pollen contains sperm cells. Sperm cells are male cells.

A long tube called a **pistil** grows up from the ovary.

A flower's colorful, sweet-smelling **petals** attract insects.

The **ovary** is the female part of a flower. Egg cells develop in the ovary. Egg cells are female cells.

When an insect visits the flower, it rubs against the top of the stamens. Pollen sticks to the insect. As the insect explores the flower, some of the pollen on the insect's body rubs off onto the pistil. The transfer of pollen from the stamens to the pistil is called **pollination** (pahl uh NAY shun). Male cells in the pollen burrow down into the ovary and join with egg cells there. The joining of egg cells and sperm cells is called **fertilization** (fur tl ih ZAY shun). The fertilized egg develops into a seed.

# Movement

See Also

Plant Behavior
pages 96–97

All organisms move in some way. Even plants move. They
bend toward light. Flower buds slowly open. And some
kinds of plants have flowers that open in the morning and
close at night.

Some animals don't seem to move at all. For example,
clams don't walk around! But they do open and close their
shells. And in one stage of their life cycle, clams swim
around in the water.

See Also

Adaptations
page 77

Different organisms use different kinds of structures to
move from one place to another. Many animals have legs.
Legs of different shapes and sizes are adapted for different
kinds of movement.

**Kangaroo**

**Cheetah**

**Tarantula**

**Koala**

Bats, some insects, and birds have wings for flying. Wings let animals move from one place to another very quickly.

Fish, alligators, and crocodiles swim by moving their tails from side to side in the water. Whales, porpoises, and dolphins swim by moving their tails up and down.

Mammals page 151

Birds page 152

Reptiles page 153

Amphibians page 154

Fish page 155

A squid moves by squirting water out of its head end. This makes the squid move backwards.

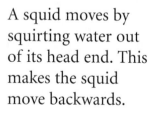 

# Sensing the Environment

To survive, animals must know what is happening in their environment. They get this information by using sense organs, such as eyes and ears. **Sense organs** are body structures that take in information from the environment. They send the information to the brain, and the brain figures out what the information means.

Adaptations
page 77

Nervous System
pages 124–125

Many animals have the same kinds of sense organs that you do.

Hawks fly slowly high above the ground. They use their eyes to spot small animals they can catch and eat.

A rabbit uses its eyes to watch out for hunting hawks.

Other animals have sense organs that you do not have.

Grasshoppers and other insects have two long structures called *antennae* (an TEN ee) on their heads. They use their antennae to feel and smell things in their environment.

A snake's tongue senses chemicals in the air. The snake can tell what is near it by "tasting" the air.

# Responding to the Environment

Organisms sense changes in their environment. They respond to those changes by doing something.

**See Also**

Hibernation
page 93

Migration
page 94

**The Outer Environment** Organisms respond to changes in the weather, the seasons, and the climate. When the seasons change from summer to fall, days grow shorter. Trees respond to this change. Their leaves turn color, die, and fall off. Some animals respond to the colder season by moving someplace where they can find more food.

Organisms also respond to other organisms in their environment. They compete with each other for food, water, and space. Animals compete for mates and for good places to raise their young. Some animals hunt and kill other animals for food. The other animals respond by hiding or running away or fighting back.

Plants compete for water, space, and light. If many trees start to grow close together, some will grow taller. The taller trees will shade the shorter trees. Over time, only the tallest trees will get enough light, and the shorter trees will die.

**The Inner Environment** Organisms respond to changes inside them. When an animal feels thirsty or hungry, it searches for water or food. When it feels tired, it sleeps. Animals also respond to germs that enter their bodies. Specialized blood cells attack and kill the germs. This protects the animals against disease.

# Animal and Plant Behavior

See Also

Adaptations
page 77

A **behavior** is something that an organism does. For example, some kinds of birds fly south when days become shorter in the fall. That is an animal behavior. Plant stems grow up and roots grow down. Those are plant behaviors. Many behaviors are adaptations that help organisms survive.

You can also think of a behavior as a response to a change in the organism's environment. Something that makes an organism act in a certain way is called a **stimulus** (STIM yuh lus). What the organism does when it senses the stimulus is called a **response.**

A pat on the head is a stimulus.
A wagging tail is a response.

# Animal Behavior

Some animal behaviors are instinctive (in STINGK tiv). An **instinctive behavior** is a behavior that an animal inherits from its parents. The animal is born with the behavior. For example, a newborn colt struggles to its feet, stands, and walks. The colt is very wobbly, but it doesn't have to be taught to stand and walk.

Later, the colt may learn to wear a saddle and bridle and carry someone on its back. These are learned behaviors. A **learned behavior** is a behavior that an animal develops by observing other animals or by being taught.

Some behaviors are a combination of instinct and learning. For example, young cheetahs have the instinct to hunt. At first, they don't know how to sneak up on another animal. But they watch their mother when she hunts. They imitate her, and they practice their hunting skills. Over time, they become successful hunters.

## Hibernation

Some kinds of animals survive through the cold winter by hibernating. **Hibernation** (hy bur NAY shun) is a deep sleeplike state when an animal's body processes slow down. The animal's body temperature drops, and its breathing and heart rate become very slow. Hibernating is an instinctive behavior. It is an adaptation that helps animals survive freezing weather when food is scarce. Animals that hibernate include ground squirrels, woodchucks, and some kinds of bats.

## Migration

Some kinds of animals move from one place to another when seasons change. They travel from places where it is difficult for them to survive to places where it is easier to survive. When seasons change again, the animals move back to the first place. This pattern continues year after year.

The seasonal movement of animals from one place to another is called **migration** (my GRAY shun). Migration is an instinctive behavior. It is an adaptation that helps animals survive. Animals that migrate include sea turtles, bats, whales, monarch butterflies, and many kinds of birds. Some animals migrate thousands of miles each year.

As winter approaches, monarch butterflies migrate from North America to Mexico and Central America. In spring, the butterflies return to North America.

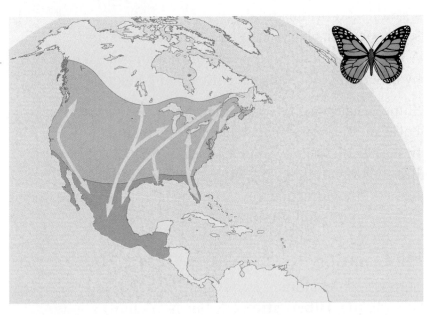

## Hunting

Hunting is a combination of instinctive behavior and learned behavior. Some animals, such as rattlesnakes, hunt alone. Others animals, such as wolves, hunt in groups. Animals that hunt in groups have to cooperate to catch and kill large animals.

## Protecting Young

Many kinds of animals
protect their young.
A mother bear will
attack anyone who gets
too close to her cubs.
Some animals that live
in herds will form a
circle around their young if a hunting animal approaches.
Birds will chase other animals away from their nests.
Protecting young is an instinctive behavior.

## Using Tools

Some animals use tools. For example, chimpanzees use
twigs to "fish" for termites. First the chimp strips leaves off
the twig. Then it pokes the twig into a hole in the termite
nest. When it pulls the branch out, termites are holding on
to it. The chimp eats the termites. Then it uses the twig
again to "fish" for more termites. Using a twig to get
termites is a learned behavior. Young chimps learn how to
do it by watching their mothers and other adult chimps.

## Plant Behavior

All plant behaviors are inherited. After all, plants can't learn! But plants do respond to a stimulus in their environment. They respond to light and gravity. Some plants respond to touch. A plant's response to a stimulus is called a **tropism** (TROH piz um).

Photosynthesis
pages 80–81

## WORD WATCH

The word *tropism* comes from the Greek word *trope,* which means "turning."

### Responding to Light

If you put a houseplant near a window, its leaves will turn toward the sunlight. This behavior is called *phototropism.* Phototropism is an adaptation that helps plants survive. Plants use the energy in sunlight to make their own food. And leaves are where the food is made. So when leaves turn toward light, they collect more energy to make food.

## Responding to Gravity

A plant can sense the pull of gravity. Its roots grow downward, toward the pull of gravity. Its stems grow upward, away from the pull of gravity. These responses are called *geotropisms*. Roots growing downward let the plant get water and nutrients from the soil. Stems growing upward raise the leaves into sunlight so they can make food for the plant.

## Responding to Moisture

Plants need water to survive. A plant's roots will grow towards moisture in the soil. If a pond or stream is nearby, the roots will grow toward the water. This response is called *hydrotropism*.

## Responding to Touch

Climbing vines respond to touch. The vine can sense contact with a wall, a tree, a fence, a trellis, or other support. The vine grabs on to the support and grows upward on it. This response to touch is called *thigmotropism*.

# Cells, Tissues, Organs, and Systems

A living thing is an **organism** (OR guh niz um). Many kinds of organisms have a body with different parts. A body part that does a certain "job" for an organism is called a **structure** (STRUK chur). The "job" that a structure does is called its **function** (FUNGK shun).

Small body parts are grouped together to form larger parts. Larger parts are grouped together to form systems. The parts and systems work together so the organism can survive, grow, and make new organisms of the same kind.

# Cells

All organisms are made of cells. A **cell** is the smallest living part of an organism. Some kinds of organisms, such as bacteria, are made of only one cell. That single cell is the organism's entire body. Many other kinds of organisms, including elephants, trees, and people, are made of trillions of cells.

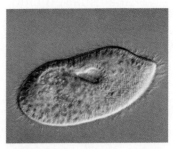

**Paramecium**

The body of a many-celled organism is made of different kinds of cells. For example, many animals have bone cells, nerve cells, muscle cells, and blood cells. Plants have leaf cells and root cells.

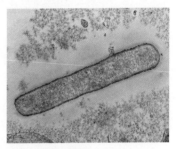

**Anthrax bacterium**

Each kind of cell in an organism performs a different function. For example, nerve cells carry messages to and from your brain. Muscle cells make parts of your body move. Blood cells carry oxygen to all your other cells. A plant's leaf cells make food for the plant.

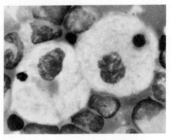

**Human bone marrow cells**

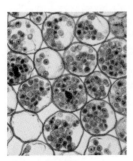

**Plant root cells**

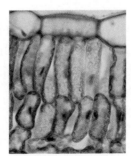

**Plant leaf cells**

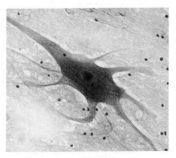

**Human nerve cell**

## Animal Cell

Plant Cell
pages 102–103

All animals, including humans, are made of different kinds of cells. This drawing shows a typical animal cell and the structures inside it. Each structure carries out a different function in the cell.

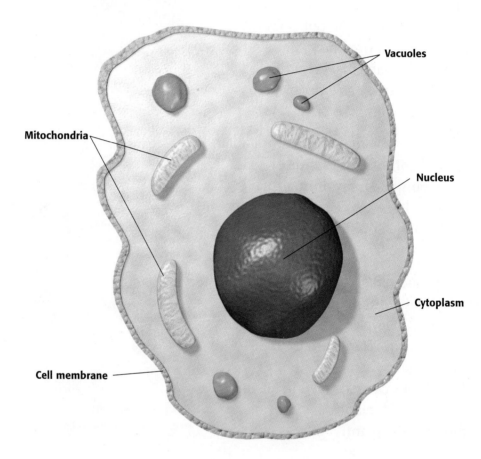

**Cell Membrane** A soft, flexible **cell membrane** surrounds the cell. It controls the movement of substances into and out of the cell. Water and other materials enter the cell, and wastes leave the cell.

Keyword: Animal / Plant Cells
www.scilinks.org
Code: GSS45040

**Cytoplasm** **Cytoplasm** (SY tuh plaz um) is a jellylike "soup" that fills most of the cell. Other cell structures float in the cytoplasm.

**Nucleus** The **nucleus** (NOO klee us) controls everything that the cell does. The nucleus "tells" the other cell structures how and when to carry out their functions. It also controls how and when the cell divides to make new cells.

Not all animal cells have all of the structures shown in the drawing. For example, red blood cells do not have mitochondria or a nucleus.

**Vacuoles** **Vacuoles** (VAK yoo ohlz) are storage spaces in the cell. They store water and nutrients until other cell structures need them. Some vacuoles store wastes until the cell can get rid of them.

**Mitochondria** **Mitochondria** (my tuh KAHN dree uh) are the "powerhouses" of the cell. They combine oxygen with the nutrients in food. This releases energy. The cell uses the energy to carry out all its activities.

Cell Respiration pages 78–79

## Plant Cell

Animal Cell
pages 100–101

All plants are made of different kinds of cells. This drawing shows a typical plant cell and the structures inside it. Plant cells have the same structures as animal cells. But plant cells also have two other structures. They are chloroplasts and a cell wall. Animal cells do not have those structures.

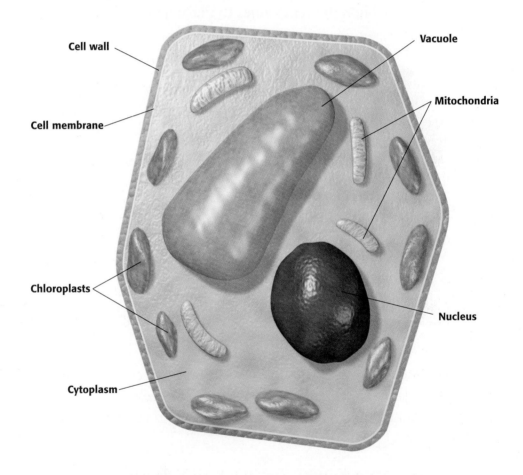

Cell wall

Vacuole

Cell membrane

Mitochondria

Chloroplasts

Nucleus

Cytoplasm

**Cell Wall** A rigid **cell wall** is the outer covering of a plant cell. It is made of a stiff material that gives plant cells a boxy shape.

Keyword: Animal / Plant Cells
www.scilinks.org
Code: GSS45040

**Chloroplasts** **Chloroplasts** (KLOR uh plasts) make food for the plant. They hold a green substance called **chlorophyll** (KLOR uh fil). Chlorophyll captures the energy in sunlight. Chloroplasts use this energy to combine carbon dioxide and water. This produces a kind of sugar called **glucose** (GLOO kohs). Glucose is the plant's food.

See
Also

Photosynthesis
pages 80–81

**Cell Membrane** The **cell membrane** surrounds the cell. It controls the movement of substances into and out of the cell. Water and other materials enter the cell, and wastes leave the cell.

**Cytoplasm** **Cytoplasm** (SY tuh plaz um) is a jellylike "soup" that fills most of the cell. Other cell structures float in the cytoplasm.

**Nucleus** The **nucleus** (NOO klee us) controls everything that the cell does. The nucleus "tells" the other cell structures how and when to carry out their functions. It also controls how and when the cell divides to make new cells.

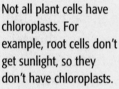

Not all plant cells have chloroplasts. For example, root cells don't get sunlight, so they don't have chloroplasts.

**Vacuoles** **Vacuoles** (VAK yoo ohlz) are storage spaces in the cell. They store water and nutrients until other cell structures need them. Some vacuoles store wastes until the cell can get rid of them.

**Mitochondria** **Mitochondria** (my tuh KAHN dree uh) are the "powerhouses" of the cell. They combine oxygen with glucose. This releases energy. The cell uses the energy to carry out all its activities.

See
Also

Cell Respiration
pages 78–79

## Tissues

A **tissue** (TISH oo) is a group of cells that work together to perform a certain function. In animals, for example, muscle cells are grouped together to form muscle tissue. In plants, certain cells are grouped together to form bark tissue. Different kinds of tissue perform different functions.

### Animal Tissues

The bodies of most animals are made of different kinds of tissues. Here are some examples.

See Also

Muscular System
pages 114–115

**Muscle Tissue**  Muscle tissue is made of many muscle cells. Muscle cells can **contract,** or get shorter. When all the cells contract at the same time, the whole tissue becomes shorter. When the cells relax, the whole tissue becomes longer again.

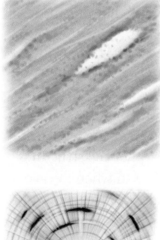

See Also

Skeletal System
pages 112–113

**Bone Tissue**  Bone tissue forms the bones in an animal's skeleton. The skeleton gives the animal its shape. When muscles pull on bones, the bones move.

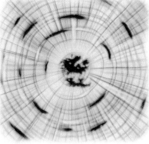

**Blood** Blood is a tissue. It contains blood cells floating in a liquid. Some blood cells carry oxygen to all parts of your body. Other blood cells fight germs that cause disease. The liquid part of your blood carries water and other materials to all the cells in your body. The liquid part also carries wastes away from your body cells.

*See Also*

Circulatory System
pages 122–123

## Plant Tissues

Plants have different kinds of tissues. Here are some examples.

**Bark** The outside of a tree or other woody plant is covered with bark. Bark helps keep water inside the plant. Bark also protects the plant against insects and diseases.

**Tubes** Some plant cells are grouped together to form tubes. One kind of tube carries water from the plant's roots to the leaves. Another kind of tube carries food from the leaves to the other parts of the plant.

*See Also*

Moving Materials Inside the Plant
page 81

## Organs

Different kinds of tissues are grouped together to form an organ. Each organ performs a different function.

### Animal Organs

Simple animals, such as earthworms and insects, have only a few simple organs. Complex animals have more kinds of organs. Here are some examples of organs that people, horses, cows, and other complex animals have.

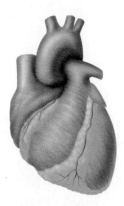

**Heart** Your heart is made mostly of muscle tissue and nerve tissue. These tissues work together to pump blood throughout your body.

**Lungs** Lungs contain tissues that form a kind of bag, tubes, tiny sacs, and blood vessels. These tissues work together to take in oxygen from the air you breathe. They also release waste gases into the air.

**Stomach** Tissues in the lining of the stomach produce chemicals that break food down. Muscle tissue in the stomach contracts and relaxes to mix the chemicals with the food.

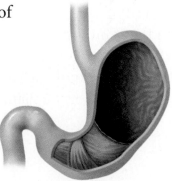

## Plant Organs

Like animal organs, plant organs are made of different kinds of tissues. You are probably most familiar with plants that have roots, stems, and leaves. Roots, stems, and leaves are plant organs. Simple plants, such as mosses, do not have these plant organs.

Photosynthesis
pages 80–81

**Leaves** The main function of these organs is to make food for the plant. Leaves also have tissues that give them their shape. Some leaf tissue forms a waxy material that coats the leaves. The waxy coat keeps leaves from losing water and drying up.

**Stems** Firm tissues in these organs hold the leaves up to the sunlight. Some tissues help move water and other materials from the roots to the leaves. Other tissues move food from the leaves to other parts of the plant.

**Roots** Roots are organs that carry out three functions for a plant. They take in water and other materials from the soil. They hold the plant in the soil. And they store extra food that the plant doesn't need right away. A different kind of tissue performs each function.

## Organ Systems

Different organs work together to form an **organ system.**
Different systems carry out different functions. For
example, a plant's roots, stems, and leaves work together to
make, transport, and store food for the plant.

Digestive System
pages 116–117

Circulatory
System pages
122–123

### Animal Systems

Different animals have different kinds of organ systems. Two
systems in complex animals are the digestive (dy JES tiv)
system and the circulatory (SUR kyuh luh tor ee) system.

**Digestive System**  The digestive system breaks food down
into simple materials that the animal's body can use. The
main organs in this
system are the
mouth, stomach,
small intestine,
large intestine, liver,
and pancreas.

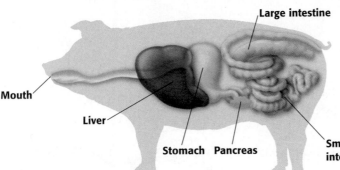

Large intestine

Mouth

Liver

Stomach  Pancreas

Small
intestine

**Circulatory System**  The circulatory system moves blood
throughout the animal's body. The organs in this system
are the heart and
blood vessels.
The heart pumps
blood through the
blood vessels.

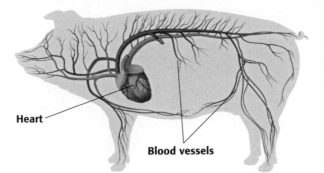

Heart

Blood vessels

## Systems Work Together

All the systems in an animal's body work together to keep the animal alive and healthy. Here is one example of how different organ systems work together.

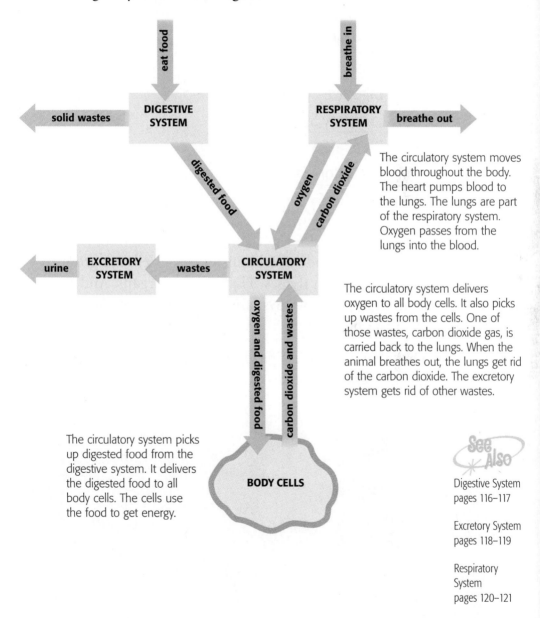

eat food

breathe in

solid wastes · **DIGESTIVE SYSTEM**

**RESPIRATORY SYSTEM** · breathe out

digested food

oxygen

carbon dioxide

The circulatory system moves blood throughout the body. The heart pumps blood to the lungs. The lungs are part of the respiratory system. Oxygen passes from the lungs into the blood.

urine · **EXCRETORY SYSTEM** · wastes · **CIRCULATORY SYSTEM**

oxygen and digested food

carbon dioxide and wastes

The circulatory system delivers oxygen to all body cells. It also picks up wastes from the cells. One of those wastes, carbon dioxide gas, is carried back to the lungs. When the animal breathes out, the lungs get rid of the carbon dioxide. The excretory system gets rid of other wastes.

The circulatory system picks up digested food from the digestive system. It delivers the digested food to all body cells. The cells use the food to get energy.

**BODY CELLS**

See Also

Digestive System
pages 116–117

Excretory System
pages 118–119

Respiratory
System
pages 120–121

Circulatory
System
pages 122–123

# Human Body Systems

Your body is made of trillions of cells. Cells are grouped together to form tissues. Tissues form organs. And organs form organ systems. Systems work together to keep you alive and healthy.

The table on the next page tells you what each system does. It also identifies the main organs in each system.

## Your Body's Systems

See Also

Systems Work Together page 109

| System | Main Organs | Functions |
|---|---|---|
| Skeletal system | bones | • Supports your body and gives it shape<br>• Protects your internal organs<br>• Helps you move<br>• Stores substances<br>• Makes blood cells |
| Muscular system | muscles | • Moves your body parts<br>• Moves food through your digestive system<br>• Pumps blood through your circulatory system<br>• Makes you breathe |
| Digestive system | mouth, esophagus, stomach, small intestine, liver, gall bladder, pancreas, large intestine, rectum, anus | • Breaks down food into simple substances that your cells can use<br>• Gets rid of solid wastes from digestion |
| Excretory system | kidneys, ureters, bladder, urethra, skin, lungs | • Removes liquid wastes and waste gases |
| Respiratory system | mouth, nose, trachea, bronchi, lungs | • Takes in oxygen from the air you breathe<br>• Gets rid of waste gases (carbon dioxide and water vapor) |
| Circulatory system | heart, arteries, veins, capillaries | • Moves blood throughout your body<br>• Delivers nutrients and oxygen to all cells<br>• Removes carbon dioxide and wastes from cells<br>• Helps fight disease |
| Nervous system organs | brain, spinal cord, nerves, sense organs | • Controls all other systems in your body<br>• Receives information about your environment<br>• Stores memories<br>• Allows you to think |

## Skeletal System

Muscular System
pages 113–114

Your body has two organ systems that work together to help you move. They are the skeletal system and the muscular system. The **skeletal system** is made of bones and cartilage. **Cartilage** (KAR tl ij) is a strong tissue that is more flexible than bone. Bones and cartilage make up the framework of your body.

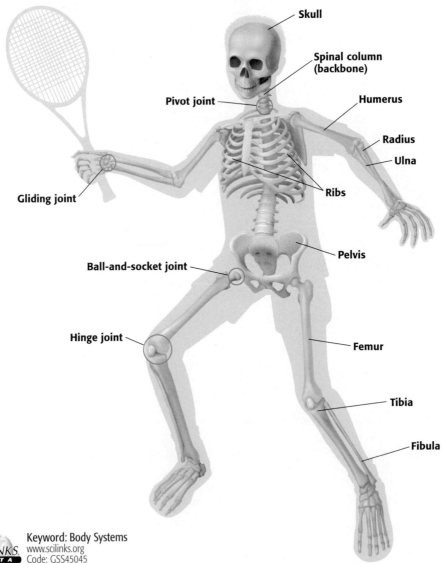

## Functions of the Skeletal System

Your skeletal system performs five important functions.

- It supports your body and gives it its shape.
- It protects your internal organs. For example, your skull protects your brain.
- It allows you to move when muscles pull on bones.
- It stores substances such as calcium.
- It makes red blood cells that carry oxygen and white blood cells that fight germs.

## Types of Joints

Two or more bones meet at a **joint.** Different kinds of joints allow different kinds of movement. For example, your shoulder joint lets you move your arm in a large circle. Your elbow joint lets you move your lower arm toward and away from your upper arm.

The bones of some joints are not moveable. For example, the bones that make up your skull are joined tightly together and do not move.

This table shows the four kinds of moveable joints.

| Kind of Joint | Where It's Found | How the Bones Move |
|---|---|---|
| Pivot joint | neck | The bones rotate around each other. |
| Gliding joint | wrist, ankle | The bones slide over each other. |
| Hinge joint | knee, elbow | The bones move back and forth like a door hinge. |
| Ball-and-socket joint | shoulder, hip | The bones move in a circle. |

## Muscular System

Your **muscular system** is made of muscles that cause parts of your body to move. Muscles move your bones. They make your heart beat. They make you breathe. They even make the pupils of your eyes become larger or smaller.

Muscles in your tongue help you speak.

Muscles in your heart pump blood through your body.

Muscles in your stomach mix food and move it along.

Muscles in your legs allow you to walk, jump, and run.

Keyword: Body Systems
www.scilinks.org
Code: GSS45045

## Functions of the Muscular System

There are three kinds of muscles in your body. Each kind has different functions.

**Skeletal muscles** move bones. For example, when you kick a soccer ball, skeletal muscles pull on the bones in your lower leg. You can control your skeletal muscles.

**Heart muscles** make your heart beat and pump blood through your body. You cannot control your heart muscles. Your heat beats automatically without your thinking about it.

**Smooth muscles** are found in many of your organs. For example, smooth muscles move food through your digestive system. They also let you breathe, cough, and sneeze. Smooth muscles work automatically, but you can control some of them. For example, you can cough on purpose if you want to.

See Also

Skeletal System
pages 112–113

Circulatory
System
pages 122–123

Respiratory
System
pages 120–121

## Some Muscles Work in Pairs

Many skeletal muscles work in pairs. When one muscle in the pair contracts, or shortens, the other muscle relaxes.

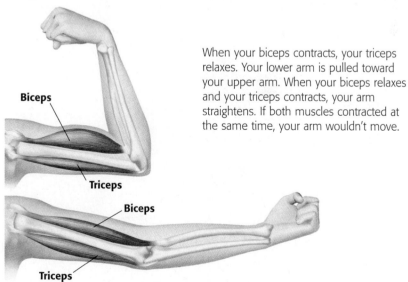

**Biceps**

**Triceps**

**Biceps**

**Triceps**

When your biceps contracts, your triceps relaxes. Your lower arm is pulled toward your upper arm. When your biceps relaxes and your triceps contracts, your arm straightens. If both muscles contracted at the same time, your arm wouldn't move.

## Digestive System

*See Also*

Cell Respiration
pages 78–79

Before your body can use the food you eat, the food has to be broken down into nutrients. A **nutrient** (NOO tree unt) is a substance that an organism needs in order to survive and grow. Breaking food down into nutrients is the function of your **digestive system.**

The digestive system breaks down food in two ways. First it grinds the food and mashes it into tiny pieces. Then it mixes the food with digestive juices. The digestive juices break the food down into nutrients.

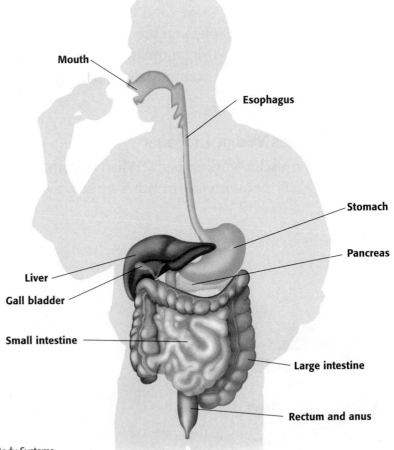

Mouth

Esophagus

Stomach

Pancreas

Liver

Gall bladder

Small intestine

Large intestine

Rectum and anus

# Organs in the Digestive System

**Mouth** Digestion begins in your mouth. Your teeth grind up food into smaller pieces. Your tongue moves the pieces around to mix them with saliva (suh LY vuh). Saliva contains a digestive juice that starts breaking down some materials in the food.

**Esophagus** When you swallow, food travels through your esophagus (ih SAHF uh gus) to your stomach.

**Stomach** Muscles in your stomach churn the food and mix it with more digestive juices. The partly digested food moves from your stomach to your small intestine.

**Liver and Gall Bladder** Your liver makes a digestive juice called bile. The bile is stored in your gall bladder. Bile passes through a tube into your small intestine.

**Pancreas** Your pancreas (PANG kree us) makes other kinds of digestive juices. They pass through a tube into your small intestine.

**Small Intestine** Here, digestive juices from your liver and pancreas finish digesting the food. Nutrients from the digested food move into your blood. Undigested materials move into your large intestine.

**Large Intestine** Your large intestine removes water from the undigested material. The water passes into your blood. The solid wastes move into your rectum.

**Rectum and Anus** Your rectum stores solid wastes until you are ready to get rid of them. The wastes leave your body through the anus.

See Also

Systems Work Together page 109

# Excretory System

See Also

Systems Work
Together
page 109

As your cells function, they produce wastes. The function of the **excretory** (EK skreh tor ee) **system** is to move these wastes out of your body. The parts of the excretory system that do this job include your urinary system, your skin, and your lungs.

## Urinary System

The urinary (YUR uh ner ee) system is made of different organs with different functions.

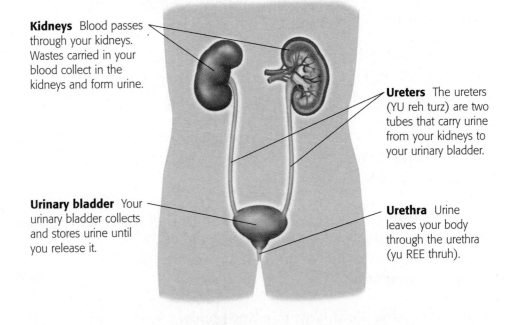

**Kidneys** Blood passes through your kidneys. Wastes carried in your blood collect in the kidneys and form urine.

**Ureters** The ureters (YU reh turz) are two tubes that carry urine from your kidneys to your urinary bladder.

**Urinary bladder** Your urinary bladder collects and stores urine until you release it.

**Urethra** Urine leaves your body through the urethra (yu REE thruh).

See Also

Digestive System
pages 116–117

## Science Alert!

The excretory system and the digestive system get rid of different kinds of wastes. The excretory system gets rid of wastes that your cells produce. The digestive system gets rid of solid wastes that are left over when you digest food.

Keyword: Body Systems
www.scilinks.org
Code: GSS45045

## Skin

Your skin is the largest organ in your body. It is the outer covering that protects your other organs and tissues. Your skin is also an excretory organ. Water and wastes leave your skin in perspiration (pur spuh RAY shun).

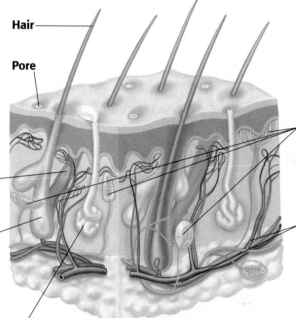

**Hair**

**Pore**

**Muscles** Tiny muscles in your skin give you "goose bumps" when you are cold. The muscles make the hair on your skin stand up.

**Oil gland** These glands produce oil. The oil keeps your skin soft. It also helps protect your skin against germs.

**Sense organs** These organs sense pressure, pain, cold, and heat. A different kind of sense organ senses each thing.

**Blood vessels** Blood vessels carry oxygen and nutrients to all the cells in your skin. Blood also carries some wastes to the skin. The wastes are eliminated in perspiration.

**Sweat gland** These glands release perspiration through pores to the surface of your skin. There, the perspiration evaporates. The evaporation of perspiration helps keep your body from overheating. Perspiration also contains wastes.

## The Lungs

Your cells produce wastes. Two of those wastes are carbon dioxide gas and water. Carbon dioxide and water leave your cells and enter your blood. The blood travels through blood vessels to your lungs. There, the carbon dioxide and water leave your blood and enter your lungs. The liquid water changes to water vapor, which is a gas. Every time you breathe out, carbon dioxide gas and water vapor leave your body.

See Also

Respiratory System pages 120–121

# Respiratory System

**See Also**

Cell Respiration
pages 78–79

Systems Work
Together
page 109

The Oxygen and
Carbon Dioxide
Cycle page 132

Your **respiratory** (RES pur uh tor ee) **system** takes in oxygen and gets rid of waste gases. When you inhale, you take air into your lungs. The air contains oxygen. Your body cells need oxygen to release energy from the nutrients in food.

**WORD WATCH**

*Inhale* means "breathe in." *Exhale* means "breathe out."

In your lungs, the oxygen passes into tiny blood vessels. Red blood cells pick up the oxygen and carry it to cells throughout your body.

As your cells use oxygen, they produce two wastes. The wastes are carbon dioxide and water. These wastes leave your cells and enter your blood. Your blood carries the carbon dioxide and water to your lungs.

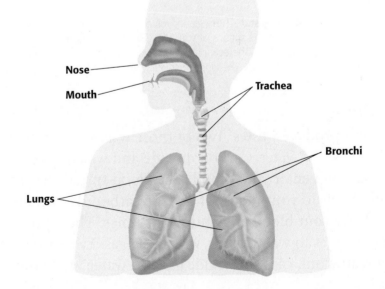

Nose

Mouth

Trachea

Bronchi

Lungs

In your lungs, carbon dioxide and water leave your blood and pass into your lungs. The liquid water changes to water vapor, which is a gas. When you exhale, carbon dioxide gas and water vapor leave your body.

## Organs in the Respiratory System

**Mouth and Nose**  Air enters your body through your nose and mouth. Waste gases from your lungs also leave the same way.

**Trachea**  Air travels through the trachea (TRAY kee uh) toward your lungs. Wastes gases from your lungs also travel through this tube to the outside

**Bronchi**  The trachea branches into two tubes called bronchi (BRONG kee). One tube leads to each lung.

**Lungs**  When you inhale, your lungs take in air. Oxygen in the air moves into your blood. Waste gases move out of your blood into your lungs. When you exhale, these gases leave your body.

### Did You Know?

You can't see the water vapor in your breath when you exhale. But if you're outside on a cold day, your breath makes a "cloud" in the air. The cloud is made of tiny droplets of water. The cold air made the water vapor in your breath change to liquid water.

SCi LINKS
NSTA
Keyword: Body Systems
www.scilinks.org
Code: GSS45045

## Circulatory System

Your **circulatory** (SUR kyuh luh tor ee) **system** moves blood throughout your body. The organs in your circulatory system are your heart and blood vessels.

Your blood carries oxygen from your lungs to all your cells. Blood also carries nutrients from your digestive system to your cells.

Systems Work Together
page 109

Excretory System
pages 118–119

Respiratory System
pages 120–121

Your blood picks up wastes that your cells produce. It carries these wastes to your kidneys and lungs. Your kidneys are part of your excretory system. Your lungs are part of your respiratory system. But your lungs also function as part of your excretory system. Together, your kidneys and lungs move wastes out of your body.

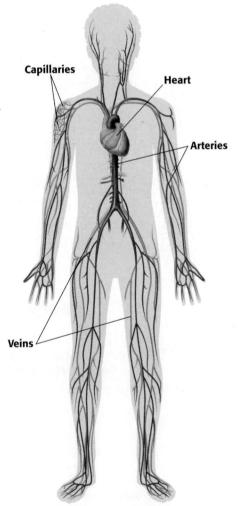

Capillaries

Heart

Arteries

Veins

Keyword: Body Systems
www.scilinks.org
Code: GSS45045

## The Heart

Your heart is an organ about the size of your fist. Its function is to pump blood through your blood vessels.

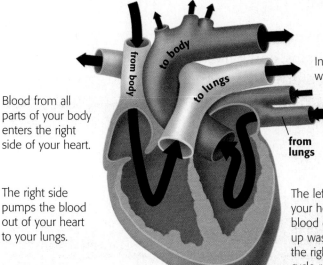

Blood from all parts of your body enters the right side of your heart.

In your lungs, the blood releases wastes and picks up oxygen.

The blood goes from your lungs to the left side of your heart.

The right side pumps the blood out of your heart to your lungs.

The left side pumps the blood out of your heart to all parts of your body. The blood delivers oxygen to cells and picks up wastes. Then the blood returns to the right side of your heart again. The cycle repeats over and over.

## Blood Vessels

Blood travels away from the heart in **arteries.** The arteries nearest the heart are very large. They get narrower as they branch out to different parts of the body. The narrowest blood vessels are called **capillaries.** The capillaries connect arteries to veins. **Veins** carry blood back to the heart.

## Blood

Your blood is made up of solid and liquid parts. The solid parts include red blood cells, white blood cells, and platelets. The liquid part is **plasma.**

Platelets plug holes in injured blood vessels. The "plugs" are blood clots.

Red blood cells carry oxygen to all parts of the body.

White blood cells fight germs that cause disease.

## Nervous System

Your **nervous system** controls all of your body's activities. None of your other systems would function without your nervous system.

The organs in your nervous system are your brain, spinal cord, sense organs, and nerves. Nerves from your sense organs carry information to your brain and spinal cord. Your brain and spinal cord control how you respond to the information.

**Brain** Your brain is the control center of your body. It gets information from your senses. It controls how you respond to the information. It allows you to think. It stores memories.

**Spinal Cord** Your spinal cord is a long bundle of nerves. It runs from your brain down your back. It is protected by your backbone. Messages to and from your brain travel through your spinal cord. The spinal cord can also receive and send some messages by itself.

**Nerves** Nerves are made of nerve cells that transmit messages. They carry messages from all parts of your body to your spinal cord and brain. They carry messages away from your spinal cord and brain to all parts of your body.

SCLINKS
Keyword: Body Systems
www.scilinks.org
Code: GSS45045
NSTA

## The Brain

Your brain is made of three main parts. Each part has different functions.

**Cerebrum** The cerebrum (suh REE brum) controls body movements that you decide to make. It also controls learning, thinking, memory, and imagination. The cerebrum is the part of your brain that receives information from your sense organs.

**Cerebellum**
The cerebellum (ser uh BEL um) coordinates the movements of your muscles. It also helps you keep your balance.

**Brain Stem** The brain stem controls your breathing, heartbeat, and movements inside your digestive system. This part of the brain functions automatically, even when you are sleeping.

## Sense Organs

Your **sense organs** are your eyes, ears, nose, tongue, and skin. They get information about your environment and send the information to your brain. Your brain then figures out what the information means and how you should respond.

Skin page 119

### Your Senses

| Sense | Sense Organ | What It Does |
| --- | --- | --- |
| Sight | Eye | Detects light and color |
| Hearing | Ear | Detects sound |
| Smell | Nose | Detects odors |
| Taste | Tongue | Detects sweet, salty, sour, and bitter tastes |
| Touch | Skin | Detects pressure, pain, heat, and cold |
| Balance | Inner ear | Detects body position |

# Ecology

If you walk through a forest, you'll see many things. Some of those things are alive. A living thing is called an **organism** (OR guh niz um). Others things in the forest are not alive. But all are interacting with each other. The study of how living and nonliving things interact is called **ecology.**

## Habitats

In autumn, a flying hawk can hardly see a sparrow perched on a tree branch. The sparrow is the same color as the branch and leaves. Its color is one of the sparrow's adaptations to its environment. An **adaptation** (ad ap TAY shun) is a characteristic that helps an organism survive in its environment. An organism's adaptations allow it to survive in a particular kind of environment.

The specific environment that meets an organism's needs is known as its **habitat** (HAB ih tat). Some needs are met by other organisms. For example, the trees in the forest provide shelter and a source of food for woodpeckers. Other needs are met by nonliving things. For example, plants need minerals in the soil, carbon dioxide, water, and sunlight to grow.

See
Also

Adaptations
page 77

A habitat can keep only a certain number of organisms alive. The number depends on how well the habitat provides for the organisms' needs. For example, the habitat must have enough food and water for all the animals to survive. If there isn't enough food or water, the animals will have to move somewhere else or they will die.

Each kind of habitat meets the needs of a different mix of organisms. A pond in California meets the needs of fish, frogs, and turtles. Cold areas in Alaska meet the needs of polar bears, caribou, and arctic foxes.

Different kinds of organisms eat different foods. They live in different parts of a habitat. They interact with their environment in different ways. All of these are part of an organism's role in its habitat. The role that an organism plays in its habitat is called its **niche** (NEESH).

## Species, Populations, and Communities

Organisms interact with each other. They interact with organisms of the same kind. For example, robins compete with other robins for good nesting places. They also interact with organisms of a different kind. Robins eat earthworms.

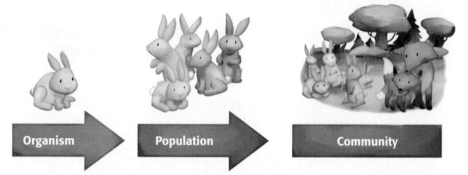

**Organism** ➤ **Population** ➤ **Community**

Two or more organisms of the same kind living in the same place make up a population. Different populations living in the same place make up a community.

### Species

A **species** (SPEE sheez) is a group of organisms that can mate and produce offspring like themselves. The offspring also can mate and produce organisms like themselves.

For example, a male gray squirrel and a female gray squirrel can mate and produce offspring. The young gray squirrels look like their parents. When the young gray squirrels become adults, they can mate and produce more gray squirrels.

Some organisms that look alike are not the same species. For example, a goose and a duck look alike. They both have feathers, webbed feet, and flat bills. But a goose and a duck can't mate to produce offspring. They are members of different species.

Keyword: Populations, Communities, Ecosystems
www.scilinks.org
Code: GSS45050

## Populations

All the organisms of the same species
that live in the same place at the same
time are a **population.** All Canada
geese are members of the same species.
The Canada geese that live at the same
lake in the summer form a population.
Mallard ducks that live at the lake form another
population. Lake trout that live in the lake form a third
population. Cattails that grow around the edge of the lake
form another population.

**Canada geese**

## Communities

Populations that live in the same place at the same time
make up a **community.** A lake community could have
populations of Canada geese, mallard ducks, lake trout,
cattails, and many other species.

The populations in a community interact
with each other. For example, mallard ducks interact with
the insects they eat. They also interact with raccoons that try
to steal their eggs. Populations also compete with each other.
Both Canada geese and mallard ducks eat insects. They both
build nests in hidden places around the edge of the lake.

## Ecosystems

The populations in a community interact with nonliving things in their environment. Nonliving things include soil, air, water, and sunlight. All the populations and nonliving things interacting in an environment form an **ecosystem** (EE koh sis tum).

**Air** Air contains two gases that different organisms need—oxygen and carbon dioxide. Both animals and plants need oxygen to release the energy in food. Plants need carbon dioxide to make their own food.

**Water** The cells of animals and plants are made mostly of water. Without water, organisms would dry up and die. Plants also need water to make their own food. Animals need water to help move digested food throughout their bodies.

**Sunlight** The energy for all living things starts with the sun. Plants use energy from the sun to make their own food. Some animals, such as rabbits, capture this energy by eating plants. Other animals, such as foxes, get this energy by eating animals that eat plants.

See Also

Cell Respiration
pages 78–79

Photosynthesis
pages 80–81

**Soil** Most plants anchor themselves in soil. Soil contains water and other substances that plants need. Some animals dig holes in the soil to stay warm and dry or to protect themselves from other animals that hunt them. Moles, earthworms, bacteria, and other organisms live in the soil all the time.

See Also

Soil
pages 168–169

## The Oxygen and Carbon Dioxide Cycle

Air contains carbon dioxide and oxygen. Organisms use these gases over and over again. The movement of carbon dioxide and oxygen between organisms and the air is called the **oxygen and carbon dioxide cycle.**

Carbon dioxide

Oxygen

| Decomposition | Cell respiration | Photosynthesis |

Photosynthesis
pages 80–81

**Photosynthesis** Plants and some other organisms take in carbon dioxide from the air. They use the carbon dioxide to make their own food. They release oxygen back into the air as a waste product.

Cell Respiration
pages 78–79

**Cell Respiration** Most organisms use oxygen to release the energy in food. This process produces carbon dioxide as a waste product. The organisms release carbon dioxide back into the air.

Decomposers
page 136

**Decomposition** Some organisms get energy by breaking down the wastes and remains of other organisms. Decomposition produces carbon dioxide. The organisms release carbon dioxide into the air.

## Living Things in Ecosystems

Every organism can be classified as a producer, a consumer, or a decomposer. Scientists classify an organism into one of these groups according to its role in an ecosystem. An organism's role includes the way it gets energy. Energy enters most ecosystems as sunlight.

**Producers**  Organisms that make their own food are called **producers** (pruh DOO surz). Producers capture the energy in sunlight. They use the energy to make their own food. Plants are producers. The green scum that grows on a pond is made of simple organisms that make their own food. They are producers, too. Some bacteria are producers. And so are some one-celled organisms that live in water. When producers make their own food, the energy that came from sunlight is stored in their bodies.

See Also

Photosynthesis pages 80–81

Plants page 142

Protists page 144

Bacteria page 145

Plants, pond scum, and some one-celled organisms make their own food. These organisms are producers.

## Consumers

Organisms that get energy by eating other organisms are called **consumers** (kun SOO murz). Scientists classify consumers into three groups—herbivores, carnivores, and omnivores.

**Herbivores** Organisms that eat only plants and plant products are called **herbivores** (HUR buh vorz). They get energy by eating roots, stems, leaves, flowers, fruits, and even plant sap. Herbivores range in size from huge elephants to tiny insects. Gorillas, deer, cows, and rabbits are herbivores. So are grasshoppers, snails, and the caterpillars of moths and butterflies.

**Carnivores** Animals that eat other animals are called **carnivores** (KAR nuh vorz). Carnivores get energy by eating the bodies of other organisms. But not all carnivores eat what you think of as meat. For example, a ladybug eats the entire body of any insect it catches. Ladybugs are carnivores. So are spiders and praying mantises.

Many carnivores have adaptations that make them good hunters. For example, lions have strong legs for chasing animals, and sharp claws and teeth for grabbing them. They also have good eyesight, hearing, and sense of smell for locating animals to hunt. And lions' sharp teeth let them tear apart their catch. Other examples of carnivores are sharks, hawks, hyenas, killer whales, owls, and wolves.

**Omnivores** Animals that eat both plants and animals are called **omnivores** (AHM nuh vorz). Bears are one of the largest omnivores. In the spring, Alaskan grizzly bears feed on salmon that are swimming up rivers. In the summer and fall, the grizzlies eat huge amounts of fruits and berries. Other examples of omnivores include cockroaches, crows, raccoons, coyotes, and humans.

See Also

Fungi page 143

Bacteria page 145

Animals With Soft Bodies page 147

**Decomposers** Some organisms don't make their own food or eat living organisms. They feed on dead plants, dead plant parts, and dead animals. They also feed on animal wastes. Organisms that get energy by feeding on dead materials and wastes are called **decomposers** (dee kum POH zurz).

Decomposers break down wastes and dead materials into simpler materials. Some decomposers break large pieces of material into smaller pieces. For example, earthworms, centipedes, and pill bugs break dead leaves into tiny pieces as they feed. Other decomposers then break the smaller pieces into simple substances. These decomposers include molds, mushrooms, and bacteria.

The simple substances enter the soil. Plants cannot take in the undigested substances, but they can take in the simple substances. So decomposers provide nutrients for plants. Decomposers also keep an ecosystem from being overloaded with dead organisms and wastes.

## Food Chains

All organisms need energy. The main source of energy on Earth is sunlight. Producers capture the energy in sunlight to make their own food. They use the food to make new cells and tissues. In this way, producers store energy in their bodies.

Think about a grasshopper and a plant. When a grasshopper eats a plant, the grasshopper gets the energy that was stored in the plant. The grasshopper uses this energy to carry out all its activities. But some of the energy is stored in the grasshopper's body.

If a shrew eats the grasshopper, the shrew gets the energy that was stored in the grasshopper's body. Some of that energy is stored in the shrew's body. If an owl eats the shrew, the owl gets energy. In this way, energy passes from the plant to the grasshopper, to the shrew, and then to the owl.

This path of energy from one organism to another is called a **food chain.** You can think of each organism as a link in the food chain. A food chain always starts with a producer. That's because producers are the only organisms that can make their own food. The second organism in a food chain is always a consumer that eats the producer. All the other organisms in the chain are also consumers.

This diagram shows the food chain that started with the plant and ended with the owl.

*See Also*

Photosynthesis
pages 80–81

Producers
page 133

*See Also*

Consumers
pages 134–135

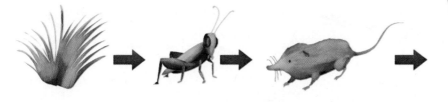

Keyword: Food Chains and Food Webs
www.scilinks.org
Code: GSS45055

## Food Webs

Food Chains
page 137

Most food chains overlap. For example, both birds and shrews eat grasshoppers. And both owls and foxes eat birds and shrews. Overlapping food chains form a food web. A **food web** shows different pathways for the flow of energy in an ecosystem.

Producers
page 133

Consumers
pages 134–135

Decomposers
page 136

The food web on this page shows overlapping food chains in a forest ecosystem. Energy moves through each food chain from producers to consumers and then from one consumer to another consumer.

When organisms die or produce wastes, energy moves to decomposers. These organisms break materials down into simple substances that plants can use. The decomposers get energy from the materials they break down.

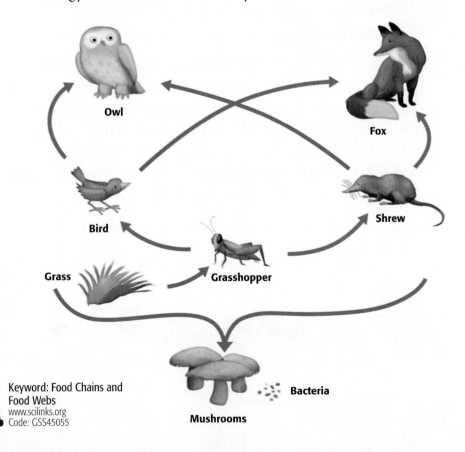

Owl

Fox

Bird

Shrew

Grass

Grasshopper

Mushrooms

Bacteria

SCiLINKS
NSTA
Keyword: Food Chains and Food Webs
www.scilinks.org
Code: GSS45055

# Classifying Organisms

Do you collect coins? Baseball cards? Shells? Rocks? Other things? If you do, you probably group them in some way.

Scientists do the same with organisms. An **organism** (OR guh niz um) is a living thing. Scientists put similar organisms in the same group. The grouping of organisms is called **classification** (klas uh fih KAY shun). Organisms can be classified in different ways.

## Kingdoms

One way that scientists classify organisms is to group them into kingdoms. A kingdom includes many different kinds of organisms.

**A Classification System of Kingdoms**

| Kingdom | Characteristics |
|---|---|
| Animals | • made of many cells<br>• most can move from place to place<br>• feed on other organisms<br>• reproduce with eggs or live birth |
| Plants | • made of many cells<br>• do not move from place to place<br>• make their own food<br>• reproduce with seeds or spores |
| Fungi | • most made of many cells; some made of one cell<br>• most do not move from place to place<br>• absorb food from dead organisms and wastes |
| Protists | • most made of one cell; some made of many cells<br>• some make their own food; others feed on other organisms<br>• some can move from place to place |
| Bacteria | • made of single cells<br>• cells do not have a nucleus<br>• some make their own food; others feed on other organisms<br>• some can move from place to place |

# Animals

All animals share certain characteristics. Their combination of characteristics sets them apart from organisms in other kingdoms.

- Animals cannot make their own food. All animals feed on other organisms.

- Animals can move from place to place, at least at some time during their lives.

- Animals are made of many cells. Animals' bodies have different kinds of cells. Each kind of cell has a different function.

- Animal cells do not have a cell wall. Their cells' outer covering is a flexible membrane.

- Animals take in oxygen and give off carbon dioxide.

- Some animals reproduce by laying eggs. Other animals reproduce by giving birth to live young.

- Animals are adapted for living on land or in water.

See
Also

Cells page 99

Animal Cell
pages 100–101

Cell Respiration
pages 78–79

The Oxygen and
Carbon Dioxide
Cycle page 132

Reproduction
page 82

Adaptations
page 77

**Box Turtle**   Box turtles live on land. The turtle's shell is a boxy shape. Its feet have claws for gripping the ground.

**Sea Turtle**   Sea turtles spend most of their lives in water. The turtle's shell is streamlined for moving through the water. Its feet are shaped like flippers.

## Plants

You might think that grass, trees, and moss don't have much in common. But they are all members of the plant kingdom. All plants share the following characteristics.

Photosynthesis
pages 80–81

- All plants make their own food. They do this through a process called **photosynthesis** (foh toh SIN thih sis). In photosynthesis, plants use the energy in sunlight to change water and carbon dioxide into a kind of sugar called glucose (GLOO kohs). Glucose is food for the plant.

- Plants do not move from place to place.

Cells page 99

Plant Cell
pages 102–103

The Oxygen and
Carbon Dioxide
Cycle page 132

Reproduction
page 82

Plant Life Cycles
pages 86–87

Adaptations
page 77

- All plants are made of many cells. A plant has different kinds of cells. Each kind of cell has a different function.

- A plant cell has a stiff outer covering called the cell wall.

- Plants take in carbon dioxide from the air and give off oxygen into the air.

- Most kinds of plants reproduce with seeds. The seeds develop in flowers or cones. Ferns and mosses reproduce with spores.

- Plants are adapted for living on land.

## Fungi

If you leave a piece of fruit out in the air too long, a fuzzy green or black material will grow on it. The material is mold. Mold is a member of the fungi kingdom.

Other members of the fungi kingdom include yeasts, mushrooms, and puffballs. Although these organisms do not look alike, all fungi have these characteristics in common.

**WORD WATCH**

*Fungi* can be pronounced either "FUHNG jy" or "FUHNG jee." *Fungi* is the plural form of the word *fungus*.

- Fungi cannot make their own food. Most fungi feed on dead plants and animals or their wastes.

- Fungi cannot move from place to place.

- Some fungi are made of a single cell. Other fungi are made of many cells.

- Like plant cells, fungi cells have a cell wall. But fungi cell walls and plant cell walls are made of different materials.

- Fungi reproduce with spores.

- Fungi are adapted for living on land.

### Did You Know?

Some fungi feed on live organisms. For example, itchy "athlete's foot" is caused by a kind of fungus.

**See Also**

Decomposers
page 136

## Protists

If you have a fish tank, you know you have to keep it free of algae (AL jee). Algae can cloud the water and coat the rocks with green slime. Algae belong to the protist kingdom. Some algae, such as seaweed, are made of many cells strung together in ribbons.

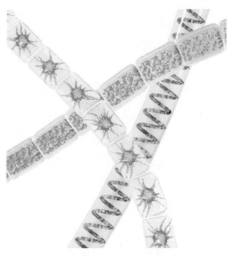

Most members of the protist kingdom are one-celled organisms. They are so tiny that you can see them only with a microscope.

Protists have the following characteristics in common.

Photosynthesis pages 80–81

- Algae and some other protists can make their own food by carrying out photosynthesis.

- Other protists, such as the amoeba, cannot make their own food. They must feed on other organisms.

- Some protists can move from place to place. For example, *Euglena* moves by whipping its tail back and forth. Other protists cannot move from place to place.

**Euglena**

- Some algae are made of many cells. Other algae and most other protists are made of only one cell.

## Bacteria

If you have a sore throat and it hurts to swallow, you might have an infection called "strep throat." Strep throat is caused by a kind of bacteria (bak TEER ee ah). Other kinds of bacteria cause diseases, too. But most bacteria are harmless to humans.

**See Also**

Science and Technology Work Together page 361

Some bacteria are helpful to people. Bacteria that live in your intestines help you digest food. Some of those bacteria make vitamins you need. People use bacteria to make yogurt, cheese, sauerkraut, and other products. Bacteria that live in soil break down dead plants, animals, and wastes into simple substances that plants can use. Some bacteria can decompose oil and are used to help clean up oil spills.

**See Also**

Decomposers page 136

All bacteria share these characteristics.

- All bacteria are made of only one cell.
- Bacteria cells do not have a nucleus.
- Bacteria cells have a cell wall.
- Some bacteria make their own food. But most bacteria feed on other organisms.
- Most bacteria need oxygen to survive. But some bacteria cannot live where there is oxygen.

Bacteria are classified into three groups according to their shape.

**Round shape**

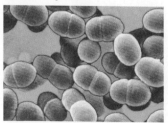

These bacteria cause infections in people.

**Spiral shape**

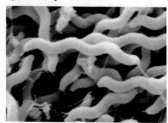

These bacteria cause most food poisoning cases.

**Rod shape**

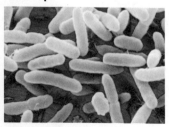

These bacteria also cause food poisoning.

# Vertebrates and Invertebrates

**See Also**

Skeletal System
pages 112–113

Scientists classify all animals into two main groups, vertebrates and invertebrates. **Vertebrates** (VUR tuh brits) are animals that have a backbone. **Invertebrates** are animals that do not have a backbone.

> The words *vertebrate* and *invertebrate* come from the word *vertebra*. A vertebra is one of the bones that form your backbone.

## Invertebrates

Invertebrates include sponges, worms, snails, jellyfish, clams, starfish, crabs, insects, and spiders. You might not think that these organisms are animals, but they are.

**Ladybug beetle**

Many invertebrates have very simple bodies. For example, a jellyfish has only one opening in its body. Food passes into the body and wastes pass out of the body through that one opening.

Earthworms have two body openings. Food enters the body through one opening, and wastes leave through the other opening. Earthworms also have a circulatory system. Insects have a circulatory system, too. Some invertebrates, such as octopuses, have a nervous system with a brain.

**Sponge**

**Jellyfish**

**Animals With Soft Bodies**  Some invertebrates have bodies that do not have any hard parts. These invertebrates include earthworms, jellyfish, slugs, and octopuses. Some kinds of soft-bodied invertebrates live on land, and other kinds live in water.

Earthworms move by contracting muscles in their tubelike bodies. They feed mainly on dead plants and plant parts.

Octopuses use their tentacles to move quickly over rocks and to catch crabs and other animals for food.

**Animals With Hard Shells**  If you've ever walked on a beach, you've probably seen seashells. The shells are all that is left of invertebrates that had hard shells. You might even have eaten these invertebrates! Clams, mussels, oysters, scallops, and snails are invertebrates with hard shells. The shells protect the animal's soft body inside.

Most animals with hard shells live in water. Some, such as the garden snail, live on land. Snails have a soft foot that they can stick out of the shell. The foot lets the snail slide very slowly across surfaces. Clams use their foot to burrow

into the sand. Mussels use their foot to anchor themselves to rocks and other objects. They don't move at all.

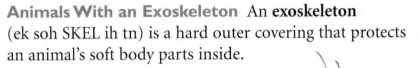

**Animals With an Exoskeleton** An **exoskeleton** (ek soh SKEL ih tn) is a hard outer covering that protects an animal's soft body parts inside.

Invertebrates with an exoskeleton include lobsters, crabs, crayfish, shrimp, ticks, scorpions, insects, and spiders. All of these animals belong to the largest group of invertebrates, called arthropods (AR thruh pahdz). **Arthropods** are invertebrates that have legs with joints. Arthropods also have sense organs such as eyes.

There are about one million different kinds of arthropods on Earth. Most of them are insects. Insects have two antennae (an TEN ee) on the front of the head. The antennae are sense organs that can feel and smell things in the environment.

Many people think that spiders are insects, but they're not. Spiders and insects have very different body parts. This table tells you some of the differences.

**Main Differences Between Spiders and Insects**

| Characteristic | Spiders | Insects |
| --- | --- | --- |
| Body parts | 2 | 3 |
| Legs | 8 | 6 |
| Wings | none | none, 2, or 4 |
| Eyes | up to 8 | 2 |
| Antennae | none | 2 |

Wolf spider

Giant ant

## Vertebrates

**Vertebrates** (VUR tuh brits) are animals that have a backbone. All vertebrates have an internal skeleton called an **endoskeleton** (en doh SKEL ih tn).

Vertebrates are classified into five main groups. The groups are mammals, birds, reptiles, amphibians, and fish. Different groups have different kinds of skeletons.

Each kind of skeleton is an adaptation to the group's environment. For example, the bones of birds have many air spaces and are very lightweight. This helps birds fly. Heavy animals that live on land have the largest and strongest bones. Large, strong bones support more weight than smaller, more delicate bones.

See Also

Skeletal System pages 112–113

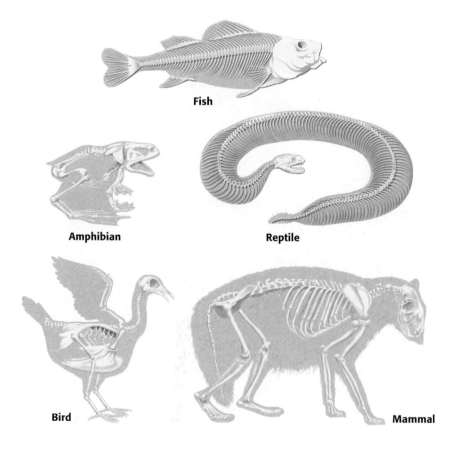

Fish

Amphibian

Reptile

Bird

Mammal

# Vertebrate Groups

Scientists classify vertebrates into five groups. This table shows the major characteristics of each group.

**Five Vertebrate Groups**

| Group | Characteristic |
|---|---|
| Mammals | • live on land and in water<br>• have hair or fur<br>• mothers nurse young with milk<br>• breathe air with lungs<br>• almost all give birth to live young; a few lay eggs |
| Birds | • live on land; some spend time in water<br>• have feathers<br>• breathe air with lungs<br>• lay eggs with hard shells<br>• most can fly |
| Reptiles | • live on land and in water<br>• have scales<br>• breathe air with lungs<br>• lay eggs with leathery shells or give birth to live young |
| Amphibians | • young live in water; adults live on land<br>• have smooth, moist skin<br>• young breathe with gills in water; adults breathe with lungs and through skin as adults<br>• lay jellylike eggs with no shells |
| Fish | • live in water<br>• most have scales<br>• breathe oxygen in water with gills<br>• lay eggs without shells or give birth to live young |

Keyword: Vertebrates and Invertebrates
www.scilinks.org
Code: GSS45060

# Mammals

Mammals come in all sizes, from the tiny pygmy shrew to the gigantic blue whale.

Pygmy shrews are the smallest land animals on Earth. A pygmy shrew can be less than 4 centimeters long and weigh as little as $\frac{1}{2}$ ounce.

Blue whales are the largest animals on Earth. A blue whale can be 33.5 meters long and weigh up to 209 tons.

**Body Covering** Mammals are the only animals that have hair or fur on their bodies. On some mammals, the hair is just short, stiff bristles. Hair or fur and a layer of fat under the skin help mammals stay warm.

**Reproduction** Almost all mammals develop inside the mother's body and are born live. All female mammals have body structures that produce milk. Mammals are the only animals that nurse their young with milk.

**Breathing** All mammals breathe air with lungs. Whales and other mammals that live in water have to swim to the surface to breathe.

**Movement** All mammals have four limbs. A *limb* is a leg or arm. Some mammals, including humans, use their front limbs as arms. The front limbs of bats are adapted for flying. Whales and other mammals that live in water have flippers for front legs.

## Birds

All birds have feathers, wings, and lightweight bones. These adaptations allow birds to fly. Birds eat seeds, insects, fruits, and other animals. They live all over the world, even in the icy Antarctic.

A hummingbird's wings can beat up to 80 times per second.

Penguins use their wings as flippers for swimming.

**Body Covering** Birds are the only animals with feathers. Long, smooth feathers help a bird fly. Small, fluffy feathers trap warm air close to the bird's body.

**Reproduction** All birds lay eggs with a hard shell. The shell protects the young bird that is developing inside. The shell keeps water out of the egg and holds liquid parts inside.

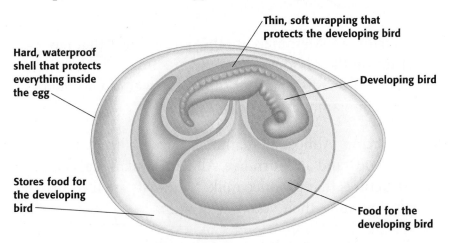

Thin, soft wrapping that protects the developing bird

Hard, waterproof shell that protects everything inside the egg

Developing bird

Stores food for the developing bird

Food for the developing bird

**Breathing** All birds breathe with lungs. Some of the air goes from their lungs into large air sacs. Birds have air sacs so they can breathe efficiently when flying.

**Movement** Birds' feet are adapted for different kinds of movement. Ducks and other water birds have webbed feet for swimming. Chickadees and other perching birds have feet that can grab onto branches.

# Reptiles

Reptiles include snakes, lizards, turtles, tortoises, alligators, and crocodiles.

**American anole**

**Nile crocodile**

**Body Covering** Some reptiles are covered with dry, leathery skin. Others are covered with scales. Turtles and tortoises also have a hard bony shell.

**Reproduction** Most reptiles lay eggs. The shell of a reptile egg is leathery and flexible, not hard like the shell of a bird's egg. The shell protects the developing reptile inside and keeps it moist. Some snakes and lizards give birth to live young.

**Breathing** All reptiles breathe with lungs. Reptiles that spend most of their time in the water have to swim to the surface to breathe.

**Movement** Many reptiles use legs to walk or swim. Turtles that live in the ocean have flippers instead of legs. Snakes do not have legs. They use muscles attached to their ribs to pull themselves along the ground.

## Amphibians

Amphibians live in water when they are young and on land when they are adults. Frogs, toads, and salamanders are amphibians.

**Body Covering** Amphibians have thin skin—so thin that air can pass through it!

Frogs have smooth, moist skin.

Toads have dry, bumpy skin.

Frog Life Cycle
page 85

**Reproduction** Most amphibians lay jellylike eggs in water or very moist places. The eggs do not have shells. A few kinds of amphibians give birth to live young.

Adaptations
page 77

**Breathing** When young amphibians live in water, they have gills. **Gills** are structures that remove oxygen from water. When adult amphibians live on land, they breathe with lungs. Some adult salamanders don't have lungs. They breathe with gills or take in oxygen through their skin.

**Movement** Frogs and toads use their hind legs to move on land. Frogs move with long jumps. Toads move with short hops. A frog's hind feet are webbed. This is an adaptation for swimming. Salamanders run across the ground on four legs. When frogs are young tadpoles, they swim by wiggling their tails back and forth.

# Fish

Fish are adapted for living in water throughout their entire lives. Most kinds of fish have a bony skeleton. Sharks, rays, and skates have a skeleton made of cartilage. **Cartilage** (KAR tl ij) is a strong material that is more flexible than bone.

**Brook trout**

**Great white shark**

**Body Covering** Most fish are covered with slippery scales. The scales let fish move easily through water. Sharks have rough skin.

Adaptations
page 77

**Reproduction** Some fish lay eggs. The eggs do not have shells. Other fish give birth to live young.

**Breathing** All fish breathe with gills. **Gills** are structures that remove oxygen from water. Lungfish also have lungs for breathing.

A lungfish can breathe air if the water dries up.

**Movement** Fish have streamlined bodies. This shape lets them glide smoothly through water. Most fish have two pairs of body fins and a tail fin. Fish swim by moving their tail fins. The body fins help them steer through water and keep their balance.

# Earth Science

I'm going to study *EARTH!*

How are rocks made? What wears away the land? What builds up the land? Why doesn't Earth lose its water? What causes weather? Why does the moon seem to change shape from day to day? These are only a few of the questions that earth scientists investigate. **Earth science** is the study of planet Earth and objects in space.

**Maybe you should study *FLYING* first!**

# Earth's Structure

Earth's surface, where you live, is made of a very thin layer of rock. Earth's rocky surface is called the **lithosphere** (LITH uh sfeer).

Above Earth's surface is a mixture of gases that make up the air you breathe. The air surrounding Earth is called the **atmosphere** (AT muh sfeer).

Earth's water makes up the **hydrosphere** (HY druh sfeer). The hydrosphere includes all the liquid water and ice on Earth's surface, liquid water in the ground, and water vapor in the atmosphere.

If you think of Earth as an apple, the lithosphere is like the apple's outer skin.

See Also

Water Cycle
pages 188–189

The lithosphere, atmosphere, and hydrosphere interact with each other. For example, water evaporates from a lake and enters the atmosphere. Some of this water falls back to Earth as rain. The rain fills streams and rivers. Moving water wears away Earth's rock surface.

## Earth's Layers

Earth is shaped like a sphere, a round ball. But Earth is not perfectly round. It bulges a little at the equator.

Imagine you are traveling from your home to Earth's center. Your trip will be about 6,380 kilometers long. As you travel, you pass through Earth's four main layers. You discover that each layer has a different thickness and a different temperature. And you find that each layer is made of different materials.

**CRUST**
**Thickness:** 5–70 km
**Materials:** solid rocks
**Temperature:** cool at top, about 870°C at bottom

**MANTLE**
**Thickness:** about 2,900 km
**Materials:** melted rock that flows like oatmeal
**Temperature:** 2,800°C to 3,200°C

**OUTER CORE**
**Thickness:** about 2,250 km
**Materials:** liquid iron and nickel
**Temperature:** 4,400°C to 5,000°C

**INNER CORE**
**Thickness:** about 1,280 km
**Materials:** solid iron and nickel
**Temperature:** estimated at 6,000°C
Even though the inner core's temperature is very high, the iron and nickel do not melt. The inner core is kept solid by the pressure of the layers above it.

## Minerals

If you look at a rock carefully, you might see tiny grains that are different colors. You might see small or large crystals. Each grain or crystal is a mineral. A rock is a mixture of minerals.

A **mineral** is

- a solid material that is formed by nature in or on Earth's crust.

- a material that has a crystal form.

- a material that has its own set of properties.

- a material that is not formed by a living thing.

Some minerals are made of one element. Other minerals are made of two or more elements joined together.

See Also

Elements
page 250

**WORD WATCH**

A **crystal** is a solid material found in nature that has straight edges and flat sides or that breaks into pieces with straight edges and flat sides.

**Sulfur**
Sulfur is made of only one element. Sulfur crystals are different shapes.

**Rock salt (halite)**
Rock salt is made of two elements. Rock salt crystals are cube-shaped.

**Emerald**
Emerald is made of four elements. Emerald crystals are long.

## Properties of Minerals

Each mineral has its own set of properties. No two minerals have the same set of properties.

**Color**  A mineral may be one color or different colors.

**Luster**  Luster is how a mineral's surface reflects light. A mineral can be shiny, glassy, dull, metallic, or oily looking.

**Graphite**
Graphite has a metallic luster.

**Turquoise**
Turquoise has a dull luster.

**Hardness**  A mineral may be very hard, very soft, or somewhere in between. Diamond is the hardest mineral. Talc is the softest.

See
Also
Mohs Hardness
Scale page 162

**Streak**  Streak is the color of the mark that a mineral makes when it is scraped on a white tile. A mineral always makes the same color mark.

**Chalcopyrite**
Chalcopyrite
(kal kuh PY ryt) is
a brassy yellow
color, but its streak
is dark green.

**Cleavage and Fracture**  These words describe how a mineral breaks. Cleavage means breaking along a smooth, flat surface. Fracture means breaking along a rough or jagged surface.

## Identifying Minerals

Suppose you found a large crystal jutting out of a rock. How would you begin to identify it? You might start by finding its hardness. **Hardness** is the ability of a material to resist being scratched.

**Green/purple tourmaline crystal in white quartz**

Harder materials scratch softer ones. A German scientist named Friedrich Mohs invented a way of comparing the hardness of minerals. This system is called the Mohs hardness scale.

To begin identifying your crystal, you could try to scratch it with the minerals in the Mohs scale. For example, if fluorite didn't scratch the crystal but apatite did, your crystal would have a hardness of between 4 and 5. You could also try to scratch the crystal with the common objects listed in the chart.

### Mohs Hardness Scale

| Hardness | Mineral | Common Material |
|:---:|---|---|
| 1 | Talc | |
| 2 | Gypsum | Fingernail: 2.5 to 3 |
| 3 | Calcite | Copper coin: 3 |
| 4 | Fluorite | |
| 5 | Apatite | Glass, steel knife blade: 5.5 to 6 |
| 6 | Feldspar | Steel file: 6.5 to 7 |
| 7 | Quartz | |
| 8 | Topaz | |
| 9 | Corundum | |
| 10 | Diamond | |

The table below shows some common minerals and some of their properties. It can help you identify an unknown mineral. You can also use a field guide to rocks and minerals.

For example, suppose you find a mineral with a hardness of 6. According to the chart, it could be amphibole, feldspar, hematite, pyrite, or pyroxene. If it has a nonmetallic luster, you can eliminate hematite and pyrite. If its color is white, you can eliminate amphibole and pyroxene. Feldspar is the only one left, but just to be sure, check its streak. If the streak is white, you have feldspar.

## Properties of Minerals

| Mineral | Luster | Hardness | Color | Streak |
|---------|--------|----------|-------|--------|
| Amphibole | glassy | 5 to 6 | green to black | gray-green |
| Calcite | glassy | 3 | colorless, white, yellow | white |
| Feldspar | glassy | 6 | white, pink, gray | white |
| Fluorite | glassy | 4 | purple, green, yellow | white |
| Galena | dull metallic | 2.5 to 3 | silver gray | gray, black |
| Gypsum | glassy | 1.5 to 2 | colorless, white | white |
| Halite | glassy | 2 | colorless, white | white |
| Hematite | dull metallic | 6.5 | steel gray | red, reddish-brown |
| Mica | glassy | 2 to 3 | colorless, light tint | white |
| Pyrite | metallic, shiny | 6 to 6.5 | brassy yellow | greenish-black |
| Pyroxene | glassy | 5 to 6 | black, green | white, gray-green |
| Quartz | glassy | 7 | colorless, white, pink, smoky, purple | white |

## Rocks

**See Also**

The Rock Cycle
page 165

Identifying Rocks
pages 166–167

Rocks are mixtures of minerals. Scientists classify rocks according to how they formed.

**Igneous Rocks** Deep under ground, temperatures are high enough to melt rocks. Melted rock is called **magma.** When magma cools, it hardens to form rock. Magma that flows out of the ground onto Earth's surface is called **lava.** Above ground, the lava cools and hardens. Rocks that formed from cooled magma or lava are called **igneous** (IG nee us) **rocks.**

**Granite**
Granite is an igneous rock.

**Sedimentary Rocks** **Sediments** (SED uh munts) are bits of rock, shells, and the remains of plants and animals. Over millions of years, sediments are buried under ground. There, they are pressed and cemented together to form sedimentary (sed uh MEN tuh ree) rocks.

**Limestone**
Limestone is a sedimentary rock.

**Metamorphic Rocks** Forces within Earth's crust can change igneous rocks and sedimentary rocks into metamorphic (met uh MOR fik) rocks. **Metamorphic rocks** are formed from existing rocks that have been squeezed and heated deep inside Earth's crust.

**Marble**
Marble is a metamorphic rock made from limestone.

**Gneiss**
Gneiss (NYS) is a metamorphic rock made from granite.

# Rock Cycle

Forces inside Earth and on its surface constantly change one kind of rock into another kind. The process of rocks changing into other kinds of rock is called the **rock cycle.**

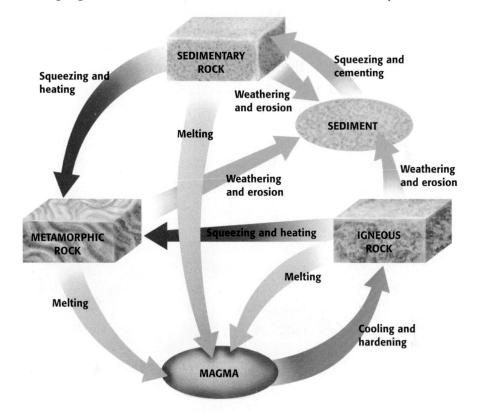

## The Rock Cycle

| | |
|---|---|
| Melting | Deep below Earth's surface, all three kinds of rock are melted to form magma. |
| Cooling and hardening | On or below Earth's surface, magma cools and hardens to form igneous rock. |
| Weathering and erosion | Weathering breaks existing rock into tiny particles, forming sediment. Erosion moves the sediment to other places, where it is deposited. |
| Squeezing and cementing | The sediment is squeezed together and cemented to form sedimentary rock. |
| Squeezing and heating | Heat and pressure change sedimentary rock and igneous rock into metamorphic rock. |

## Identifying Rocks

How can you tell whether a rock is sedimentary, metamorphic, or igneous? The rock holds clues to its origin. The clues are hidden in the properties of the rock, and you can learn to read those clues.

Texture is one property that helps tell you how a rock formed. You might think of texture as something you feel. But you can figure out the texture of a rock just by looking at it.

For example, rocks made of large grains or large crystals have coarse-grained textures. Rocks made of small grains or small crystals have fine-grained textures.

**Mica schist**
A coarse-grained metamorphic rock

**Shale**
A fine-grained sedimentary rock

Igneous, sedimentary, and metamorphic rocks have other properties that can help you identify them.

**Igneous Rocks** Many kinds of igneous rocks have large or small crystals that you can see. Some of the crystals can only be seen with a microscope. Some igneous rocks have holes made by gas bubbles.

**Sedimentary Rocks** Many sedimentary rocks have flat layers you can see. Some contain fossils, such as the imprints of shells. Sedimentary rocks are usually softer than igneous or metamorphic rocks that look similar.

**Metamorphic Rocks** Some metamorphic rocks, such as slate and schist, have layers that look like dark and light bands. In schist, the bands are often wavy. These rocks will break along the bands. Other metamorphic rocks, such as marble and quartzite, do not have crystals arranged in bands.

**Key to Rock Identification**

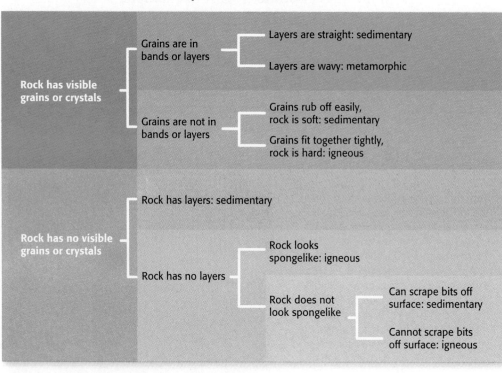

*Not all rocks can be identified using this key.*

## Soil

*See Also*

Weathering
page 171

Erosion and
Deposition
pages 172–173

**Soil** is made of tiny pieces of rock, minerals, and decayed plant and animal matter. The tiny pieces of rock and the minerals came from large rocks that were weathered. **Weathering** is the wearing away of rock. For example, water in a river makes rocks bang against each other, breaking pieces off. Water also dissolves some of the minerals that make up rocks.

If you have ever seen a deep hole dug in soil, you may have noticed that soil is made of layers. Each layer has different properties. The layers of some soils may be very different from the layers of other soils. For example, desert soil is different from forest soil. This picture shows the layers you might find in a forest soil.

**Undecayed layer** This layer contains mostly dead and decaying leaves, twigs, animal remains, and animal wastes. Decaying material in soil is called **humus** (HYOO mus).

**Topsoil** Topsoil is loose, rich soil near the top. It is rich because it holds lots of humus and minerals. Humus provides many substances that plants need. Topsoil soaks up and stores water well.

**Subsoil** Subsoil holds many minerals that rainwater has washed down from the topsoil. This layer is where you might find clay. Clay is made of the smallest particles of rock. Water does not flow easily through clay.

**Rock** Below the subsoil are large pieces of weathered rock. Below the weathered rock is rock that has not been weathered.

# Properties of Different Soils

Different areas of the United States have different kinds of soil. Each kind of soil forms under different conditions and has different properties.

Soil page 329

**Forest soil**  Forest soil contains very little humus. The topsoil layer is thin. Because of heavy rains, forest soil is not rich in nutrients.

**Grassland soil**  This soil is rich in humus and holds water well. The topsoil is thick. It is very fertile soil where corn, wheat, and many other crops are grown.

**Desert soil**  There are not many plants in a desert, so the soil contains very little humus. But it does contain lots of minerals. That's because low rainfall doesn't wash the minerals deep into the ground. When desert soil is watered, it can be very fertile.

**Tropical soil**  Year-round rain and warm temperatures mean that soil forms quickly in the tropics. This makes tropical soil thick. But thick does not mean fertile. Heavy rains wash nutrients away. Trees and other plants quickly take up any nutrients that are left in the soil.

**Arctic soil**  Lower layers of soil are always frozen in these areas. The upper layers are boggy and thin. Water cannot drain into the frozen layers below.

**Mountain soil**  This soil is made of jagged pieces of rock, some sand, and some clay. Mountain soil often does not have a layer of topsoil. Rainwater rushing down the mountainside washes the topsoil away.

 **SCiLINKS**
N S T A
Keyword: Explore Soil
www.scilinks.org
Code: GSS45065

# Earth's Changing Surface

Earth's surface is constantly changing. For example, mountains rise where once there may have been only flat land. Wind-blown sand, crashing waves, and water freezing into ice change rocks into bits of sand and soil. Rushing rivers and creeping glaciers carve great canyons and steep valleys.

## Slow Changes

Some changes happen so slowly that you would never see them. For example, it took about six million years for the Colorado River to carve the Grand Canyon.

# Weathering

Earth's surface is exposed to water, wind, ice, and growing plants. Each of these can break down rocks into smaller pieces. This breaking down of rocks is called **weathering.**

**Water**  Some of the minerals in rocks dissolve in water. When this happens under ground, huge caverns can form. Moving water that carries rough pieces of sand can also chip away rocks.

Weathering by water formed Carlsbad Caverns in New Mexico.

**Wind**  If you have ever seen workers sandblasting a building, you have an idea how wind can weather rocks. Wind that contains sand wears away rock like sandpaper wears away wood.

**Ice**  Liquid water collects in cracks in a rock. When the water freezes, it expands. The expanding ice pushes apart the rock and breaks it.

**Plants**  If you look carefully at the side of a cliff, you might see a plant sprouting from a crack in the rock. What you can't see is the plant's roots spreading inside the crack and pushing it apart. This process loosens and breaks off bits of the rock.

## Erosion and Deposition

**Erosion** (ih ROH zhun) carries weathered materials away from a place. **Deposition** (dep uh ZISH un) drops the materials in a new place. Erosion and deposition destroy old landforms and create new ones. Moving water, wind, and moving ice cause erosion and deposition.

**Moving Water** Rain, streams, and rivers cause erosion. As water moves across the land, it carries away soil, sand, and small rocks. When the water slows down, the materials fall out and are deposited. Deposition forms deltas and beaches.

A butte is a steep hill that stands alone in a flat area. Water eroded the land around the butte.

A delta is a large flat area of land at the mouth of a river. This is the Mississippi Delta, the largest delta in the United States.

**Wind** Wind can move and deposit particles of rock, soil, and sand. Wind makes the most changes when it blows over open areas such as deserts, plowed fields, and beaches. The amount of erosion caused by wind depends on the speed of the wind and how long it blows. The higher the wind's speed and the longer the wind blows, the greater the erosion. Wind builds land when it deposits materials.

Wind erodes sand from one side of a dune and deposits it on the other side.

**Moving Ice** In mountains and in cold parts of the world, glaciers may form. A **glacier** (GLAY shur) is a large body of moving ice. Glaciers that form in mountain valleys move downward very slowly. As they move, they scrape away pebbles, rocks, and even huge boulders. These materials cut away more land as the glacier drags

A glacier picks up pebbles, rocks, and boulders and carries them along in the ice.

them along. If a glacier melts and shrinks, the materials are deposited. At its front end and its sides, the glacier leaves behind a ridge of rocks called a **moraine** (muh RAYN).

## Mountain Building

Where the Rocky Mountains stand today, the land was once flat. This is also true of the Sierra Nevada Mountains of California. Over millions of years, forces in Earth's crust pushed up these mountains in two different ways.

The Rocky Mountains are an example of folded mountains.

**Folded mountains** are produced when land is squeezed together. Think of the land as a sheet of very thin paper. Hold one end of the sheet down with your right hand. Use your left hand to push the other end of the sheet toward your right hand. The paper will fold or wrinkle upward. Forces in Earth act like your left hand. They push on the land, forcing it upward. The Appalachians in North America, the Andes in South America, and the Alps in Europe are other examples of folded mountains.

The Sierra Nevada Mountains in California are an example of fault-block mountains.

**Fault-block mountains** are produced when blocks of rock slide upward or downward along a fault. A **fault** is a crack in Earth's crust. Land moves along a fault in one of three ways.

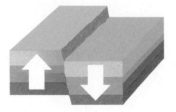

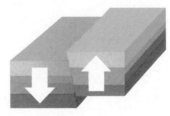

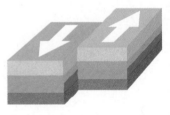

At a **normal fault,** a block of land drops downward. This process can form valleys with steep walls.

At a **reverse fault,** a block of land is pushed upward. This is how California's Sierra Nevada Mountains were formed.

At a **strike-slip fault,** blocks of rock move sideways past each other. The San Andreas Fault in California is a strike-slip fault.

## Earth's Moving Plates

Earth's crust is not one solid piece. It is broken into sections, like a cracked eggshell. The sections are called **plates.** The plates are always moving, although very slowly.

Volcanoes
pages 178–179

Earthquakes
pages 180–181

Some plates crunch into each other. Others move away from each other. Most earthquakes and volcanoes occur at or near the boundaries between plates. Movements at the boundaries can produce earthquakes. Weak spots in the crust at the boundaries can allow melted rock to reach the surface. This produces a volcano.

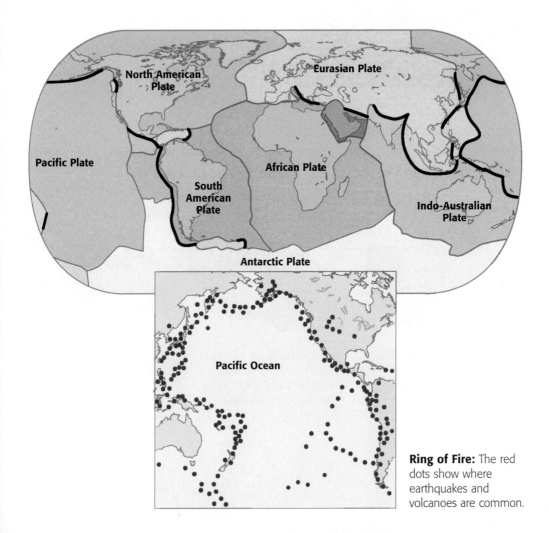

North American Plate

Eurasian Plate

Pacific Plate

African Plate

South American Plate

Indo-Australian Plate

Antarctic Plate

Pacific Ocean

**Ring of Fire:** The red dots show where earthquakes and volcanoes are common.

About 100 years ago, a German scientist named Alfred Wegener noticed something curious about the map of Earth. Some continents fit together like the pieces of a jigsaw puzzle.

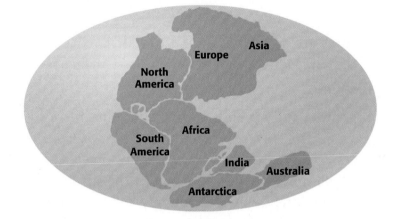

This observation led Wegener to suggest a new idea: The continents were once part of a single chunk of land that split apart millions of years ago. Over millions of years, the continents moved to their present locations.

Scientists have found evidence to support the idea that continents moved. For example, rocks found on the east coast of South America are the same as rocks found on the west coast of Africa. And these rocks are different from rocks found in other places on Earth.

More evidence came from fossils. Fossils of an animal that could not live in ocean water were found in both South America and Africa. Scientists reasoned that these animals must have walked between South America and Africa when the two continents were joined.

See Also

Fossils pages 185–186

All the evidence supported the idea that continents had moved. But no one could figure out *how* they moved. The discovery of Earth's moving plates solved the mystery. The continents are part of the plates, and they move with them.

## Rapid Changes

Volcanoes, earthquakes, landslides, and floods can change Earth's surface very quickly.

### Volcanoes

Temperatures are so high at the bottom of Earth's crust that rocks melt. Melted rock below Earth's surface is called **magma.**

Earth's Moving Plates pages 176–177

As magma heats and expands, it pushes in all directions. It moves to Earth's surface where the crust is weakest. Many weak places exist where Earth's rocky plates meet. At these places, magma may shoot or pour out of the surface in an eruption. Magma that reaches the surface is called **lava.**

An eruption can also throw hot boulders, ash, gases, and cinders into the air A **volcano** is a mountain built up from hardened lava, rocks, and ash that erupted out of Earth.

Some eruptions occur slowly. The volcanoes of Hawaii produce slow eruptions. The magma rises to the surface and forms lakes of lava. During an eruption, the lakes overflow and lava flows down the sides of the volcano.

Kilauea in Hawaii

Other eruptions occur quickly as explosions. Mount St. Helens is a volcanic mountain in the Cascade Range in Washington State. In 1980, the mountain exploded.

Magma and gases had built up and were trapped inside the mountain. The pressure grew to be enormous. It became so great that in an instant it blew away one side of the mountain. The explosion was so powerful that it knocked down trees 25 kilometers away. It shot steam and ash 20 kilometers into the sky.

**Mount St. Helens**

Keyword: How Do Volcanoes Form?
www.scilinks.org
Code: GSS45070

## Earthquakes

An **earthquake** happens when huge slabs of rock move against each other deep below Earth's surface. The slabs touch at a fault. A **fault** is a crack in Earth's crust.

The rock slabs do not move slowly and steadily along the fault. Instead, they stick together until the forces pushing on them become very great. Then one of the slabs suddenly moves a short distance. This jolt produces waves in the crust like ripples in a pond. These waves can be felt as an earthquake.

In some places, land may drop during an earthquake. In other places, land may rise. So earthquakes can build up or destroy land.

Mountain
Building
pages 174–175

**Fault**
Slabs of rock move
along a fault.

**Epicenter**
The epicenter is the point
on Earth's surface directly
above the focus.

**Waves**
Waves move out in all
directions from the focus.

**Focus**
The focus is the point deep
below the surface where
the earthquake starts.

All earthquakes are not alike. Some release more energy than others. Some are more destructive than others. The strength of an earthquake can be measured by the energy it releases or by the destruction it produces.

In 1935, an American scientist named Charles Richter developed a way of comparing the strengths of earthquakes. His invention is called the Richter Scale.

The Richter scale has the numbers 1 through 9. Number 1 is the weakest earthquake, and number 9 is the strongest.

Each larger number means an earthquake 10 times stronger than the number before it. For example, an earthquake that measures 3.0 on the Richter Scale is 10 times stronger than an earthquake that measures 2.0. An earthquake that measures 4.0 is 10 times stronger than one that measures 3.0 and 100 times stronger than one that measures 2.0.

**Richter Scale**

| Strength | Effects |
|---|---|
| 1–3 | Not felt by people |
| 3–4 | Felt by some people; little damage |
| 5 | Felt by most people; causes slight damage near epicenter |
| 6 | Damage caused to weak buildings and other structures within about 10 km of the epicenter |
| 7 | Great damage to structures up to 100 km from the epicenter |
| 8 | Very destructive; may injure and kill people more than a few hundred kilometers from the epicenter |
| 9 | Very rare; great damage to areas up to 1,000 km from the epicenter |

**Tsunamis** A tsunami (tsoo NAH mee) is a giant ocean wave caused by an undersea earthquake. When an earthquake occurs on the ocean floor, it releases a lot of energy. The energy travels through the water and produces a small wave on the surface.

The wave moves outward in all directions. Far out at sea, the wave may be less than a meter tall. But as it nears land, it piles up into a huge, tall wave. When it hits the shore, it may be more than 20 meters tall.

People sometimes call tsunamis "tidal waves." But tsunamis have nothing to do with tides.

## Landslides and Floods

The force of gravity can cause rapid changes in the land. For example, gravity pulls downward on the rocks and soil on the slope of a hill. During a rainstorm, earthquake, or volcanic eruption, the rocks and soil can be loosened. Then the force of gravity pulls the rocks, soil, and mud down the hill in a **landslide.**

Landslides destroy structures such as hills and cliffs. But new land is built up at the bottom of the landslide. The land is quickly worn away, or eroded. But just as quickly, it is deposited somewhere else.

In many parts of the world, farmers plant crops on the sides of steep hills. To help prevent landslides, they dig terraces into the hills. Planting trees also helps prevent landslides. The trees' roots hold on to the soil.

See Also
Erosion and Deposition pages 172–173

Floods also change the land suddenly. They sweep land away from one place and deposit it in another place, such as at the mouth of a river.

River floods are usually caused by long, steady, heavy rains or by rapid melting of large amounts of snow. The soil cannot absorb the water fast enough. The water runs into rivers, which then overflow.

**Ohio River flood in 1997**

A heavy rainstorm can cause a sudden flood called a flash flood. In a flash flood, water enters a stream very rapidly. The stream cannot carry away the water fast enough. The water flows over the banks of the stream or fills a steep-sided canyon.

Not all river floods can be prevented. But dams, levees, and other flood-control measures can help prevent damage.

## Earth's History and Fossils

If you could cut a slice into Earth's crust, you would see layers of rock. Some layers might be made of sedimentary rock, some might be made of metamorphic rock, and some might be made of igneous rock. But no matter what the layers are made of, you can be sure of one thing. In general, the layers near the surface are younger than the layers farther down.

Each layer is like a page in a history book. The last page—the top layer—tells about the present. The first page—the bottom layer—tells about the distant past. In between, the pages fill in the history from past to present. The layers usually don't tell you exactly when an event took place in Earth's history. And they do not tell you the whole story. They only tell you the order in which some events took place.

Youngest —

Oldest —

A layer of sedimentary rock on top of a layer of igneous rock might tell you this: First there was a volcano here. It erupted, and lava hardened into igneous rock. Much later, an ocean covered the igneous rock. Sediments drifted to the ocean floor. Over millions of years, the sediments formed sedimentary rock that covered the igneous rock.

## Fossils

Organisms have lived on Earth for at least 3.5 billion years. During that time, organisms and the environment have changed many times. Fossils hold clues to those changes. **Fossils** are the remains or traces of organisms that lived long ago.

Most fossils are found in sedimentary rock. The original organisms were trapped in sediments. When the sediments hardened into rock, signs of the organisms stayed in the rock.

**Fossils Give Clues to the Environment** Today, Antarctica is the coldest continent on Earth. About 35 years ago, scientists found fossils of trees and large animals in Antarctic rock. The trees and animals could only have lived in a warm climate. The fossils were about 250 million years old. That meant Antarctica had a warm climate at that time.

**Fossils Give Clues to Organisms** Fossils can show the history of an organism. For example, ancestors of today's horses lived about 50 million years ago. Fossils show that these animals were about the size of dogs. And they had four toes on their front feet instead of hooves.

**Ancient horse**          **Modern horse**

The small animal was the ancestor of today's horses.

**Kinds of fossils** Fossils form in different ways. They also record different information about the organisms they preserve.

Whole insects were trapped in tree sap. The sap hardened into a substance called amber.

Footprints were preserved when a dinosaur or other animal walked in mud, and the mud hardened into rock. Footprints, tracks, and burrows made by organisms and preserved in rock are called **trace fossils.**

A **mold** is a space pressed into rock. When an organism died, its body lay on mud. The mud hardened into rock. The mold has the shape of the organism.

A **cast** is a mold that was filled in with minerals or grains of rock, then turned into solid rock.

A **petrified fossil** formed when the hard parts of an organism were replaced by minerals. The fossil looks like a bone or tree trunk, but it is made of rock.

# Water on Earth

About 75 percent of Earth's surface is covered with water. Some of this water is fresh water. Most rivers, streams, lakes, and ponds hold fresh water. Mountain glaciers and the ice sheets at the North and South Poles are also made of fresh water. The rest of the water on Earth is salt water. Most of Earth's salt water is in the oceans. A tiny percentage of water is in Earth's atmosphere as water vapor or water droplets.

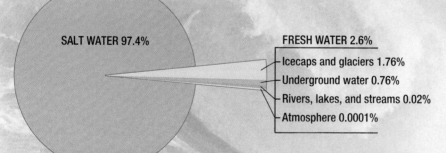

SALT WATER 97.4%

FRESH WATER 2.6%
- Icecaps and glaciers 1.76%
- Underground water 0.76%
- Rivers, lakes, and streams 0.02%
- Atmosphere 0.0001%

*Source: U.S. Geological Survey 2012*

# Water Cycle

**See Also**

States of Matter
pages 262–263

Changing States
of Matter
pages 264–265

Suppose snow falls in your area early on a winter morning. Then the temperature rises and the solid snow turns to puddles of liquid water. By the time you come home from school, some of the puddles have vanished. When the puddles evaporated, the water became a gas. During this day, water existed in three states—solid, liquid, and gas.

The change of water from one state to another and its movement from one place to another on Earth is called the **water cycle.** The changes and movement of water during the water cycle are driven by the sun's energy. For example, heat from the sun causes liquid water to become a gas.

**Condensation**
Water vapor in the atmosphere condenses into tiny water droplets. The droplets form clouds.

**Precipitation**
Liquid or frozen water droplets fall to Earth as precipitation.

**Evaporation**
Liquid water evaporates from Earth's surface and enters the atmosphere as water vapor.

SCILINKS

Keyword: Water Cycle
www.scilinks.org
Code: GSS45075

## Evaporation, Condensation, Precipitation

During **evaporation** (ih vap uh RAY shun), liquid water changes to a gas called water vapor. Water vapor enters the air above Earth's surface. Heat from the sun speeds up evaporation.

The atmosphere always holds some water vapor. When the air gets cooler, water vapor changes to tiny droplets of liquid water. The change from water vapor to liquid water is called **condensation** (kahn dun SAY shun). Water droplets clump together to form a cloud.

Water vapor is fresh water. When salty ocean water evaporates, it leaves salts behind. Only fresh water enters the air.

As condensation continues, the water droplets get larger and larger. When the drops become too large and heavy, they fall to Earth's surface. Water that falls to Earth's surface is called **precipitation** (prih sip ih TAY shun). Precipitation falls as rain, snow, hail, or sleet.

See Also

Changing States of Matter pages 264–265

## Fresh Water

Imagine all the water on Earth in a 1-liter bottle. Less than three teaspoons would be fresh water. Of that, only about half a teaspoon would be liquid water. The rest of Earth's fresh water would be ice.

Almost all of Earth's ice is in polar icecaps and in glaciers. **Icecaps** are the sheets of ice that cover areas around the North and South Poles. A **glacier** (GLAY shur) is a large body of moving ice.

Without liquid water, life on Earth would not be possible. All living things need liquid water to carry out their life processes.

### Bodies of Fresh Water

Earth's fresh water collects on the surface in streams, rivers, ponds, lakes, swamps, and marshes.

A **stream** is a narrow body of flowing water. Some streams are steep. In mountain areas, streams collect water from melting snow or ice. Streams usually flow into large bodies of water such as rivers and lakes.

**Rivers** are wide bodies of slowly moving water. They are fed by streams and flow down to the ocean. Many rivers are used to transport goods and people.

**Ponds** and **lakes** are bodies of still water. They are fed by streams. People used them for recreation such as swimming, boating, and fishing. Lakes are deeper than ponds. Some lakes are used for drinking water.

The water in **swamps** and **marshes** is shallow and still or very slow-moving. These bodies of water are dotted with large and small plants. They are home for many different kinds of animals.

## Groundwater

Water that collects underground is called **groundwater.** Less than one percent of Earth's fresh water is under ground. That makes groundwater a very limited but valuable resource. People dig or drill wells to get groundwater. In many areas, groundwater is the only supply of clean fresh water for drinking, bathing, cooking, washing, and farming.

If you've ever hiked outdoors, you may have seen a spring bubbling water from the side of a hill. A spring is a natural source of groundwater. Pressure from groundwater higher on the hill forces water out of the ground at the spring.

When rain falls or snow and ice melt, water soaks into the ground.

**Rock layer with cracks and spaces**

Water moves down through spaces in the soil and rocks until it reaches a layer of waterproof rock. The water is trapped there.

**Waterproof rock layer**

A well reaches the trapped groundwater.

A spring appears where the groundwater level reaches the surface of the land.

**Well**

**Waterproof rock layer**

**Waterproof rock layer**

**Spring**

**Groundwater**

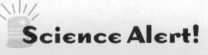

## Science Alert!

There are very few underground lakes, streams, or ponds. Most groundwater is trapped in spaces between rock grains or in cracks in the rock.

## Oceans

Oceans, seas, and bays cover almost three-quarters of Earth's surface. They hold a little more than 97 percent of Earth's water.

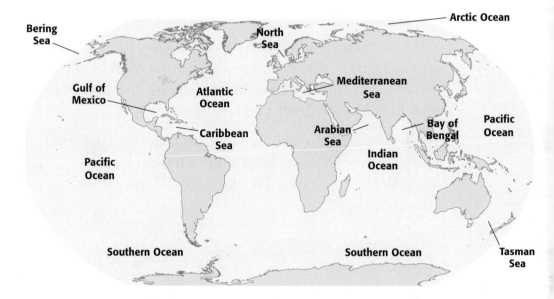

## Ocean Water

Earth's ocean water holds many dissolved salts. Most of the salt is sodium chloride, the same kind of salt you sprinkle on food.

The temperature of Earth's oceans varies from top to bottom, from place to place, and from season to season. Temperatures are highest near the surface and lowest near the bottom. Oceans are saltier in some places and less salty in other places.

Organisms live in all parts of all oceans. But seaweed and other organisms that use sunlight to make their own food can live only near the surface. That's because sunlight reaches only about 100 meters deep in the water.

Photosynthesis
page 80

Producers
page 133

## Waves and Currents

Friction
page 274

Force, Mass, and
Motion page 278

Forms of Energy
page 285

As the wind blows over the ocean's surface, it pushes against the water. This pushing transfers energy from the wind to the water. The energy moves through the water in waves. The water itself does not move forward. Only the energy moves forward.

The size of an ocean wave depends on three things. They are the speed of the wind, the distance the wind blows, and the length of time it blows. As wind speed, distance, and time increase, waves get larger.

When a wave crashes on the shore, its energy is transferred to objects on the shore. Sand is moved from place to place. Rocks are broken. People and buildings can be knocked down.

Ocean currents are like rivers in the ocean. Different currents have different properties and effects. Some currents are warm. Other currents are cold.

The climate of a coastal region is affected by the currents that pass close by. For example, a warm current keeps the land near it warm. A cold current cools the nearby land.

Climate
pages 216–217

# Tides

If you visit an ocean beach, you'll see something curious. At certain times, the water comes up higher on the beach. At other times, it is lower. What you are seeing are high and low tides. Tides are caused mostly by the pull of gravity between Earth and its moon.

Each day, the beach will have a high tide, a low tide, another high tide, and another low tide. About six hours will pass between high and low tide. That's how long it takes Earth to make one quarter turn on its axis. Each quarter turn positions Earth and its moon differently. The different positions cause different tides.

The highest tides occur when Earth, the moon, and the sun are lined up. In this position, the sun's gravity adds to the gravity of Earth and the moon to make the tides higher and lower. This happens when the moon is in its new or full phase.

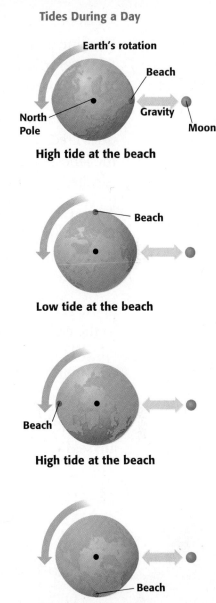

**Tides During a Day**

High tide at the beach

Low tide at the beach

High tide at the beach

Low tide at the beach

The combination of the moon's gravity and Earth's gravity makes the ocean water bulge outward at two places. It bulges outward on the part of Earth that faces the moon and on the part that faces away from the moon. These bulges cause a high tide in both places. The parts of Earth that do not face the moon or do not face away from the moon have low tides at that time.

## Features of the Ocean Floor

Imagine you can walk into the ocean and across the ocean floor. Your journey starts at the shoreline. The **shoreline** is the area where the ocean meets the land.

If you wait on the shoreline for several hours, you'll see tides creep forward and back along the beach. The part of the land that is constantly covered and uncovered by tides is called the **intertidal** (in tur TYD l) **zone.**

As you walk farther into the ocean, the bottom slants downward very gradually. You are on the continental shelf. The **continental** (kahn tuh NEN tl) **shelf** is the underwater part of a continent.

Suddenly, the bottom slopes down steeply. You have come to the end of the continent. You are now moving down its edge. The sharp drop at the edge of a continent is called the **continental slope.**

Down you go, perhaps 4 to 5 kilometers. You find yourself on a flat plain. The flat plain on the ocean floor is called the **abyssal** (uh BIS ul) **plain.**

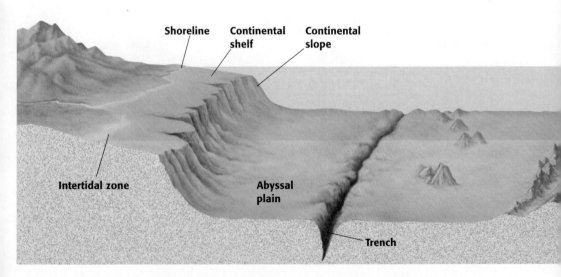

Shoreline    Continental shelf    Continental slope

Intertidal zone

Abyssal plain

Trench

You move along carefully because you know a trench might be ahead. A **trench** is a steep crack in the ocean floor. Trenches are the deepest places in the ocean.

You cross the trench safely and move on. Soon you see a huge underwater mountain range ahead. You've come to the mid-ocean ridge. The **mid-ocean ridge** is a chain of mountains that runs down the middle of an ocean.

Halfway across the mid-ocean ridge, you find yourself looking down at a deep valley. You've come to a rift valley. A **rift valley** is a deep valley that runs down the middle of a mid-ocean ridge.

You walk down into the rift valley and then up and down the mountains on the other side. Now you're back on the abyssal plain.

After nearly endless kilometers, you spot a group of mountains that poke above the ocean's surface. The mountains form a volcanic island chain. A **volcanic island chain** is made of volcanoes that built up from the ocean floor.

As you keep on walking, you come to another steep slope and then another gentle slope. You've reached another continent on the other side of the ocean.

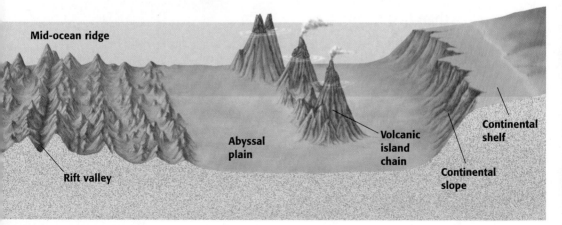

Mid-ocean ridge

Rift valley

Abyssal plain

Volcanic island chain

Continental slope

Continental shelf

# Weather and Climate

Suppose it is raining and cool where you are. That's your weather today. If you live in a desert area, most days it is dry and warm. That's your climate. Weather and climate are conditions in the air around you.

## Earth's Atmosphere

See
Also
Earth's Layers
page 159

Earth's **atmosphere** is the air around you and above you. The atmosphere is a mixture of gases. The gases stretch more than 600 kilometers above Earth.

Other gases 1%
(carbon dioxide, water
vapor, argon, neon,
helium, krypton,
xenon, methane,
hydrogen, ozone)

Oxygen
21%

Nitrogen
78%

Keyword: Weather
www.scilinks.org
Code: GSS45080

# Layers of the Atmosphere

Earth's atmosphere has five layers. Each layer has different properties, such as temperature and air pressure. **Air pressure** is the push of air against objects in all directions. As air heats and cools, it moves into and out of different layers.

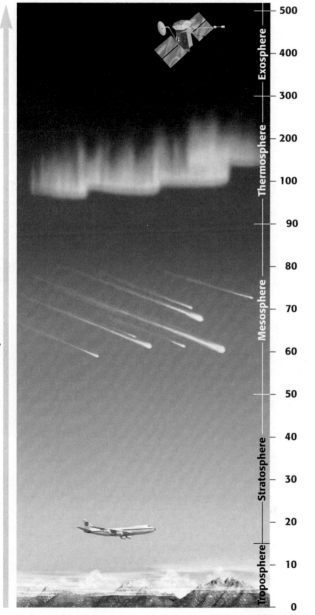

**Exosphere** (300 km to more than 600 km)
- Many satellites orbit here.
- Air pressure is lowest here.
- Temperature goes up as altitude increases.

**Thermosphere** (90 km to 300 km)
- Shimmering curtains of light called *auroras* happen here.
- Air pressure is lower than mesosphere.
- Temperature goes up as altitude increases.

**Mesosphere** (50 km to 90 km)
- Meteors, or "shooting stars," burn up here.
- Air pressure is lower than stratosphere.
- Temperature goes down as altitude increases. This is the coldest layer of the atmosphere.

**Stratosphere** (16 km to 50 km)
- Jets cruise near the bottom of this layer.
- Air pressure is lower than troposphere.
- Temperature goes up as altitude increases.

**Troposphere** (0 km to 16 km)
- All weather happens here.
- Air pressure is highest in this layer.
- Temperature goes down as altitude increases.

Air pressure decreases

Altitude (km)

## Weather

Should you wear a sweater today or just a T-shirt? Should you carry an umbrella? You ask yourself questions like these every day. What you are really asking is, *What will the weather be like today?*

**Weather** is the condition of the atmosphere in a certain place at a certain time. Weather can change from day to day, hour to hour, or even minute to minute. A number of conditions in the atmosphere affect weather.

### Temperature

Heat Energy
pages 289–291

Transfer of
Heat Energy
pages 292–294

The land and water on Earth's surface absorb heat energy from the sun. Some of this heat energy then warms the atmosphere above the surface. The amount of heat that is absorbed by Earth's surface and then released into the atmosphere changes from hour to hour and day to day.

This diagram shows the positions of the sun from sunrise to sunset on the first day of summer.

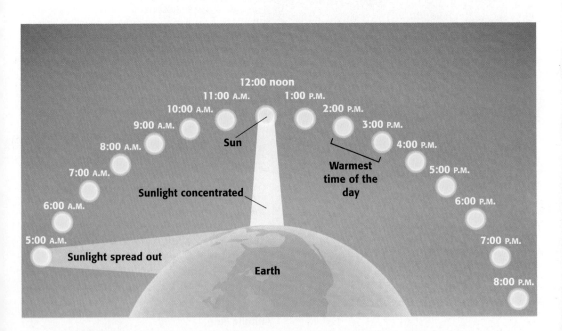

The sun is lowest in the sky early in the morning. When the sun is low in the sky, sunlight strikes Earth's surface at a low angle. The sunlight is spread out so the ground warms up less. At noontime, when the sun is highest in the sky, sunlight strikes Earth's surface like a more focused beam. The light is more concentrated. Earth's surface heats up more. A few hours later, much of this heat has warmed the atmosphere. That's why temperatures are usually highest in mid-afternoon.

Away from the equator, temperatures in the summer are warmer than temperatures in the winter. This difference is also caused by the position of the sun in the sky. In summer, the sun rises higher into the sky than it does in winter. So the sun's rays are more concentrated on Earth's surface on a summer day than on a winter day.

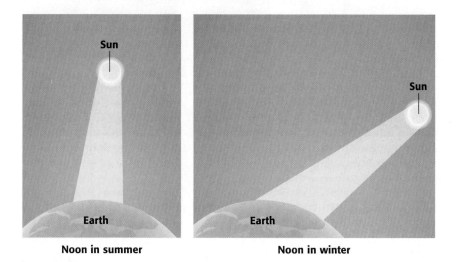

Noon in summer          Noon in winter

Different surfaces heat up at different rates. Grass heats up very slowly and does not hold heat well. That's why grass feels cool to your bare feet on a hot day. Water heats up slowly but holds heat longer than grass. Roads, especially black tar roads, heat up quickly and can get very hot on a sunny day. They cool down quickly during the night.

Measuring Temperature page 49

Heat Energy page 289

## Wind

**Wind** is moving air. Air moves because Earth's surface is heated unevenly. On a hot summer day at the beach, the land heats up faster than the water. The air above the land becomes warmer than the air above the water. The warmer air above the land rises. It is replaced by cooler air moving in from above the water. This wind is called a sea breeze.

After sunset, the land cools faster than the water. Now the air above the water is warmer than the air above the land. The warm air above the water rises. It is replaced by cooler air moving in from above the land. This wind is called a land breeze.

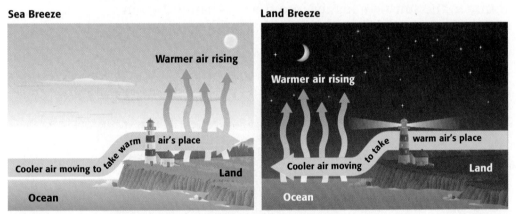

**Sea Breeze**

Warmer air rising

Cooler air moving to take warm air's place

Ocean • Land

**Land Breeze**

Warmer air rising

Cooler air moving to take warm air's place

Ocean • Land

Air movements like these can take place anywhere there is uneven heating of Earth's surface. Uneven heating produces most winds.

Wind direction is shown by a **wind vane.** Wind speed is measured with an **anemometer** (an uh MAHM ih tur).

**Wind vane**
The arrow points to the direction the wind is coming from. In this picture, the wind is blowing from north to south, so the arrow points north. The wind in the picture is called a north wind.

**Anemometer**
The wind pushes against the cups and makes them spin around. The faster the wind is blowing, the faster the cups spin.

# Air Pressure

Air has mass. Because it has mass, it has weight. **Air pressure** is the weight of air pressing on everything around it. Air presses on objects from all sides, not just down on them.

Air pressure is measured with a **barometer** (buh RAHM ih tur). There are two main types of barometers. One is a liquid barometer, and the other is an aneroid (AN uh royd) barometer.

Air pressure can change as time passes. Three conditions affect air pressure.

- **Water Vapor** Water vapor makes air moist. Air that is moister has lower air pressure. Air that is drier has higher air pressure.

- **Temperature** When air gets warmer, its pressure goes down. When air gets cooler, its pressure goes up.

- **Altitude** Air at high altitudes is thinner than air at low altitudes. "Thinner" means that the air molecules are more spread out. As altitude gets higher, air pressure goes down.

When the air pressure changes, you can tell that the weather will change. Rising air pressure means clearer weather is coming. Falling air pressure means unsettled or wet weather is coming.

**Liquid barometer**
Air presses on liquid inside the barometer. The air pressure forces the liquid up a tube. The greater the air pressure, the higher the liquid rises. The level of the liquid shows the air pressure measurement.

**Aneroid barometer**
Air presses on parts inside the barometer. The parts move a pointer. The pointer shows the air pressure measurement.

See Also

Layers of the Atmosphere page 199

Highs and Lows page 210

## Humidity

On a very humid day, your skin may feel damp. That's because the air holds a lot of water vapor. Water vapor in the air is called **humidity** (hyoo MID ih tee).

Water Cycle
pages 188–189

Water vapor enters the air when liquid water on Earth's surface evaporates. Most water vapor comes from Earth's oceans, lakes, and rivers. Some comes from damp soil. Some comes from plants and animals. Humidity changes when more or less water evaporates from these sources. Humidity also changes if water vapor in the air condenses and falls to Earth's surface.

You may have heard a weather forecaster say, "The relative humidity is 60 percent." **Relative humidity** is the amount of water vapor that the air *is* holding compared with the amount that it *could* hold at that temperature. A relative humidity of 100 percent means that the air is holding all of the water vapor it can hold at that temperature.

Relative humidity is measured with a **hygrometer** (hy GRAHM ih tur). The hygrometer in this picture is made with a hair!

**Hair hygrometer**
A hair is attached to a pointer. When humidity goes down, the hair shrinks and the pointer moves down. When humidity goes up, the hair lengthens and the pointer moves up. The numbers show the humidity measurements.

### Did You Know?

The hair on your head also shrinks and lengthens as the humidity changes. That's why some people's hair gets curlier when it's humid.

# Precipitation

The atmosphere contains water vapor. When air gets cooler, water vapor condenses. That means it changes to tiny droplets of liquid water. Water droplets clump together to form a cloud.

As more water vapor condenses, the droplets grow larger. When the drops get too large and heavy, they fall to Earth's surface. Water that falls to Earth's surface is called **precipitation** (prih sip ih TAY shun). There are different types of precipitation.

See Also

Water Cycle
pages 188–189

States of Matter
pages 262–263

Changing States
of Matter
pages 264–265

### Types of Precipitation

| Type | Characteristics |
| --- | --- |
| Drizzle | liquid drops about 1 mm in diameter |
| Rain | liquid drops 1 mm to 3 mm in diameter |
| Snow | ice in the form of six-sided crystals |
| Hail | chunks or balls of ice from 5 mm to 75 mm in diameter |
| Sleet | pellets of ice no more than 5 mm in diameter |

Rainfall is measured with a **rain gauge** (GAYJ). A rain gauge is a clear container with marks that show inches, just like a ruler.

There are snow gauges, too. A snow gauge works just like a rain gauge.

**Rain gauge**
As rain falls, water collects in the container. The mark that the water level reaches shows how much rain fell.

## Clouds

Water Cycle
pages 188–189

Precipitation
page 205

A cloud forms when water vapor in the atmosphere condenses and changes to tiny droplets of liquid water. The droplets clump together to form a cloud. If the air is cold enough, the droplets freeze to form ice crystals.

If you look up at the sky on different days, you'll see different kinds of clouds. Each kind of cloud tends to go with a different kind of weather. Each kind gives a clue about the weather that might be coming.

Clouds are not made of water vapor. They are made of droplets of liquid water or crystals of ice.

**Naming clouds** Scientists use a few basic words to describe the shapes of clouds. When you observe clouds, you can use these terms to identify what kind of cloud you are seeing.

- **Cirrus** (SEER us) means "feathery" or "tufted."
- **Stratus** (STRAT us) means "sheets" or "layers."
- **Cumulus** (KYOOM yuh lus) means "piled up."

Other words tell what the cloud may produce. For example, **nimbus** (NIM bus) means "rain cloud." So a cumulonimbus cloud is a piled up rain cloud. A nimbostratus cloud is a layered or flat rain cloud.

The word part *alto-* means "middle height." So an altostratus cloud is a layered cloud at middle height in the atmosphere.

Clouds are classified by their shape and their height above the ground.

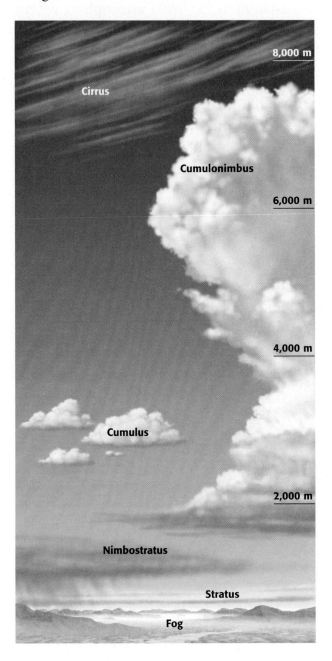

**Cirrus** clouds are high, feathery clouds at 6,000 meters to 12,000 meters above Earth's surface. These clouds are made of ice crystals. Cirrus clouds may be followed by rain or snow in a few hours.

**Cumulonimbus** clouds are huge vertical clouds. They stretch from 2,000 meters to 6,000 meters above Earth's surface. These clouds produce thunderstorms, so they are also called "thunderheads."

**Cumulus** clouds are puffy and white with flat bottoms. They are usually found between 2,000 meters and 6,000 meters above Earth's surface. These are "fair-weather" clouds.

**Nimbostratus** clouds are low, gray rain clouds or snow clouds. They are found at the same height as stratus clouds.

**Stratus** clouds are flat, gray, layered clouds that cover the whole sky. They usually are less than 2,000 meters above Earth's surface. They can bring light rain and drizzle.

**Fog** is a stratus cloud that forms close to the ground. The cloud is made of very small water droplets.

# Weather Systems and Maps

See Also

Highs and Lows
page 210

A **weather system** is an area in the lower atmosphere where the air is moving around a high or low. A high-pressure system has a high at the center. A low-pressure system has a low at the center. A weather system covers a large area.

Low-pressure systems often include weather fronts. A **front** is where one air mass meets and pushes aside another air mass. An **air mass** is a large "bubble" of air that has about the same characteristics all through it.

The numbers and symbols on a weather map tell you the characteristics of an air mass. These characteristics include air pressure, air temperature, cloud cover, wind speed, wind direction, and precipitation. The map also tells which direction the front is moving and whether it is a warm front or a cold front. Some weather maps show colored areas. Areas of the same color have similar temperatures.

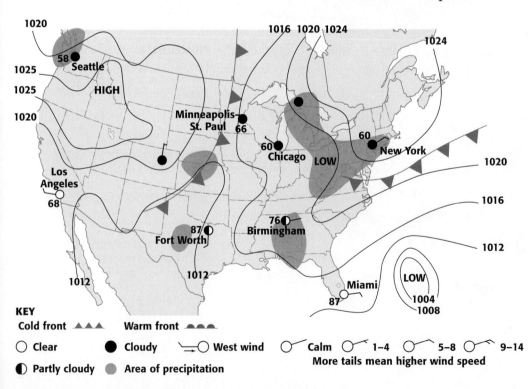

## Air Masses

An air mass has the same weather from end to end and top to bottom. The main characteristics of an air mass are its temperature and humidity. Humidity is a measure of the moisture in the air. An air mass can be cold and dry, warm and dry, cold and moist, or warm and moist.

## Weather Fronts

There are different kinds of fronts. The leading edge of a moving mass of cooler air is a **cold front.** The leading edge of a moving mass of warmer air is a **warm front.**

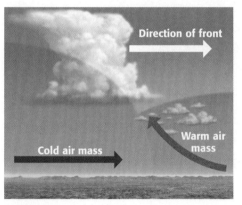

Cold front

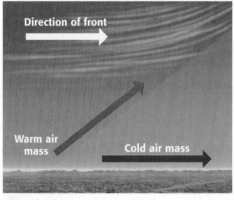

Warm front

Weather changes at fronts. For example, tall storm clouds such as thunderheads usually form at cold fronts. As the front moves through, cool fair weather is likely to follow. Warm fronts bring rain, showers, and low flat clouds. As the front passes, temperatures rise and the air becomes moister.

**Cold front**          **Warm front**

A line shows the boundary of a front. A cold front is shown by a line with triangles. A warm front is shown by a line with half circles. The triangles or half circles point in the direction that the front is moving.

## Highs and Lows

You may see the words HIGH and LOW on a weather map or just the letters H and L. These words or letters tell the locations of centers with high air pressure and centers with low air pressure. **Air pressure** is the weight of air pressing on everything around it.

Air Pressure
page 203

In a high-pressure center, air pressure is higher than in the surrounding air. In a low-pressure center, air pressure is lower than in the surrounding air.

Fair weather is usually found in areas where air pressure is high. Clouds and precipitation are usually found in areas where air pressure is low. Winds tend to blow from high-pressure areas to low-pressure areas. The greater the difference between the two areas' air pressure, the stronger the winds.

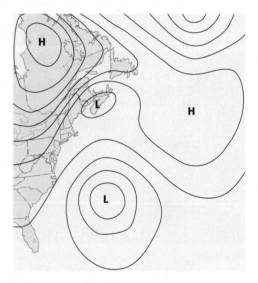

## Global Winds and Weather Systems

If you live in the northeastern part of the United States and you want to know what your weather will be like tomorrow, check today's weather in the Midwest. Why? In the United States, weather generally moves from west to east. And it usually takes about a day for weather in the Midwest to reach the northeastern part of the country.

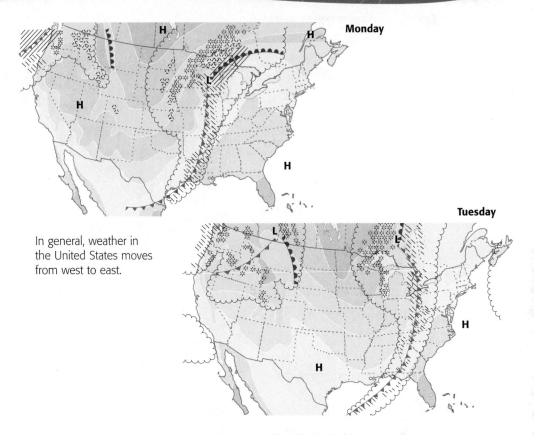

Monday

Tuesday

In general, weather in the United States moves from west to east.

**Jet stream** A steady worldwide wind called the **jet stream** blows from west to east. This wind is 6,000 to 12,000 meters above Earth's surface. Its speed is usually about 250 kilometers per hour. And it is 160 to 400 kilometers wide.

The jet stream tends to flow west to east through the middle of the United States. But it can dip farther to the south or slip higher to the north. The jet stream separates cooler air to the north from warmer air to the south. The jet stream usually shifts southward in winter and northward in summer. In winter, it can bring freezing weather as far south as Florida. The jet stream can produce low-pressure areas and local storms in the air below it.

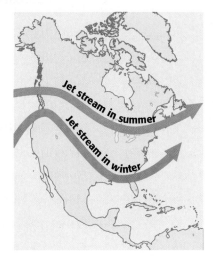

## Severe Weather

### Thunderstorms

When a cold front moves into a warm, moist air mass, the cold air slides under the warm air. The warm, moist air rushes upward along the cold front. This builds tall cumulonimbus clouds called thunderheads. These clouds can produce a huge amount of rain in just a few minutes.

This builds up electrical charges. The charges are released in lightning. The heat of the lightning makes the air around it expand explosively.

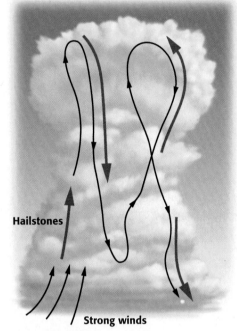

Hailstones

Strong winds

Hailstones form in a high part of a cloud where the air temperature is below freezing. Then they fall to a warmer part of the cloud. There, they pick up a layer of water. Winds blowing upward in the cloud move the hailstones up, where the water layer freezes. As winds keep moving the hailstones up and down, they grow larger and larger. Finally, the hailstones get too heavy and fall to the ground.

### How to Stay Safe in a Thunderstorm

Lightning is the main danger in a thunderstorm. Follow these tips to stay safe if a thunderstorm strikes.

- Find shelter in a building or a car.
- Don't go under a tree to find shelter.
- If you are swimming, get out of the water. If you are in a small boat, get off.
- Do not stand in an open field. Crouch.
- If you are on a bike, get off.

## Tornadoes

A **tornado** is a dark funnel of strong winds that spiral upward. Tornadoes are very powerful. A tornado's winds can reach speeds of 500 kilometers per hour.

Air pressure inside the tornado's funnel is much lower than the air pressure outside. This makes the tornado act like a huge, powerful vacuum cleaner. It can pick up or knock down trees, houses, cars, and other large objects.

In the United States, most tornadoes occur in the spring, and most occur in the Mississippi Valley and the Great Plains. They happen when a warm, moist air mass from the Gulf of Mexico runs into a cold front moving east from the Rocky Mountains.

### How to Stay Safe When a Tornado Is Coming

The main danger from a tornado is the powerful winds. Follow these tips to stay safe if a tornado strikes.

- Find shelter in a basement or a tornado cellar.
- Stay clear of outside walls, windows, and doors.
- Get away from cars, mobile homes, and other objects that might be flipped over or thrown by winds.
- If you are outdoors, find shelter in a ditch, ravine, or cave. Cover your head with your arms.

Keyword: Severe Weather
www.scilinks.org
Code: GSS45085

## Hurricanes

**Hurricanes** are very large and violent tropical storms. They can be hundreds of kilometers wide. To be called a hurricane, the winds of a tropical storm must be greater than 117 kilometers per hour.

Hurricanes start as small thunderstorms over warm water. Heat from the water fuels the storm. Winds and moisture swirl upward and increase the storm's strength.

Hurricanes usually form in late summer when the sun heats huge masses of moist air.

The calm center of a hurricane is called the eye.

High clouds move clockwise around the eye.

### Staying Safe in a Hurricane

The major dangers from a hurricane are high winds, flooding, and pounding waves. Follow these tips to stay safe if a hurricane is coming.

- Leave areas that are in the path of a hurricane well before it strikes.
- If you are caught in a hurricane, find shelter in a strong brick or stone building on high ground.
- Stay away from windows and doors.
- Keep extra food and water, a flashlight, a battery-operated radio, and, if possible, a cell phone with you.

## Blizzards

A **blizzard** is a snowstorm with winds greater than 56 kilometers per hour and air temperature below −7°C at ground level. Blizzards usually include heavy snowfall.

Blizzards often form in winter when a warm air mass runs into a cold air mass. Clouds form, the cold air freezes the moisture in the warm air mass, wind speed increases, and snow falls. If the storm gets stuck in one place, snow can fall for many hours or even a few days.

### Staying Safe in a Blizzard

A blizzard's main dangers are its strong winds, freezing temperatures, and deep snow. Follow these tips to stay safe if a blizzard strikes your area.

- Find shelter indoors.
- Stay away from windows and doors.
- If you are stuck in a car with the engine running to stay warm, keep the windows open a little bit. This will let poisonous carbon monoxide escape from the inside of the car.
- Keep extra food and water, a flashlight, a battery-operated radio, and, if possible, a cell phone with you.
- If you are trudging through deep snow, keep moving. Do not lie down to rest.
- If you are caught outdoors, use clothing to cover your face and as much of your skin as you can.

See Also

Air Masses
page 209

Weather Fronts
page 209

## Climate

**Climate** is the general weather of an area over a long period of time, such as many years. **Weather** is the condition of the atmosphere at a place for a short period of time, such as a few days.

Scientists identify three basic climates on Earth. The climates are tropical, temperate, and polar.

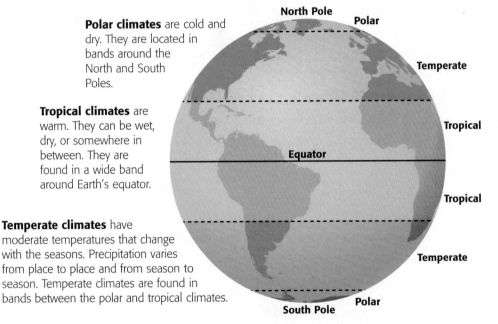

**Polar climates** are cold and dry. They are located in bands around the North and South Poles.

**Tropical climates** are warm. They can be wet, dry, or somewhere in between. They are found in a wide band around Earth's equator.

**Temperate climates** have moderate temperatures that change with the seasons. Precipitation varies from place to place and from season to season. Temperate climates are found in bands between the polar and tropical climates.

Earth's tilt on its axis is mainly responsible for these climate bands. For example, in December the North Pole is tilted away from the sun. Sunlight doesn't reach the North Pole, and temperatures plunge. Even in June, sunlight is at a low angle and does not heat the land much. So this region stays cold all year round.

Revolution and Seasons pages 220–221

Sunlight hits the temperate regions more directly in summer and less directly in winter. So these regions become warmer and cooler and warmer again as the seasons pass. The tropical regions get the most direct sunlight all year. So they are warm all year.

A region's climate is affected by many things. These include the region's latitude, elevation, nearness to large bodies of water, and nearby ocean currents.

See Also

Waves and Currents page 194

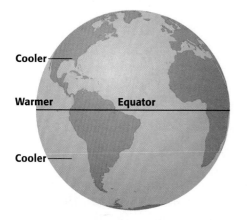

**Latitude** is the distance from the equator. In general, the farther away from the equator a region is, the cooler its climate is.

**Elevation** is the height above sea level. In general, the higher the region's elevation, the cooler its climate is.

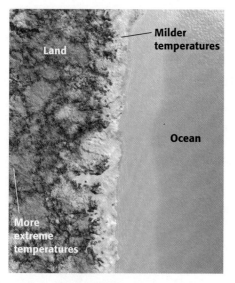

**Large bodies of water** In general, temperatures are milder near large bodies of water such as oceans, seas, and large lakes. Where winds usually blow inland, the climate is wetter.

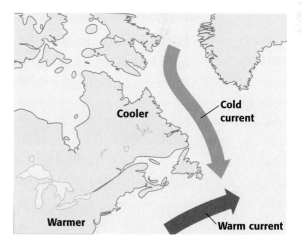

**Ocean currents** Cold currents make nearby land cooler. Warm currents make nearby land warmer.

# Earth and Its Moon

Scientists Are
Affected by Their
Societies
pages 368–369

Earth and its moon move in different ways. Earth revolves around the sun. The moon revolves around Earth. Both Earth and the moon also rotate like a spinning top. These movements are predictable and regular.

## Earth's Rotation

Earth rotates once on its axis every 24 hours. Earth's **axis** (AK sis) is an imaginary line that passes through Earth's center from the North Pole to the South Pole.

One rotation of Earth equals one day. At any time, half of Earth faces the sun. That half has daytime. At the same time, the other half of Earth faces away from the sun. That half has nighttime.

Earth rotates from west to east on its axis. This makes the sun, moon, and stars look as though they are moving from east to west. The sun, moon, and stars rise in the east and set in the west.

The length of daylight changes during the year. The shortest amount of daylight is on the first day of winter. That is December 21 in the Northern Hemisphere. The longest amount of daylight is on the first day of summer, June 21. From June 21 to December 21, the days grow shorter. From December 21 to June 21, the days grow longer.

These changes are caused by Earth's tilt on its axis and its revolution around the sun. On June 21, the Northern Hemisphere is tilted the most toward the sun. As Earth rotates, places in the Northern Hemisphere are in daylight longer than places in the Southern Hemisphere.

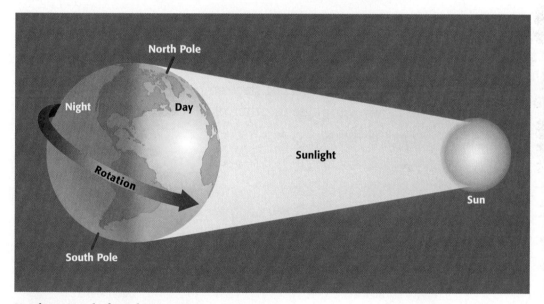

**Northern Hemisphere in summer**

On June 21 in the Northern Hemisphere, places farthest from the equator are in daylight the longest. In the Southern Hemisphere, places farthest from the equator are in darkness the longest. On June 21, the area around the North Pole has daylight 24 hours a day. At the same time, the area around the South Pole is in darkness 24 hours a day. At the equator, daylight and darkness are about equal in length.

Revolution and Seasons
pages 220–221

# Revolution and Seasons

A **revolution** (rev uh LOO shun) is a complete trip around the sun. One revolution equals one year. Earth makes one revolution in $365\frac{1}{4}$ days. But your calendar shows that most years are only 365 days long. The missing quarters of a day add up year after year. In four years, one whole day has been added. The "extra" day is shown on the calendar as February 29. That year has 366 days and is called a leap year.

Earth's path around the sun is called its **orbit.** Earth's orbit is not a circle. It is a shape called an ellipse (ih LIPS). Think of an ellipse as a flattened circle that is longer than it is wide.

Earth is tilted $23\frac{1}{2}$ degrees on its axis. Because of this tilt, different parts of Earth have different amounts of daylight and darkness at the same time of the year. And sunlight strikes different parts of Earth more directly in some places and at a lower angle in other places. These differences cause Earth's seasons.

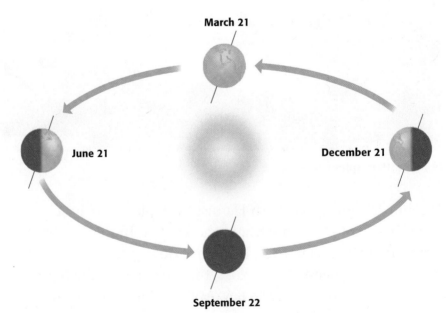

March 21

June 21

December 21

September 22

Summer is when the Northern Hemisphere is warmest. In July, August, and September, sunlight strikes the Northern Hemisphere more directly and for more hours each day than it does in January, February, and March. So the Northern Hemisphere has summer from July until September.

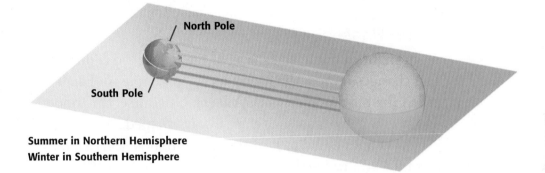

North Pole

South Pole

**Summer in Northern Hemisphere**
**Winter in Southern Hemisphere**

Seasons are opposite in the Northern Hemisphere and the Southern Hemisphere. The first day of summer in the Northern Hemisphere happens when the Northern Hemisphere is most tilted toward the sun. As that same time, the first day of winter comes to the Southern Hemisphere. On this day, the Southern Hemisphere is most tilted away from the sun.

See
Also

Climate
pages 216–217

When it is fall in North America, it is spring in South America. When it is spring in North America, it is fall in South American. On the first day of fall and spring, Earth isn't tilted either away from or toward the sun. Day and night are about equal in length.

The seasons aren't caused by how close Earth is to the sun. In fact, Earth is closer to the sun in January than it is in July!

## Moon Motions

The moon rotates on its axis and revolves around Earth. One rotation and one revolution take the same amount of time, about 28 days. Because of this, the same side of the moon always faces Earth.

### Moon Phases

From night to night, the shape of the moon looks different. The changes in how the moon looks to people on Earth are called the moon's **phases** (FAYZ ez). Of course, the moon doesn't really change shape. It's always shaped like a ball. What changes is the part of the moon that reflects light from the sun to Earth.

Sometimes the moon looks like a full circle. That phase is called a full moon. At two other times in a month, the moon looks like a half circle. Those phases are called the first quarter and the last quarter. The first quarter comes about 7 days before a full moon. The last quarter comes about 7 days after a full moon. The same phase of the moon repeats about every $29\frac{1}{2}$ days.

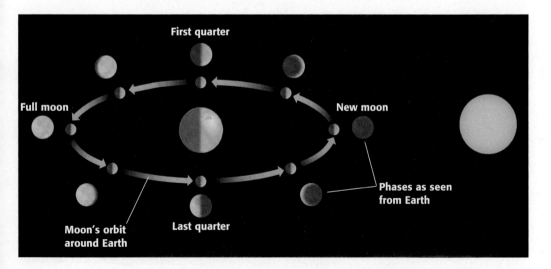

First quarter

Full moon

New moon

Phases as seen from Earth

Moon's orbit around Earth

Last quarter

The moon doesn't have any light of its own. The light we see is sunlight that hits the moon and is reflected to Earth.

The shape of the part of the moon that reflects light to Earth depends on two things. One is the moon's position in its orbit around Earth. The other is the position of the sun. In every phase of the moon, the lit part faces the sun. Even if you can't see the sun, you can tell where it is by how it lights the moon. For example, when you see a first-quarter moon with the lighted side to your right, the sun is to your right. When you see a full moon, the sun is behind you.

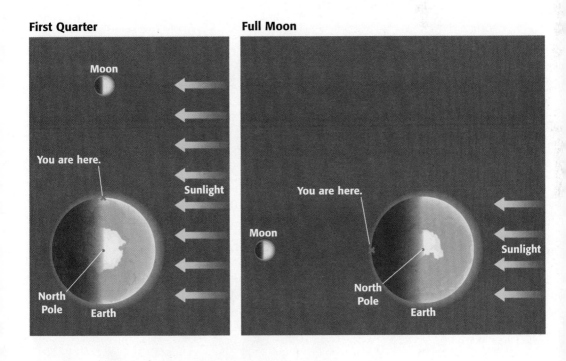

**First Quarter**

Moon

You are here.

Sunlight

North Pole    Earth

**Full Moon**

You are here.

Moon

Sunlight

North Pole

Earth

## Science Alert!

In some phases, you can see the moon during part of the day.

## Eclipses

Imagine you were in an ancient city and suddenly, in the full light of day, a shadow began to creep across the sun's surface. What would you think was happening? About two hours later, the shadow would have covered the entire sun. Ancient civilizations were often terrified of these shadows, but all they would have seen was an eclipse of the sun.

An **eclipse** (ih KLIPS) happens when one object in space casts a shadow on another object in space. At least twice a year, Earth casts a shadow on the moon. This occurrence is called an eclipse of the moon.

**Eclipse of the moon**
An eclipse of the moon happens when Earth comes between the sun and the moon.

Sun     Earth     Moon

In an eclipse of the sun, the moon casts a shadow on Earth. People in this shadow see the sun slowly blotted out by the moon passing between it and Earth.

**Eclipse of the sun**
An eclipse of the sun happens when the moon comes between Earth and the sun.

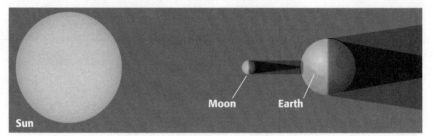

Sun     Moon     Earth

During an eclipse of the sun, the moon's shadow on Earth is small. That's because the moon's diameter is so much smaller than Earth's diameter. It's like holding up a penny between a lamp and your hand. The penny casts a shadow over only part of your hand. During an eclipse of the moon, it's as if your hand is between the lamp and the penny. Your hand casts a large shadow over the penny.

## Properties of the Moon

In some ways, the moon is like Earth. In other ways, it is much different from Earth.

### Properties of the Moon and Earth

| Property | Moon | Earth |
| --- | --- | --- |
| Diameter | 3,476 km | 12,756 km |
| Shape | almost a round ball | almost a round ball |
| Atmosphere | none | 78% nitrogen, 21% oxygen, 1% other gases |
| Surface | rocky; many craters; mountains; plains; dry | rocky; 70% covered by water; very few craters; mountains; plains |
| Rotation | 27 days, 7 hours, 43 minutes | 23 hours, 56 minutes, 4 seconds |

U.S. astronauts explored the moon in the late 1960s and early 1970s. They haven't been back since then.

# The Solar System and Beyond

Our **solar system** includes the sun, eight planets and their moons, comets, large space rocks called asteroids (AS tuh roydz), dwarf planets, and small space rocks called meteoroids (MEE tee uh roydz). Beyond our solar system are stars and groups of stars called galaxies.

## The Sun

See Also

Gravity and Orbits page 227

Asteroid Belt page 230

Comets and Meteoroids page 233

The sun is an average-size star at the center of our solar system. Everything in the solar system revolves around the sun. Everything is kept in orbit by the pull of the sun's gravity.

The sun is a huge yellow ball made mostly of fiery hydrogen gas. This fiery ball produces the heat and light that stream 150 million kilometers through space to Earth.

The sun rotates on it axis. The sun completes one rotation in 25 days. One rotation of Earth takes a little less than 24 hours.

## Gravity and Orbits

**Gravity** is a force that pulls objects toward each other. All objects produce a force of gravity. The more mass an object has, the greater its force of gravity. The sun has much more mass than Earth, so the sun's gravity is much greater than Earth's gravity.

Mass page 244

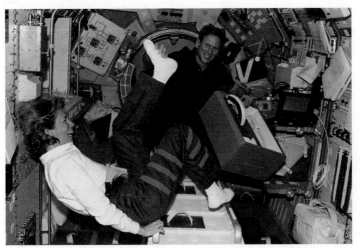

The force of Earth's gravity tends to pull objects toward Earth. At the same time, the outward movement of an object in orbit tends to move it away from Earth. When these forces balance, the object doesn't move either toward or away from Earth. It just floats in space, like an astronaut in an orbiting space shuttle. The object is said to be "weightless."

As the distance between objects increases, the force of gravity between them decreases. If Earth were farther away from the sun, the force of gravity between Earth and the sun would be less.

The sun's gravity keeps the planets and other objects in the solar system in orbit around the sun. An **orbit** is the path one object takes around another object. If it were not for the sun's gravity, planets and other objects in the solar system would speed off into outer space. The gravity of a planet keeps its moons in orbit around it.

Keyword: Solar System
www.scilinks.org
Code: GSS45090

## The Planets

Eight planets revolve around the sun. Each planet is a different distance from the sun. This diagram shows the planets' distances from the sun. The sizes of the planets are not shown to scale.

Earth is the third planet from the sun. The distance between Earth and the sun is almost 150 million kilometers.

Each planet's orbit around the sun is a flattened circle called an **ellipse** (ih LIPS). Each planet takes a different and predictable amount of time to complete one trip around the sun. One trip around the sun is called a **revolution** (rev uh LOO shun). The time it takes for a planet to make one revolution around the sun is the planet's **year.** The closer a planet is to the sun, the shorter the planet's year is.

The planets are much smaller than the sun. The largest planet in the solar system is Jupiter. But Jupiter's diameter is only about one-ninth the diameter of the sun. This picture shows the relative sizes of the sun and the planets. The distances between planets are not shown to scale.

## Mercury

Mercury is the closest planet to the sun. Its surface is rocky and pockmarked with craters. There is no water on Mercury, and it has almost no atmosphere. Because Mercury is so close to the sun, its daytime temperatures can reach about 450°C. But because Mercury has almost no atmosphere, heat from the sun is lost very quickly at night. At night, Mercury's temperatures plunge to below −180°C.

**A Quick Look at Mercury**

| | |
|---|---|
| Diameter | 4,900 km |
| Length of day (Earth time) | 59 days |
| Length of year (Earth time) | 88 days |
| Distance from the sun | 58 million km |
| Number of known moons | 0 |

## Venus

Venus is the second closest planet to the sun. Its surface is rocky. Craters dot the surface. Large plains stretch over parts of the surface, and tall mountains rise from it. There is no liquid water on Venus. It has a very thick atmosphere made mostly of carbon dioxide. The temperature at the surface is about 470°C.

**A Quick Look at Venus**

| | |
|---|---|
| Diameter | 12,000 km |
| Length of day (Earth time) | 243 days |
| Length of year (Earth time) | 225 days |
| Distance from the sun | 108 million km |
| Number of known moons | 0 |

## Mars

Mars is the fourth planet from the sun. Its surface is rocky. It has craters, mountains, and canyons. There is no liquid water on Mars, but ice covers its North Pole area in winter. Mars has a thin atmosphere made mostly of carbon dioxide. Temperatures range from about 20°C to –123°C.

### A Quick Look at Mars

| | |
|---|---|
| Diameter | 6,800 km |
| Length of day (Earth time) | 25 hours |
| Length of year (Earth time) | 687 days |
| Distance from the sun | 228 million km |
| Number of known moons | 2 |

### Did You Know?

People call Mars the Red Planet because its surface has a reddish color. You can even see the color from Earth without using a telescope.

## Asteroid Belt

There is a large space between the orbit of Mars and the orbit of the next planet, Jupiter. In this space is a belt of small and large rocks called **asteroids** (AS tuh roydz). Most asteroids are about 1 kilometer in diameter. The largest is 940 kilometers in diameter. Asteroids do not have an atmosphere.

This asteroid is named Ida. It is the first asteroid with a moon that scientists have discovered.

# Jupiter

Jupiter is the fifth planet from the sun. It is the largest planet in the solar system. Scientists think that Jupiter's surface is an ocean of liquid hydrogen. Jupiter's atmosphere is very thick and made mostly of hydrogen gas. Temperatures in Jupiter's atmosphere fall to about −160°C.

**A Quick Look at Jupiter**

| | |
|---|---|
| Diameter | 143,000 km |
| Length of day (Earth time) | 10 hours |
| Length of year (Earth time) | 112 years |
| Distance from the sun | 778 million km |
| Number of known moons | 63 |

# Saturn

Saturn is the sixth planet from the sun. It is the second largest planet in the solar system. It has the largest set of rings of any of the planets. Its surface is probably a mixture of liquid or slushy substances. Saturn's atmosphere is very thick and made mostly of hydrogen. Temperatures in Saturn's atmosphere fall to about −190°C.

**A Quick Look at Saturn**

| | |
|---|---|
| Diameter | 121,000 km |
| Length of day (Earth time) | 10 hours |
| Length of year (Earth time) | 29.5 years |
| Distance from the sun | 1,430 million km |
| Number of known moons | 62 |

## Uranus

Uranus is the seventh planet from the sun. Scientists think its surface is a mixture of frozen materials. Uranus's atmosphere is very thick and made of hydrogen, helium, and methane gases. The planet's axis points almost directly at the sun, so you might think of Uranus as rotating on its side. Temperatures in Uranus's atmosphere are as low as about −220°C.

### A Quick Look at Uranus

| | |
|---|---|
| Diameter | 51,100 km |
| Length of day (Earth time) | 17 hours |
| Length of year (Earth time) | 84 years |
| Distance from the sun | 2,870 million km |
| Number of known moons | 27 |

## Neptune

Neptune is the eighth planet from the sun. Evidence suggests that Neptune's surface may be made of rock, frozen water, and frozen ammonia. Neptune's atmosphere is very thick and made of hydrogen and methane gases. The coldest temperature in the atmosphere of Neptune is a little below −220°C.

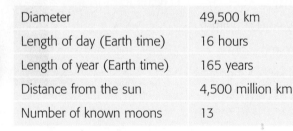

### A Quick Look at Neptune

| | |
|---|---|
| Diameter | 49,500 km |
| Length of day (Earth time) | 16 hours |
| Length of year (Earth time) | 165 years |
| Distance from the sun | 4,500 million km |
| Number of known moons | 13 |

## Pluto

For nearly 80 years, Pluto was considered to be the ninth planet of the solar system. It is very far away from Earth, and no space probes have visited it. In 2006, scientists decided that for an object to be a planet, it had to be in a clear orbit around a star. Because Pluto is not in a clear orbit around the sun, scientists reclassified it as a "dwarf planet."

### A Quick Look at Pluto

| | |
|---|---|
| Diameter | 2,300 km |
| Length of day (Earth time) | 6 days, 9 hours |
| Length of year (Earth time) | 248 years |
| Distance from the sun | 5,900 million km |

## Comets and Meteoroids

**Comets** are mountain-size chunks of ice and dust that orbit the sun. They streak towards the sun from beyond Pluto and then back into outer space. Some comets orbit the sun again and again. Others crash into the sun. And some make one trip around the sun and never return.

**Comet**

**Sun**

As a comet orbits the sun, the sun's radiation sweeps some of it into a tail millions of kilometers long. A comet's tail always points away from the sun.

**Meteoroids** (MEE tee uh roydz) are small space rocks that orbit the sun. Sometimes a meteoroid enters Earth's atmosphere and burns up. The streak of light made by a burning meteoroid is called a **meteor** (MEE tee ur). Meteoroids that strike Earth's surface are called **meteorites** (MEE tee uh ryts).

## Stars

A **star** is an object in space that produces its own heat and light. Space is filled with many trillions of stars. Some stars are 1,000 times the size of our sun. Some stars are as small as 16 kilometers in diameter. That's 87,000 times smaller than our sun's diameter. Our sun is an average-size star.

Stars are made mostly of hydrogen and helium gas. Stars are different colors—blue, white, yellow, red, and red-orange.

The Sun
pages 226–227

Some stars are brighter than others. A star's brightness is described in two ways. One is its actual brightness. That is the actual amount of light the star gives off. The other is how bright a star *looks* to people on Earth. If two stars have the same actual brightness but one is farther away, the one that is closer will look brighter.

Space stretches out beyond our solar system for at least 100 sextillion kilometers! That's the numeral 1 followed by 23 zeros.

## Galaxies

A **galaxy** (GAL uk see) is a group of between 1 million and 1 trillion stars. Our sun and solar system are part of the Milky Way Galaxy. The Milky Way Galaxy contains 100 to 200 billion stars.

From above, the Milky Way Galaxy would look like a spiral. So it is called a spiral galaxy. From the side, it would look a little like a dinner plate. Different galaxies have different shapes and sizes.

Space is filled with several billion galaxies. The nearest galaxy to the Milky Way Galaxy is so far away that its light takes almost two million years to reach Earth.

**There are three main types of galaxies.**

**Spiral galaxy**

**Elliptical galaxy**

**Irregular galaxy**

## Constellations

A **constellation** (kahn stuh LAY shun) is a group of stars that ancient people thought formed a picture in the sky. Many constellations are named for animals, heroes, or other characters in ancient tales.

Today's astronomers identify 88 constellations. Some can be seen only from Earth's Northern Hemisphere. Others can be seen only from the Southern Hemisphere. The stars in a constellation are really far apart in space. From Earth, the stars *look* as if they are close together because they are so far away.

Astronomers use the constellations as a map of the sky. For example, the planets are in different places in the sky at different times. To help you find a planet in the sky, an astronomer might tell you to look at stars in a certain constellation.

As Earth revolves around the sun, constellations appear in different parts of the sky in different seasons. Some constellations rise high in the night sky in one season and disappear below the horizon in another season.

Polaris (puh LAR is), called the North Star, is always seen directly above Earth's North Pole. You can use the "pointer stars" in the Big Dipper to find Polaris. Then you can tell which direction is north.

Little Dipper

Polaris (North Star)

Big Dipper

Pointer stars

These are the constellations you can see from the middle latitudes of the Northern Hemisphere in winter and summer.

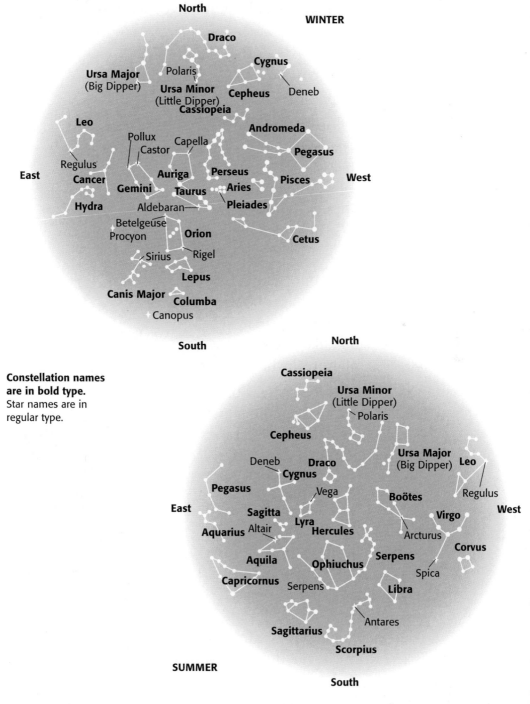

Constellation names are in bold type.
Star names are in regular type.

## Observing Space

Astronomers use different tools to observe objects in space. These tools include light telescopes, radio telescopes, and satellites.

### Light Telescopes

Light telescopes use lenses and mirrors to capture light from distant objects in space.

- Light telescopes collect much more light than you can see with just your eyes. Objects that are too dim for you to see with your eyes can become visible with a light telescope.

- Light telescopes allow astronomers to see objects that are very close together. What may look like one star to your eyes might really be two stars.

- Light telescopes make objects in space look larger and closer. For example, you can see craters on the moon that you can't see with just your eyes.

The larger the lens or mirror in the telescope, the more you can see with it. The largest mirror for a light telescope is 980 centimeters in diameter. It has 36 separate mirrors that fit together. A hobby telescope might have a mirror that is 15 centimeters in diameter.

See Also

Mirrors and Reflection page 313

Lenses and Refraction page 314

**Light rays**
**Large lens**
**Small eyepiece lens**

**Refracting telescope**
A refracting telescope has two lenses.

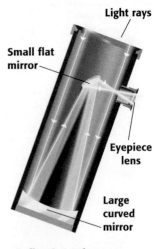

**Light rays**
**Small flat mirror**
**Eyepiece lens**
**Large curved mirror**

**Reflecting telescope**
A reflecting telescope has one lens and two mirrors.

## Radio Telescopes

A radio telescope uses a large "dish" to collect radio waves from outer space. Radio waves are invisible. Radio telescopes collect information that cannot be seen. Scientists have detected radio waves coming from places in the sky that are totally dark.

The largest single-dish radio telescope in the world is located at Arecibo, Puerto Rico. Its dish is more than 300 meters wide.

## Satellites

Some satellites that orbit Earth carry instruments that are used to observe objects in space. These instruments receive clearer pictures of distant objects than the pictures that astronomers can get from Earth. That's because Earth's atmosphere interferes with light and other forms of energy arriving from space. Satellites orbit above most of the atmosphere.

Layers of the Atmosphere page 199

The most famous satellite telescope is the Hubble Space Telescope. It orbits 610 kilometers above Earth's surface. Pictures taken by this telescope are beamed to Earth as radio waves.

# Physical Science

*HOW* does this coaster work?

What is a roller coaster car made of? What makes it creep up a hill? What makes it plunge down the other side? What makes it stop? The science that answers questions like these is physical science. **Physical science** is the study of matter, forces, motion, and energy.

# Matter

In science, the "stuff" that everything is made of is called **matter.** You are made of matter. A basketball is made of matter. Water is matter. So is the air in a balloon and the air around the balloon. All objects and substances are made of matter.

You can use your senses to detect matter. You can feel the shape and roughness of a rock. You can taste the juice of an orange. You can smell popcorn. You can see the crowd at a ball game.

But some kinds of matter, such as air, are invisible. And they don't have a taste or odor. So how do you know that air is made of matter? You know because when air moves, you can feel it. You can see it blow leaves across the ground. You can see a kite lifted high by the wind. And you can feel the kite pull against the string as the wind blows it.

Some bits of matter, such as viruses and the cells that make up your body, are too small to see with just your eyes. The only way you can see most cells is to look at them through a microscope. But even when something is too tiny to see, it is still made of matter.

## Properties of Matter

Both sugar and salt are white, grainy substances. You know that sugar tastes sweet and salt tastes salty. But could you tell these substances apart without tasting them? Yes, if you knew some of their other properties.

States of Matter
pages 262–263

**Properties** are the characteristics of a substance. The way a substance tastes is one of its properties. The way it smells is another property. So is its color. Other properties include whether it is attracted to a magnet, whether it dissolves in water, and whether it is a solid, a liquid, or a gas at room temperature. No two substances have exactly the same set of properties.

Three major properties of all matter are mass, volume, and density.

**Mass** All matter has mass. **Mass** is the amount of matter in an object or substance. Your mass is greater than the mass of a brick. That's because your body contains more matter than a brick does.

Mass is measured in kilograms (kg), grams (g), and milligrams (mg). The mass of an object can be measured with a balance.

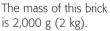

Using a Two-
Pan Balance
page 47

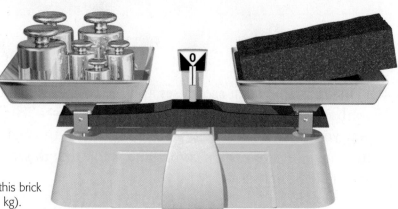

The mass of this brick
is 2,000 g (2 kg).

**Volume** All matter takes up space. The amount of space that an object or substance takes up is its **volume** (VAHL yoom). You have a larger volume than a brick. Your body takes up more space than a brick does.

**See Also**

Useful Equations
pages 384–385

The volume of block-shaped objects, such as bricks, boxes, and rooms, is measured in cubic centimeters (cm³) and cubic meters (m³). To find the volume of a block-shaped object, first you have to measure its length, width, and height. Then multiply those measurements to find the volume.

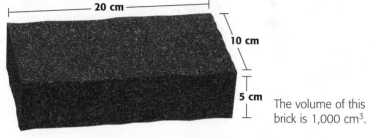

10 cm

5 cm   The volume of this brick is 1,000 cm³.

**20 cm × 10 cm × 5 cm = 1,000 cm³**

The volume of liquids and powders is measured in milliliters (mL), liters (L), and kiloliters (kL). Measuring cups and graduated cylinders are used to measure the volume of liquids and powders.

**See Also**

Measuring the Volume of Liquids
pages 44–45

**Density** The amount of mass in a known volume of an object is the object's **density** (DEN sih tee). To find the density of an object, divide its mass by its volume.

The brick's density is 2 g/cm³ (two grams per cubic centimeter).

**brick's density = 2,000 g ÷ 1,000 cm³**

## Physical and Chemical Properties

All matter has two kinds of properties—physical properties and chemical properties. A **physical property** is a property that can be observed, measured, or changed without changing the substance itself. The first table on the next page lists some physical properties of matter.

Physical Changes
page 261

States of Matter
pages 262–263

Changing States
of Matter
pages 264–265

Chemical
Changes
pages 266–267

For example, you can measure the mass and length of a nail. You can bend the nail. You can test it to see if it's attracted to a magnet. You can cut it into little pieces. You can melt it. Measuring the nail, bending it, testing it with a magnet, cutting it up, and melting it don't change the substance that makes up the nail.

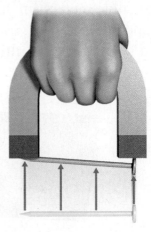

Being magnetic is a physical property of the nail.

A **chemical property** is the ability of a substance to change into a new substance with different properties. For example, if you leave a nail outdoors where it can get wet, the nail rusts. Iron in the nail combines with oxygen in the air to form rust. The properties of rust are different from the properties of iron and the properties of oxygen. The rust is a new substance. The second table on the next page lists some chemical properties of matter.

The ability of iron to combine with oxygen and form rust is a chemical property of iron.

## Physical Properties

| Property | What It Means | Example |
|----------|---------------|---------|
| color | the color of a substance | Iron is gray. Rust is red. |
| texture | how a substance feels or looks | Sandpaper is rough. Glass is smooth. |
| odor | how a substance smells | Water has no odor. Vinegar has a sharp odor. |
| conducts heat | how easily heat moves through a substance | Metals conduct heat well. Plastics do not conduct heat well. |
| conducts electricity | how easily electricity moves through a substance | Copper is a good conductor of electricity. Rubber is not. |
| magnetic | is attracted to a magnet | Iron is magnetic. Aluminum is not. |
| floats or sinks in water | is more dense or less dense than an equal volume of water | Lead sinks in water. Oil floats on water. |
| solubility | the ability to dissolve in another substance | Sugar dissolves in water. Sand does not. |
| boiling point | the temperature at which a substance begins to turn from a liquid to a gas | The boiling point of water is 100°C. |
| melting point | the temperature at which a substance begins to turn from a solid to a liquid | The melting point of frozen water is 0°C. |

## Chemical Properties

| Property | What It Means | Example |
|----------|---------------|---------|
| burns | flames when heated | Paper burns. Iron does not. |
| rusts | forms rust when exposed to air and water | Iron rusts. Aluminum does not. |
| reacts with acids | changes when exposed to an acid | Baking soda gives off carbon dioxide bubbles when exposed to vinegar. |

## Atoms

How many pieces can you divide a pure substance into? You can divide it until you just have one atom of it. An **atom** is the smallest particle of a substance that has all the properties of the substance.

Gold is made of atoms of gold. All gold atoms are alike. All gold atoms have the same properties. Silver is made of atoms of silver. All silver atoms are alike. They are not like gold atoms or the atoms of any other substance.

Atoms are very tiny. They are tinier than the cells in your body. They are tinier than germs. They are too small to be seen with ordinary microscopes.

It would take about 100 million of the smallest atoms laid end-to-end to stretch across your thumbnail!

**Hydrogen atom**
The smallest atom, a hydrogen atom, is 1,000 times smaller than a flu virus.

**Flu virus**
A flu virus is 10 times smaller than the germ that causes strep throat.

**Strep germ**
The germ that causes strep throat is 10 times smaller than one of your red blood cells.

**Red blood cell**
$1,000 \times 10 \times 10 = 100,000$
A hydrogen atom is 100,000 times smaller than one of your red blood cells.

## Parts of an Atom

An atom is made up of still smaller parts. These parts determine what the atom is, its mass, and how it behaves. The parts are protons (PROH tahnz), neutrons (NOO trahnz), and electrons (ih LEK trahnz). Protons and neutrons are packed together in the atom's center, called the **nucleus** (NOO klee us). Electrons are in the space outside the nucleus. All protons, neutrons, and electrons are the same, no matter what kind of atom they are in.

**Protons** are positively charged particles in the nucleus of an atom. The number of protons tells what kind of atom it is. For example, atoms with one proton are hydrogen atoms. Atoms with two protons are helium atoms. The atom in this drawing has three protons. It is an atom of a light metal called lithium.

**Nucleus**

**Neutrons** are also in the nucleus of an atom. They are not charged. Neutrons add mass to an atom. The number of neutrons in an atom is usually the same as the number of protons. But some atoms of the same kind may have different numbers of neutrons. The number of neutrons does not change what kind of atom it is.

**Electrons** are negatively charged particles. The number of electrons in an atom is usually the same as the number of protons. Electrons are in spaces called "clouds" outside the nucleus. The number and arrangement of electrons determine how an atom will interact with other atoms. In other words, electrons determine an atom's chemical properties.

*See Also*

Physical and Chemical Properties pages 246–247

Keyword: Inside the Atom
www.scilinks.org
Code: GSS45095

# Elements

An **element** is a pure substance made of only one kind of atom. Gold is an element. So are iron, hydrogen, and oxygen. Water is not an element because it is made of hydrogen and oxygen atoms joined together.

All the atoms of an element are alike. Different elements have different kinds of atoms. For example, all atoms of hydrogen are alike. All atoms of oxygen are alike. Atoms of hydrogen are different from atoms of oxygen.

There are well over 100 known elements on Earth and in the universe. Of these, 94 elements occur naturally on Earth, on other planets, and in the stars. The rest have been made by scientists in laboratories.

The bodies of all living things, including you, are made mostly of four elements—oxygen, carbon, hydrogen, and nitrogen. If you could weigh the elements in your body, you would find it is about 65% oxygen, 18.5% carbon, 9.5% hydrogen, 3.3% nitrogen, and 3.7% other elements.

**Chemical Symbols** Each element has a chemical symbol. The symbol is a short way of writing the element's name. Some symbols are the first one or two letters of the element's name or the first letter plus another letter in the name. For example, **C** is the symbol for carbon. **He** is the symbol for helium. **Mg** is the symbol for magnesium. Some symbols come from an element's Latin name. The Latin name for iron is *ferrum*. The chemical symbol for iron is **Fe**.

Chemical symbols are used to show the elements in the periodic table of the elements. The **periodic table of the elements** lists all the elements arranged by properties and by atomic number. An element's atomic number equals the number of protons in one atom.

# Periodic Table of Elements

13
**Al**
Aluminum
26.98

Atomic number
Chemical symbol
Element name
Average atomic mass

**Chemical Symbol**
Solid **Na**
Liquid **Hg**
Gas

**Background**
Metals
Metalloids
Nonmetals

113
**Uut**
Ununtrium
(284)
Unconfirmed Elements

| Group 1 | Group 2 | Group 3 | Group 4 | Group 5 | Group 6 | Group 7 | Group 8 | Group 9 | Group 10 | Group 11 | Group 12 | Group 13 | Group 14 | Group 15 | Group 16 | Group 17 | Group 18 |
|---|---|---|---|---|---|---|---|---|---|---|---|---|---|---|---|---|---|
| 1 **H** Hydrogen 1.008 | | | | | | | | | | | | | | | | | 2 **He** Helium 4.003 |
| 3 **Li** Lithium 6.94 | 4 **Be** Beryllium 9.01 | | | | | | | | | | | 5 **B** Boron 10.81 | 6 **C** Carbon 12.01 | 7 **N** Nitrogen 14.01 | 8 **O** Oxygen 16.00 | 9 **F** Fluorine 19.00 | 10 **Ne** Neon 20.18 |
| 11 **Na** Sodium 22.99 | 12 **Mg** Magnesium 24.31 | | | | | | | | | | | 13 **Al** Aluminum 26.98 | 14 **Si** Silicon 28.09 | 15 **P** Phosphorus 30.97 | 16 **S** Sulfur 32.06 | 17 **Cl** Chlorine 35.45 | 18 **Ar** Argon 39.95 |
| 19 **K** Potassium 39.10 | 20 **Ca** Calcium 40.08 | 21 **Sc** Scandium 44.96 | 22 **Ti** Titanium 47.87 | 23 **V** Vanadium 50.94 | 24 **Cr** Chromium 52.00 | 25 **Mn** Manganese 54.94 | 26 **Fe** Iron 55.85 | 27 **Co** Cobalt 58.93 | 28 **Ni** Nickel 58.69 | 29 **Cu** Copper 63.55 | 30 **Zn** Zinc 65.38 | 31 **Ga** Gallium 69.72 | 32 **Ge** Germanium 72.63 | 33 **As** Arsenic 74.92 | 34 **Se** Selenium 78.96 | 35 **Br** Bromine 79.90 | 36 **Kr** Krypton 83.80 |
| 37 **Rb** Rubidium 85.47 | 38 **Sr** Strontium 87.62 | 39 **Y** Yttrium 88.91 | 40 **Zr** Zirconium 91.22 | 41 **Nb** Niobium 92.91 | 42 **Mo** Molybdenum 95.96 | 43 **Tc** Technetium (98) | 44 **Ru** Ruthenium 101.07 | 45 **Rh** Rhodium 102.91 | 46 **Pd** Palladium 106.42 | 47 **Ag** Silver 107.87 | 48 **Cd** Cadmium 112.41 | 49 **In** Indium 114.82 | 50 **Sn** Tin 118.71 | 51 **Sb** Antimony 121.76 | 52 **Te** Tellurium 127.60 | 53 **I** Iodine 126.90 | 54 **Xe** Xenon 131.29 |
| 55 **Cs** Cesium 132.91 | 56 **Ba** Barium 137.33 | 57 **La** Lanthanum 138.91 | 72 **Hf** Hafnium 178.49 | 73 **Ta** Tantalum 180.95 | 74 **W** Tungsten 183.84 | 75 **Re** Rhenium 186.21 | 76 **Os** Osmium 190.23 | 77 **Ir** Iridium 192.22 | 78 **Pt** Platinum 195.08 | 79 **Au** Gold 196.97 | 80 **Hg** Mercury 200.59 | 81 **Tl** Thallium 204.38 | 82 **Pb** Lead 207.2 | 83 **Bi** Bismuth 208.98 | 84 **Po** Polonium (209) | 85 **At** Astatine (210) | 86 **Rn** Radon (222) |
| 87 **Fr** Francium (223) | 88 **Ra** Radium (226) | 89 **Ac** Actinium (227) | 104 **Rf** Rutherfordium (261) | 105 **Db** Dubnium (262) | 106 **Sg** Seaborgium (266) | 107 **Bh** Bohrium (264) | 108 **Hs** Hassium (277) | 109 **Mt** Meitnerium (268) | 110 **Ds** Darmstadtium (271) | 111 **Rg** Roentgenium (272) | 112 **Cn** Copernicium (285) | 113 **Uut** Ununtrium (284) | 114 **Fl** Flerovium (289) | 115 **Uup** Ununpentium (289) | 116 **Lv** Livermorium (293) | 117 **Uus** Ununseptium (294) | 118 **Uuo** Ununoctium (294) |

Lanthanides

| 58 **Ce** Cerium 140.12 | 59 **Pr** Praseodymium 140.91 | 60 **Nd** Neodymium 144.24 | 61 **Pm** Promethium (145) | 62 **Sm** Samarium 150.36 | 63 **Eu** Europium 151.96 | 64 **Gd** Gadolinium 157.25 | 65 **Tb** Terbium 158.93 | 66 **Dy** Dysprosium 162.50 | 67 **Ho** Holmium 164.93 | 68 **Er** Erbium 167.26 | 69 **Tm** Thulium 168.93 | 70 **Yb** Ytterbium 173.05 | 71 **Lu** Lutetium 174.97 |
|---|---|---|---|---|---|---|---|---|---|---|---|---|---|

Actinides

| 90 **Th** Thorium 232.04 | 91 **Pa** Protactinium 231.04 | 92 **U** Uranium 238.03 | 93 **Np** Neptunium (237) | 94 **Pu** Plutonium (244) | 95 **Am** Americium (243) | 96 **Cm** Curium (247) | 97 **Bk** Berkelium (247) | 98 **Cf** Californium (251) | 99 **Es** Einsteinium (252) | 100 **Fm** Fermium (257) | 101 **Md** Mendelevium (258) | 102 **No** Nobelium (259) | 103 **Lr** Lawrencium (262) |
|---|---|---|---|---|---|---|---|---|---|---|---|---|---|

Period 1
Period 2
Period 3
Period 4
Period 5
Period 6
Period 7

**Hydrogen** Hydrogen is the lightest element. A typical hydrogen atom has only one proton and one electron. It doesn't have any neutrons.

Hydrogen is a colorless, odorless gas. It is lighter than air. Hydrogen burns very easily. Because of this chemical property, hydrogen is used as fuel in space rockets.

Hydrogen is important to living things. Most of the chemicals made by living things contain hydrogen. Almost one-tenth of your weight is hydrogen atoms.

**Carbon** Carbon is a very common element. A typical carbon atom has six protons, six neutrons, and six electrons.

Carbon is a solid material. There are different forms of carbon. For example, charcoal and soot are black forms of carbon. Graphite, which is mixed with clay to make pencils, is a gray and greasy form of carbon. Diamonds are a very hard and clear form of carbon.

Carbon is found in all living things. It is in most of the foods you eat. Carbon atoms make up about one-fifth of your body weight.

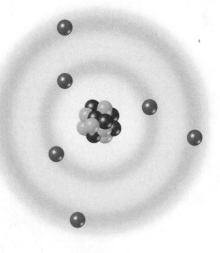

**Nitrogen**  Nitrogen is a colorless, odorless gas. A typical nitrogen atom has seven protons, seven neutrons, and seven electrons.

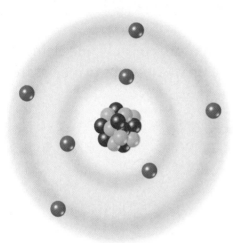

Nitrogen makes up 78 percent of the air you breathe. The bodies of all living things need nitrogen to build body parts. But most living things cannot use the nitrogen in air. They must take it in with the foods they eat. Animals get nitrogen from foods that are rich in proteins. Plants get nitrogen from substances in soil.

**Oxygen**  Oxygen is a colorless, odorless gas. A typical oxygen atom has eight protons, eight neutrons, and eight electrons.

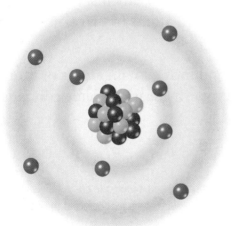

Oxygen makes up 21 percent of the air we breathe. Without oxygen, people, other animals, and plants could not survive. They need oxygen to release the energy in food.

Oxygen is also needed for materials to burn. If you place a glass upside-down over a burning candle, soon the flame will go out. That happens because the flame uses up oxygen. The upside-down glass doesn't let more oxygen reach the candle.

See Also

Cell Respiration pages 78–79

# Molecules

Atoms join together to form molecules. A **molecule** (MAHL ih kyool) is made up of two or more atoms joined tightly together.

Elements
page 250

A molecule can be made up of atoms of only one element. A molecule can also be made up of atoms of two or more different elements.

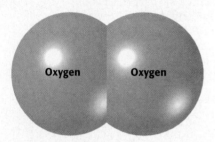

**Oxygen molecule (O₂)**
Each molecule of oxygen in the air you breathe is made up of two oxygen atoms.

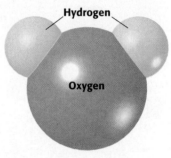

**Water molecule (H₂O)**
Each molecule of the water you drink is made up of two hydrogen atoms and one oxygen atom.

Compounds
pages
256–257

Water is a compound. A **compound** is a substance whose molecules contain atoms of different elements. For example, water molecules contain atoms of two elements—hydrogen and oxygen.

The molecules of some compounds contain atoms of more than two elements. For example, a sugar molecule contains atoms of carbon, hydrogen, and oxygen. The molecules of proteins in the foods you eat contain atoms of carbon, hydrogen, oxygen, nitrogen, and sometimes sulfur.

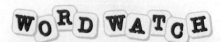

**WORD WATCH**

A compound and a molecule are not the same thing. The word *compound* refers to the entire substance. The word *molecule* refers to a small particle of a substance that has all the properties of the substance.

Carbon dioxide is another example of a compound. Carbon dioxide is a gas in air that plants need in order to make their own food. Each molecule of carbon dioxide contains one carbon atom joined with two oxygen atoms.

Photosynthesis
page 80

Scientists use numbers and the symbols for elements to describe molecules. For example, a molecule of oxygen is described as $O_2$. The **O** is the symbol for oxygen. The little $_2$ means that there are two atoms of oxygen in the molecule.

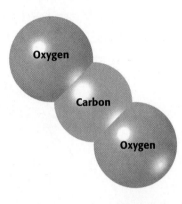

**Carbon dioxide molecule ($CO_2$)**

The carbon dioxide molecule is written as $CO_2$. **C** is the symbol for carbon. **O** is the symbol for oxygen. The little $_2$ is right after the symbol for oxygen. That means there are two atoms of oxygen in a molecule of carbon dioxide.

See Also
Chemical Symbols
page 250

Familiar Elements
page 251

In $CO_2$ for carbon dioxide, there is no number next to the symbol for carbon. No number means there is only one atom of this kind in the molecule. You don't have to write a little number $_1$ next to the symbol for carbon.

# Compounds, Mixtures, and Solutions

A bowl of oatmeal with milk and sugar contains materials that are mixed together in different ways. The mixtures are not all the same. It's easy to see the parts in some of the mixtures. But you can't see the parts in other mixtures. That's one of the properties that make one kind of mixture different from another kind.

## Compounds

A **compound** is a substance whose molecules contain atoms of different elements. The sugar in your bowl of oatmeal is a compound. Sugar is made of atoms of carbon, hydrogen, and oxygen tightly joined together.

Molecules
pages 254–255

The atoms in a compound cannot be separated by ordinary means. For example, you can't put sugar through a sifter to separate the atoms of carbon, hydrogen, and oxygen from each other. No matter how tiny the holes in the sifter are, the different kinds of atoms cannot be separated. That's because the atoms are held together very tightly in molecules. A molecule is the smallest bit of a compound.

The properties of a compound are different from the properties of the elements in its molecules. For example, sugar is made of carbon, hydrogen, and oxygen. By itself, carbon is a dark-colored solid that doesn't dissolve in water. Sugar is a white solid that does dissolve in water. By themselves, hydrogen and oxygen are tasteless gases. Sugar tastes sweet and is a solid.

Table salt is made of sodium and chlorine. Each of these elements is very poisonous by itself. But when the two elements are joined together in a compound, they form a harmless flavoring.

## Common Compounds

A bowl of oatmeal, milk, and sugar contains many common compounds. Some compounds in the oatmeal are named in the ingredients list on the box.

Table sugar is a compound called sucrose. A molecule of sucrose has 12 carbon atoms, 22 hydrogen atoms, and 11 oxygen atoms. The short way to write this is $C_{12}H_{22}O_{11}$.

Table salt is a compound called sodium chloride. A molecule of table salt has one sodium atom and one chlorine atom. The symbol for sodium is **Na**. The symbol for chlorine is **Cl**. The short way to write sodium chloride is NaCl.

**Ingredients**
Whole grain rolled oats (with oat bran), sugar, salt, brown sugar flavor blend (natural flavors, non-fat milk, salt, carob powder), calcium carbonate (a source of calcium), guar gum, caramel color, natural flavors, niacinamide, reduced iron, pyridoxine hydrochloride, vitamin A palmitate, riboflavin, thiamin mononitrate, folic acid

See Also

Chemical Symbols page 250

## Mixtures

Compounds
pages 256–257

Oatmeal, milk, and sugar form a mixture. A **mixture** is a combination of two or more substances that do not form a new substance. If the combination *did* form a new substance, it would be called a compound.

Physical and Chemical Properties
pages 246–247

Each substance in a mixture keeps its own chemical properties. For example, you can taste the sugar in your bowl of oatmeal because the sugar has not changed. It has kept its properties, including its sweet taste.

The substances in a mixture can be separated from each other easily. You can separate the oatmeal from the milk and sugar by passing all three through a strainer. The oatmeal would get trapped in the strainer, but the milk and sugar would pass through it.

How could you separate a mixture of sand and bits of cork? You could put the mixture in a jar of water. The sand would sink to the bottom, and the cork would float. You could skim the cork off the water's surface. Then you could pour out the water. The sand would be left in the jar.

How could you separate a mixture of iron filings and sand? Iron is attracted to a magnet, and sand is not. You could pass a strong magnet over the mixture. The iron filings would stick to the magnet, and the sand would be left behind.

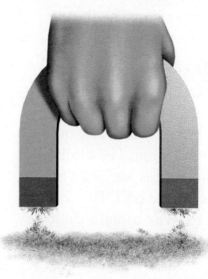

## Solutions

A solution (suh LOO shun) is a special kind of mixture. A **solution** is a mixture with one substance spread out evenly in another substance. The substances are spread out so evenly that you cannot tell one from the other. For example, when you stir sugar into milk, the sugar seems to disappear. But if you taste the milk, it tastes sweet. That means the sugar is in the milk.

The sugar hasn't changed. It has become invisible because it has dissolved in the milk. **Dissolve** means to form a solution with another substance. When sugar dissolves in milk, the sugar molecules spread out so evenly in the milk that they no longer form grains of sugar.

Sugar dissolved in milk is an example of a solid dissolved in a liquid. There are other kinds of solutions, too. These pictures show some other kinds.

Air is a solution of gases dissolved in other gases.

Most gold jewelry is made of one solid, copper, dissolved in another solid, gold.

Soda water is a gas, carbon dioxide, dissolved in a liquid, water.

# Changes in Matter

When the temperature falls below freezing, water in a pond changes from a liquid to a solid. The water hasn't changed what it is. It is still water. It has just changed to another form. Changing from one form to another form without turning into a new substance is an example of a **physical change.**

If you leave an iron nail outdoors long enough, it will rust. Rust is not iron. It is a new substance made of iron and oxygen. Changing into a new substance is an example of a **chemical change.**

# Physical Changes

You can always tell when a physical change has occurred. The object changed, but what it is made of did not change.

For example, if you cut a sheet of paper in half, you would have two smaller sheets of paper. The original sheet of paper would have changed. But both the whole sheet and the two new sheets would still be made of paper. Cutting, crushing, melting, and freezing are all physical changes. What you cut, crush, melt, or freeze looks different, but it is still the same material.

## States of Matter

Substances such as water and iron can exist as solids, liquids, or gases. Solid, liquid, and gas are **states of matter.** These states are physical properties of matter.

A substance changes state when enough heat energy is added to it or subtracted from it. If you add enough heat energy to ice, it turns into liquid water. If you add enough heat energy to liquid water, it turns into a gas called water vapor. If you cool the substance by subtracting heat energy, you can reverse these changes. You can turn a gas into a liquid and a liquid into a solid. Changing from one state to another state is an example of a physical change.

See
Also

Properties of
Matter
pages 244–245

Physical and
Chemical
Properties
pages 246–247

Water Cycle
pages 188–189

A substance changes state when its temperature changes. A change in temperature changes how the atoms and molecules in a substance move around. When heat energy is added to the substance, its particles move faster and farther apart. As they move faster and farther apart, the substance turns from a solid to a liquid and then from a liquid to a gas.

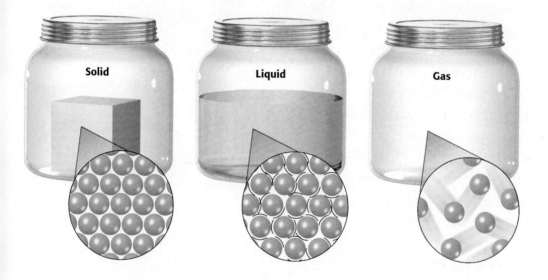

Solid

Liquid

Gas

This table tells the major characteristics of solids, liquids, and gases.

| State | Description |
|---|---|
| Solid | has a definite shape and a definite volume |
| Liquid | has a definite volume but takes the shape of its container |
| Gas | takes the shape and volume of its container |

**Solids** The particles in solids are close together and do not move around very much. This makes solids keep their shape and volume. For example, if you put a rock on your desk, the rock would hold its shape. It would not start to bulge on one side or flatten out like a pancake. And the volume of the rock would not change. It would not get smaller or larger as it sat on your desk.

**Liquids** The particles in liquids are not as close together as the particles in solids. A liquid's particles move more freely than the particles in a solid. A liquid's particles can flow around one another. The ability to flow is a physical property of all liquids.

Liquids have a definite volume, but they do not have a definite shape. A liquid takes the shape of its container. For example, suppose you pour 1 liter of water into a flat pan and 1 liter of water into a skinny vase. The pan and the vase contain the same volume of water. But the *shapes* of the spaces filled by the water are different.

Some substances seem to be partway between a solid and a liquid. For example, a lump of silicone putty holds it shape for a while, like a solid. Then it flows very slowly until it takes the shape of its container, like a liquid.

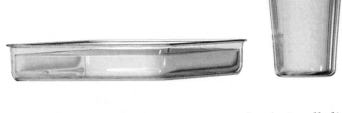

**Gases** The particles in gases move freely in all directions. They spread outward until they hit the walls of the container. For this reason, a gas has no definite volume. It takes on the volume of the container. A gas also has no definite shape. Air in a balloon takes the shape of the balloon. Air in a football takes the shape of the football.

## Changing States of Matter

**See Also**

Physical and Chemical Properties pages 246–247

States of Matter pages 262–263

Heat Energy page 289

You probably don't think that gold could ever exist as a gas. But it can! Almost all substances, including gold, can exist in all three states of matter.

You're probably most familiar with the three states of water. Water can exist as a solid, a liquid, and a gas. So can metals such as gold. All you have to do to change a substance from one state to another state is add or subtract enough heat energy.

*Did You Know?*

Water is the only common substance on Earth that exists in all three states at ordinary temperatures.

**Melting point** The **melting point** of a substance is the temperature at which it changes from a solid to a liquid. The melting point of water is 0°C. When ice is heated to 0°C, it begins to melt.

The **freezing point** of a substance is the temperature at which it changes from a liquid to a solid. A substance's freezing point is the same as its melting point. For example, ice melts at 0°C, and water freezes at 0°C.

**Boiling point** The **boiling point** of a substance is the temperature at which it changes rapidly from a liquid to a gas. The boiling point of water is 100°C. When water is heated to a temperature of 100°C, it begins to boil. Water molecules escape from the liquid and enter the air as a gas.

When molecules of water vapor are cooled, they condense and form liquid water. The **condensation** (kahn dun SAY shun) **point** of a substance is the temperature at which it changes from a gas to a liquid. A substance's condensation point is the same as its boiling point. Water boils at 100°C, and water vapor condenses at 100°C.

The melting and freezing points of a substance and its boiling and condensation points are physical properties of the substance. Every substance has its own set of these points. That's one way you can tell one substance from another.

For example, a mineral called "fool's gold" looks like real gold. But fool's gold is made of iron and sulfur. It is not valuable. You could be fooled into thinking a lump of fool's gold was real gold. But you could tell the difference if you measured the lump's melting point. Fool's gold melts at 1,171°C. Real gold melts at 1,063°C.

# Chemical Changes

A **chemical change** happens when one or more substances change into one or more new substances. The properties of the new substances are different from the properties of the original substances.

For example, baking soda is a solid. Vinegar is a liquid. Mixing baking soda with vinegar produces bubbles of a gas called carbon dioxide. Carbon dioxide has different properties from either baking soda or vinegar.

Carbon dioxide

## Chemical Reactions

Baking soda and vinegar combining to form carbon dioxide is an example of a chemical reaction. "Chemical reaction" is another way of saying that a chemical change has happened.

In some chemical reactions, two substances may exchange parts of their molecules to make new substances. This is what happens when you mix baking soda with vinegar.

See Also

Compounds
pages 256–257

In other chemical reactions, the atoms or molecules of two substances join together to form a new substance. For example, hydrogen atoms and oxygen atoms join together to make molecules of water.

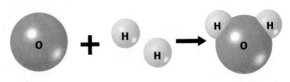

Oxygen atom          Hydrogen atoms          Water molecule ($H_2O$)

In still other chemical reactions, the molecules of one substance break apart to form molecules of other substances. This is what happens when carbonic acid breaks apart to form water and carbon dioxide.

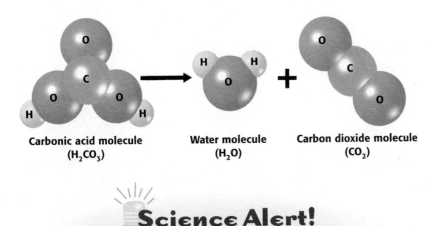

Carbonic acid molecule ($H_2CO_3$)          Water molecule ($H_2O$)          Carbon dioxide molecule ($CO_2$)

## Science Alert!

During a chemical reaction, the atoms in molecules are rearranged to form new molecules. The total number of atoms does not change.

Substances react with each other in predictable ways. For example, mixing baking soda with vinegar will always produce carbon dioxide. But you wouldn't get the same result if you mixed baking soda with water. That's because substances react only with certain other substances. For example, iron reacts with oxygen to form rust. But gold does not react with oxygen at all.

# Forces and Motion

When you kick a soccer ball, you are applying a force to the ball. When you drag a sled up a snow-covered hill, you are applying a force to the sled. A **force** is a push or pull. When you kick a soccer ball, you give it a push. When you drag a sled up a hill, you give the sled a pull. In both of these examples, the objects move when you apply the force.

SCi LINKS
N S T A

Keyword: Forces and Motion
www.scilinks.org
Code: GSS45100

A force can make an object start moving, stop moving, change speed, or change direction. Here are some examples.

When you start to skate, you apply a force to the ground. Your skates push backward on the ground. This makes you move forward.

When you catch a fly ball, you stop the ball's downward motion. You do this by applying a force to the ball. The force is the upward push of your hand.

When you hit a pitched softball, you change the direction that the ball is moving. The force you apply to the ball makes it move away from you instead of continuing toward you.

When you pedal a bicycle, you can change its speed by pedaling faster or by braking. You do this by applying force to the pedals or the brakes.

### Did You Know?

The unit of force in the metric system is the newton (N). One newton is about the force you would need to lift a small pear.

# Common Forces

Every minute of the day, forces act on you and on all the objects around you. Four main forces are gravity, buoyant force, magnetic force, and friction.

## Gravity

Gravity and Orbits page 227

All objects attract each other. The sun and Earth attract each other. The moon and Earth attract each other. You and Earth attract each other. The force that attracts objects to each other is **gravity.** Gravity keeps Earth and the other planets in orbit around the sun. It keeps the moon in orbit around Earth. On Earth, it makes objects fall to the ground.

**Factors That Affect the Force of Gravity** The force of gravity between two objects depends on two things. They are the mass of the objects and the distance between them. Objects that have greater mass produce a greater force of gravity. Objects that are closer together produce a greater force of gravity.

Mass page 244

Planet B has more mass than Planet A. The force of gravity between Planet B and its moon is greater than the force of gravity between Planet A and its moon.

Planet C and its moon are closer together. The force of gravity between Planet C and its moon is greater than the force of gravity between Planet D and its moon.

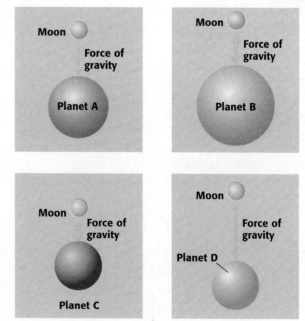

**Mass and Weight** Different planets in the solar system have different masses. Because of this, the force of gravity that the planets put on other objects is different. That makes the weight of an object different on different planets. **Weight** is a measure of the pull of gravity on an object. **Mass** is the amount of matter in an object. An object's mass is the same wherever it is. But its weight can change.

For example, suppose your mass is 30 kilograms. On Earth you would weigh about 66 pounds. The force of gravity on the moon is about one-sixth the force of gravity on Earth. So if you were on the moon, you would weigh only 11 pounds. But your mass would still be 30 kilograms.

See Also

Air Pressure
page 203

**Atmospheric Pressure** Air has mass. The pull of Earth's gravity on air gives air weight. That weight is greatest on Earth's surface. High on a mountain, the weight of air is less because there is less air pushing down from above.

**Water Pressure** Earth's gravity pulls on water, too. This produces water pressure on any objects that are in the water. Water pressure is greater at the bottom of a pool. That's because there's more water pushing down from above.

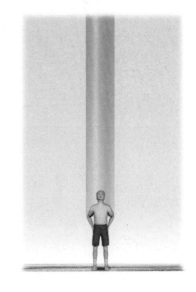

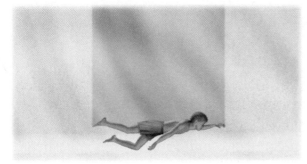

## Buoyant Force

If you drop a steel ball into water, it sinks. But if you mold the same amount of steel into the shape of a small boat, the boat floats. A steel boat floats because of buoyant (BOY unt) force. **Buoyant force** is the upward push of a liquid or gas on an object.

The upward push of the buoyant force works against the downward pull of gravity. As long as the upward push of the buoyant force is greater than the downward pull of gravity, an object will float.

The weight of a steel ball is greater than the buoyant force of water. So the ball sinks. If you mold the steel into the shape of a boat, the shape holds air. Now the weight of the steel and the air inside it is less than the buoyant force of the water. The boat floats.

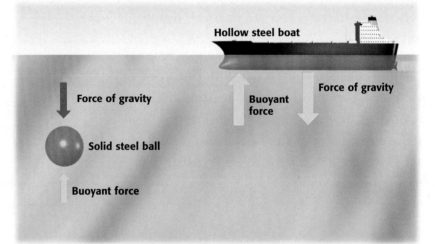

Hollow steel boat

Force of gravity

Buoyant force

Force of gravity

Solid steel ball

Buoyant force

## Magnetic Force

A magnet pulls an iron nail towards it. A **magnet** is any object that attracts iron and a few other magnetic materials. A magnet changes the motion of the nail. The magnet pulls the nail toward it. Magnetism is a force.

The force of magnetism works at a distance. For example, a magnet attracts a nail that is some distance away from it. But suppose you move the nail farther away from the magnet. When the distance between the objects increases, the force of magnetism decreases. The area around a magnet where the force of magnetism can be felt is called a **magnetic field.**

No matter what its shape, every magnet has a north pole and a south pole. Opposite poles attract, or pull on, each other. Like poles repel, or push against, each other. Magnetism is strongest near the magnet's poles.

*See Also*
Magnetism
pages 304–305

**Earth as a Magnet** Earth acts as if it had a bar magnet pushed through its center from north to south. One end of this imaginary magnet is called the north magnetic pole. The other end is called the south magnetic pole. A compass needle lines up with Earth's magnetic poles.

**Magnetic north pole**

**Compass**

*Did You Know?*

Earth has two north poles and two south poles. The magnetic north and south poles are points where Earth's magnetism is strongest. The geographic North and South Poles are points at the ends of Earth's axis. The magnetic poles and the geographic poles are not in exactly the same places.

*See Also*
Earth's Rotation
pages 218–219

## Friction

Imagine that you're riding your bicycle. Suddenly a puppy jumps in front of you. You apply the brakes. The bike's wheels stop turning. The tires rub against the ground, and you stop.

One object rubbing against another object produces a force called friction (FRIK shun). **Friction** is a force that works against motion.

The amount of friction depends on two things. One is the surfaces that are rubbing against each other. Rough surfaces produce more friction than smooth surfaces. For example, a rubber tire sliding on a cement sidewalk produces a lot of friction. But suppose you tried to stop your bike on an icy surface. You would travel much farther before stopping.

The second thing is the amount of force pushing the surfaces together. The greater this force, the greater the friction. The tires of a heavy car produce more friction with the ground than the tires of your bicycle do.

### Did You Know?

A meteor is a streak of light produced when a space rock plunges through Earth's atmosphere. The rock rubs against molecules of air. This produces friction. The friction produces heat that burns up the rock.

# Describing Motion

You know motion when you see it. One minute, a bird is perching on the branch of a tree in your yard. Then it flies to your bird feeder. The bird has changed its position. A change of position is called **motion.**

The bird could have followed different routes to the feeder. It could have flown in a straight line. It could have flown in an up-and-down curving line. Or it could have swooped down and then up again. An object in motion can follow different paths.

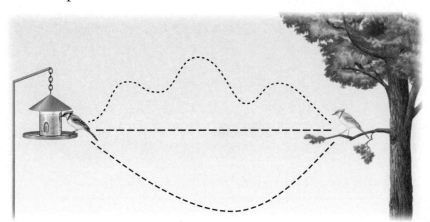

## Point of View

You see the movement of an object from your point of view, or your position. If you are standing on the corner of a busy street, you see cars move past you. But if you are riding in one of the cars, you see the buildings, the sidewalk, and people on the sidewalk move past you.

Even when you are standing still, you're moving. That's because Earth turns on its axis. As Earth turns, its surface carries you along with it. You're really traveling hundreds of kilometers per hour!

## Speed

Imagine that your mother is driving you from City A to City B. As she drives, she looks at the speedometer once in a while. The speedometer shows how fast the car is moving. How fast it is moving is its speed. **Speed** is a change in position over a period of time.

Speed is found by dividing the distance that was traveled by the amount of time it took to travel that distance. For example, suppose the distance between City A and City B is 120 miles, and you covered that distance in 3 hours. What was your average speed?

120 miles ÷ 3 hours = 40 mph (miles per hour)

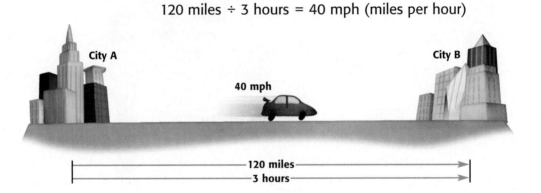

Of course, you didn't travel exactly that speed for the entire 120 miles. Your mother slowed down when traffic was heavy or when rounding a curve. She had to stop at red lights. And she drove faster than 40 mph on a highway when traffic was light. An object's speed can increase, decrease, or stay the same as it moves.

### Did You Know?

Some forms of energy travel at a constant speed. For example, the speed of light is almost 300,000 kilometers per second. The speed of sound in air is about 340 meters per second.

# Changing Motion

During a soccer game, a player starts the ball moving. Sometimes she speeds up the ball, and sometimes she slows it down. She might stop it for a moment. She passes it right or left. The ball is changing motion. A change in motion means starting or stopping, speeding up or slowing down, or moving in a different direction.

When a soccer ball isn't moving, it will stay in its position unless a force starts it moving. Once the ball is in motion, it will keep moving in the same direction unless a force acts on it to change its motion. The force might be a kick from an opposing player.

The tendency of an object to resist a change in motion is called **inertia** (ih NUR shuh). You have to overcome the inertia of a soccer ball to start it moving, stop it from moving, or change its speed or direction. A change in an object's speed or direction is called **acceleration** (ak sel uh RAY shun).

**WORD WATCH**

Many people use the word *acceleration* just to mean speeding up. But in science, the word means speeding up *or* slowing down *or* changing direction.

## Force, Mass, and Motion

The motion of an object will change only if it is pulled or pushed by something. Pulling or pushing applies a force to the object.

The amount of change in the motion of an object depends on the amount of force applied to it. For example, a football that is kicked with more force will move faster and farther than a football that is kicked with less force. A blocker that hits you from the side with more force will change your direction more than a blocker who hits you from the side with less force.

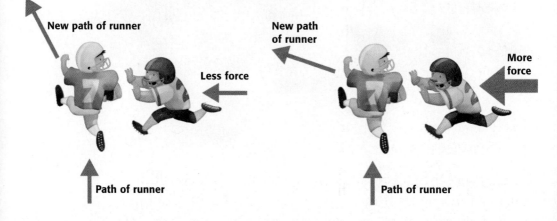

New path of runner

Less force

Path of runner

New path of runner

More force

Path of runner

The mass of an object affects the amount of force that is needed to change its direction. For example, you have to apply more force to change the motion of a 120-kg football player the same amount as the motion of a 100-kilogram football player.

See Also

Friction page 274

Gravity, friction, and other forces sometimes combine to change an object's motion. For example, being hit from the side by a blocker makes you change direction. At the same time, gravity makes you fall to the ground. When you are bowling, you apply a strong force to move the ball quickly down the alley. But as it moves, friction between the ball and the alley's surface slows the ball down.

## Gravity and Motion

Gravity is a force that pulls one object toward another object. On Earth, gravity pulls objects toward Earth's center. If you let go of an object you're holding, it will fall to the ground. The force of gravity pulls the object down. Without the force of gravity, the object would float in the air when you let go of it.

Objects of the same size and shape fall at the same speed. For example, if you drop an iron ball and a rubber ball of the same size and shape from a building, they will hit the ground at the same time.

If you drop a sheet of paper and a tack of the same weight, the tack will hit the ground first. That's because the sheet of paper has more surface area than the tack. As the paper falls, it has to push aside more air than the tack would. The paper has to overcome the resistance of the air. Remember, air is matter. It gets in the way of falling objects.

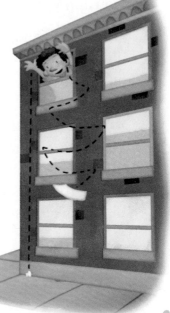

See Also

Gravity
pages 270–271

## Simple Machines

In science, the word *work* has a special meaning. **Work** happens when a force moves an object through a distance. The greater the force and the greater the distance the object moves, the more work that is done.

Work equals force times distance.

$$W = F \times d$$

A **simple machine** is a tool that makes work easier. Most simple machines let you use less force to move an object. But when you use less force, you have to apply it for a longer distance. Some simple machines let you move an object a longer distance. You have to apply more force, but you can apply it for a shorter distance.

With any kind of simple machine, the amount of work you do doesn't change. What changes is the amount of force you apply and the distance you apply it.

There are six kinds of simple machines. They are an inclined plane, a wedge, a screw, a lever, a wheel and axle, and a pulley.

### Inclined Plane

An **inclined plane** is a flat surface that slopes. Pushing a heavy box up an inclined plane takes less force than lifting the box straight up. But you have to push the box for a longer distance.

You apply less force, but you have to apply it for a longer distance.

10'    2'

## Wedge

A **wedge** is an inclined plane that moves. An ax, a knife, and scissors are examples of wedges. A wedge reduces the amount of force that is needed to split apart an object. But you have to apply the force for a longer distance.

You apply force for a long distance. The wedge moves the object's pieces a short distance.

## Screw

A **screw** is an inclined plane wrapped around a small rod. The inclined plane forms ridges on the screw. When you turn the screw, the ridges pull the board up the screw. You use less force to turn a screw than to hammer a nail of the same size into a board. But you have to turn the screw more times than you'd have to hammer the nail. You have to move the screw for the entire length of the inclined plane wrapped around it.

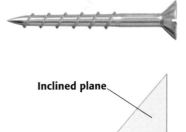

Inclined plane

You use less force to turn the screw. But you have to apply the force for a longer distance.

Keyword: Simple Machines
www.scilinks.org
Code: GSS45105

## Lever

A **lever** is a long bar or board that turns around a support that doesn't move. The support is called the **fulcrum** (FUL krum). There are three kinds of levers.

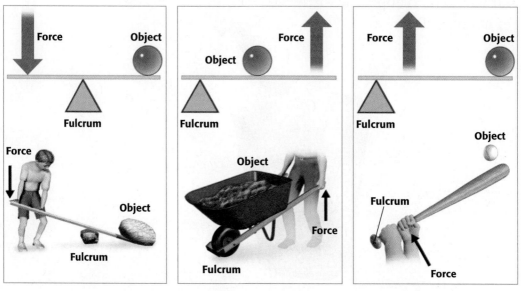

The fulcrum is between the object you are moving and the force you are applying.

The object you are moving is between the fulcrum and the force you are applying.

You apply force between the fulcrum and the object you are moving.

## Wheel and Axle

A **wheel and axle** is a wheel that turns around a rod, called the axle. The axle goes through the center of the wheel. A wheel and axle reduces the force you have to apply *or* reduces the distance you apply the force.

When you turn the handle of a screwdriver, you apply force to the wheel part of a wheel and axle. A small force on the handle is magnified into a large force on the axle.

When you pedal a bicycle, you apply force to the axle. That's where the chain is attached. Every turn of the axle makes the tire turn a greater distance.

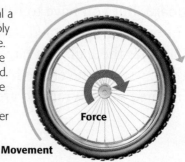

# Pulley

A **pulley** is a wheel with a rope or chain wrapped around it. Pulleys are used to lift heavy objects. For example, auto mechanics use pulleys to lift an engine out of a car. A pulley reduces the force that is needed to lift the object *or* it changes the direction of the force. There are three kinds of pulleys.

This kind of pulley changes the direction of the force you apply. You pull down, and the object moves up. The pulley does not reduce the amount of force that you have to apply.

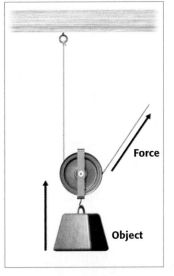

This kind of pulley reduces the amount of force that you have to apply. Some of the weight is held by the object that the rope is attached to. So you don't have to pull as hard. The pulley does not change the direction of the force. You pull up, and the object moves up.

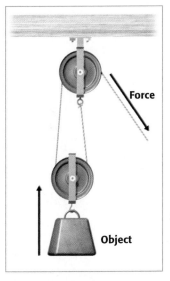

This pulley system is called a block and tackle. It's a combination of the other two kinds of pulleys. Using more than one pulley reduces the force that is needed to lift the object. But you have to pull the rope a longer distance.

# Compound Machines

A **compound machine** is made of two or more simple machines. A hand-operated can opener is a compound machine. Its two handles are levers. Its cutting part is a wedge. And you turn a wheel and axle to move the cutting part around the top of the can.

# Energy

In science, the word *energy* has a special meaning. **Energy** is the ability to do work. And *work* has a special meaning in science, too. It doesn't mean cleaning your room or mowing the lawn. In science, **work** is done when a force moves an object.

Energy can cause motion. Energy can also cause changes in matter. These pictures show some examples.

Plants use the energy in sunlight to change carbon dioxide gas and water into a simple sugar for food.

People use electrical energy to start car engines, run the headlights and taillights, and light buildings and streets.

Heat energy deep below Earth's surface makes a volcano erupt. The eruption can throw lava, rocks, and ash high into the air.

# Forms of Energy

There are different forms of energy. These forms are all around you.

## Forms of Energy

| Form | Examples |
| --- | --- |
| Heat energy | Heat from an oven, a furnace, a toaster, or the sun<br>Heat in your body |
| Light energy | Light from a light bulb, the stars, or a computer screen<br>Lightning flashing in the sky |
| Sound energy | Sound from a loudspeaker, a radio, or a TV<br>The sound of the wind, thunder, or someone's voice |
| Electrical energy | Electricity from a power plant, a car battery, or a dry cell in a flashlight |
| Chemical energy | Energy stored in the foods you eat<br>Energy stored in fuels such as wood and gasoline |
| Nuclear energy | Energy used to generate electricity in a nuclear power plant<br>Energy used to kill cancer cells |
| Mechanical energy | **Kinetic energy:** The energy of a bowling ball rolling down an alley<br>**Potential energy:** The energy of a roller coaster car at the top of a hill |

Notice that two forms of mechanical energy are listed in the table. **Kinetic** (kuh NET ik) **energy** is the energy of motion. The faster an object moves and the greater its mass, the more kinetic energy it has. A bus going 55 miles per hour has more kinetic energy than a car going 40 miles per hour.

**Potential** (puh TEN shul) **energy** is stored energy. The higher above ground an object is and the greater its mass, the more potential energy it has. A boulder at the top of a hill has more potential energy than a pebble halfway down the hill.

Keyword: Energy
www.scilinks.org
Code: GSS45110

# Energy Changes

Energy can change from one form to another. Here are just a few examples.

A roller coaster car at the top of a hill has potential energy

As the car moves downhill, potential energy changes to kinetic energy.

A hydroelectric power plant changes the kinetic energy of moving water into electrical energy.

A light bulb changes electrical energy to light energy and heat energy.

When wood burns, chemical energy stored in the wood changes to heat energy and light energy.

When gasoline burns in a car's engine, engine parts move. Chemical energy changes to kinetic energy.

## Science Alert!

Energy cannot be created or destroyed. The same amount of energy exists before and after it changes form.

# Energy From the Sun

Most of the energy on Earth comes from the sun. The sun's energy heats Earth's surface, and the surface heats the air above it. The sun's energy also heats water on Earth's surface and makes it evaporate. When water vapor cools, it forms clouds. Clouds produce rain, snow, sleet, and hail. In these ways, the sun's energy creates Earth's weather, winds, storms, and climate.

**See Also**
Water Cycle
pages 188–189

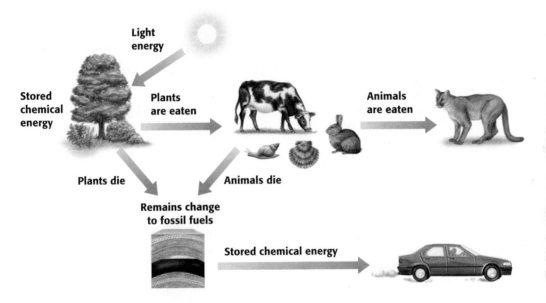

Plants use the energy in sunlight to make food. In the process, the sun's light energy is changed to chemical energy. Some of the chemical energy is stored in the plant. Animals that eat plants take in this chemical energy. And animals that eat plant-eating animals take in chemical energy, too. You and other animals use this energy to stay alive.

The chemical energy in fuels also comes from the sun's energy. Ancient plants and animals stored chemical energy in their bodies. The organisms died and decayed. Over millions of years, their bodies were changed into oil, coal, and natural gas. Today we burn these fuels to release the chemical energy that is stored in them.

**See Also**
Cell Respiration
pages 78–79

Photosynthesis
pages 80–81

Food Chains
page 137

Fossil Fuels
pages 322–323

# Heat

Atoms
pages 248–249

Molecules
pages 254–255

Air, water, rocks, plants, animals, people, the moon, the stars—everything on Earth and in space is made of atoms and molecules. These tiny particles are in constant motion. They jiggle back and forth. They bump against each other. Even the particles that make up solid objects are constantly moving.

States of Matter
pages 262–263

Changing
States of Matter
pages 264–265

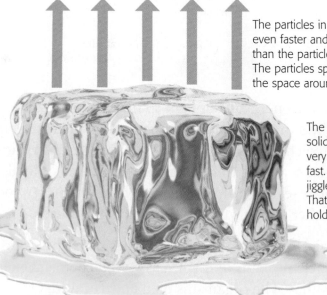

The particles in a gas move even faster and farther apart than the particles in liquids. The particles spread out in the space around them.

The particles in a solid don't move very far or very fast. They just jiggle in place. That's why solids hold their shape.

The particles in a liquid move faster and farther away from each other than the particles in solids. But the particles in a liquid still stay close to each other.

When ice melts, it changes to liquid water. When liquid water evaporates, it changes to a gas called water vapor.

# Heat Energy

Moving particles have energy. The energy of moving particles is called **heat energy.**

Heat from a stove's burner makes the particles of a metal pot start moving faster. Then the particles of the pot make the particles of water in the pot start moving faster and faster. The water particles have more and more energy. The more the water particles are heated, the faster they move. Soon they are moving with so much energy that they escape from the surface of the water. They become a gas and enter the air. That's what happens when you boil water.

Suppose you put a small pot of water and a large pot of water on the stove. You turn the two burners up to the same size flame. Which pot do you think would boil first? If you said the small pot, you're right. There aren't as many particles of water in the small pot. So less heat energy is needed to make the particles move fast enough to escape into the air.

A large amount of matter needs more heat energy to warm up than a small amount of the same kind of matter.

## Sources of Heat

Heat energy can be produced in different ways. All of these ways change another form of energy into heat energy.

Remember: Energy cannot be created. It can only be changed from one form to another form. Heat energy always comes from another form of energy.

**Heat energy**

**Stored chemical energy**

Burning changes the chemical energy stored in propane gas to heat energy.

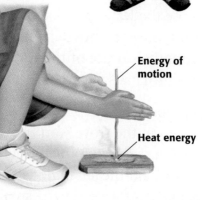

**Energy of motion**

**Heat energy**

The energy of motion can produce heat energy. Spinning a stick very fast can produce enough heat to start a campfire.

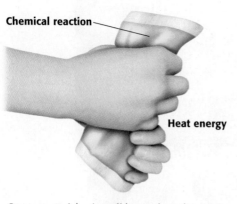

**Chemical reaction**

**Heat energy**

Some materials give off heat when they are mixed together. The chemical reaction produces heat energy. This is what happens in a chemical hot pack.

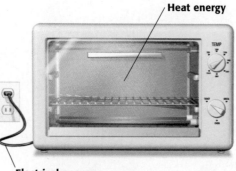

**Heat energy**

**Electrical energy**

Electricity flows through metal coils in a toaster oven. The electricity heats the coils. Electrical energy changes to heat energy.

## Temperature

Suppose you put a thermometer in a beaker of boiling water. The thermometer would read 100°C. And suppose you put a thermometer in a beaker of ice cubes and water. That thermometer would read 0°C.

The thermometers are showing the temperature of the water in the beakers. **Temperature** (TEM pur uh chur) is the average speed of the particles in a substance. The thermometer in the boiling water shows a higher temperature than the thermometer in the ice water. That means the particles in the boiling water are moving faster than the particles in the ice water.

The particles in any substance speed up when the substance is heated. But different substances' particles speed up at different rates. For example, the particles in metals speed up more quickly than the particles in water. That's why a metal pot heats up faster than the water inside the pot.

Plastics and wood also heat up more slowly than metals. Many metal pots have handles made of wood or plastic. The handles stay cool when the metal pot heats up.

Keyword: Heat and Temperature
www.scilinks.org
Code: GSS45115

# Transfer of Heat Energy

Have you ever touched a hot pot? If you have, you know that heat energy can move from one object to another object—from the pot to your hand. Heat energy also moves from one area to another area—for example, from a warm room to a cool room.

Heat energy always moves from a warmer object or area to a cooler object or area. If you hold an ice cube in your hand, heat energy moves from your hand to the ice and melts it. If you open a door on a cold winter day, heat energy moves from inside your warm house to the cold outdoors.

Heat energy moves in three different ways. They are conduction, convection, and radiation.

## Conduction

**Conduction** (kun DUK shun) is the movement of heat between objects that touch each other. For example, suppose you are cooking vegetables in a wok. Heat energy moves from the hot metal wok to the vegetables.

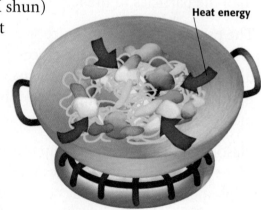

Heat energy

**Conductors and Insulators of Heat** Materials that allow heat energy to pass through them easily are called **conductors** (kun DUK turz). Iron, copper, aluminum, and some other metals are good conductors. That's why pots and pans are usually made of metal.

Conductors and Insulators of Electricity page 299

**Insulators** (IN suh lay turz) are materials that do not allow heat energy to move through them easily. Wood and plastic are poor conductors of heat. That's why the handles of pots and pans are often made of wood or plastic. They don't let the heat from the metal reach your hand.

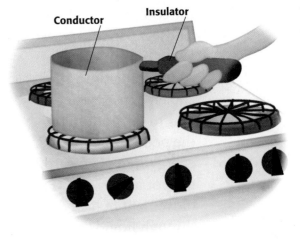

Conductor  Insulator

Cloth is also a poor conductor of heat. That's why potholders are made of thick cloth. It's also one reason that blankets and winter clothing are made of thick cloth, layers of cloth, or cloth filled with feathers. Cloth and feathers are good insulators. They keep your body's heat next to you instead of escaping into the cold outside air.

## Convection

When you heat a pot of water, the water particles near the bottom of the pot start moving faster and farther apart. The water at the bottom becomes less dense than the cooler water above it. The less dense, warmer water rises in the pot. At the same time, the cooler, denser water falls to the bottom of the pot. In this way, heat energy moves upward in the pot in currents. The movement of heat energy through liquids and gases in currents is called **convection** (kun VEK shun).

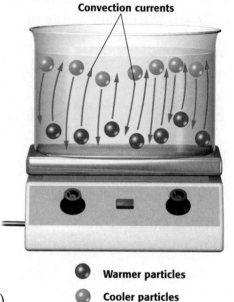

Convection currents

● Warmer particles

● Cooler particles

The heating system in your home uses convection to heat the rooms evenly. Air is heated near the floor of a room. The heated air moves up to the ceiling, and the cooler air near the ceiling moves down. Then the cooler air is heated and rises to the ceiling. These repeating currents keep the room at an even temperature.

## Radiation

Heat energy moves through space by **radiation** (ray dee AY shun). For example, energy from the sun travels to Earth by radiation. When the energy reaches Earth, it warms Earth's surface. The heated surface then heats the air above it. If you sit near a fireplace or campfire, you feel heat coming from the burning logs. The heat reaches you by radiation.

# Electricity and Magnetism

Flip a switch, and the lights go on in your room. Press a button on a remote control, and your TV springs to life. A heater and a bubbler keep the fish in your aquarium healthy. Turn a control knob, and a model train races around a track. None of these things would be possible without electricity and magnetism.

Magnetism and electricity are related to each other. You can use one to produce the other. Electric generators use magnetism to produce electricity. Motors of all kinds use electricity to produce magnetism that makes the motor go. Magnetism and electricity are both caused by charged particles called electrons.

Parts of an Atom page 249

## Electricity

If you were in the northeastern part of the United States on August 14, 2003, you learned how important electricity is to you. A huge blackout happened that night. People from Michigan to New England had no electricity for hours. But what exactly was it that they didn't have? What *is* electricity?

**Electricity** (ih lek TRIS ih tee) is a form of energy that is produced when electrons move from one place to another place. What makes electrons move is the charges that different particles have.

Parts of an Atom page 249

**Charged Particles** Atoms are made up of electrons, protons, and neutrons. Neutrons have no charge. Electrons have a negative charge. Protons have a positive charge.

Like charges repel, or push against, each other. Unlike charges attract, or pull on, each other. Electrons repel other electrons, but they are attracted to protons. Protons repel other protons, but they are attracted to electrons.

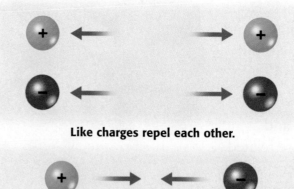

**Like charges repel each other.**

**Unlike charges attract each other.**

These forces of attraction and repulsion make electrons move away from areas with a negative charge and toward areas with a positive charge. This movement of electrons is electricity.

## Static Electricity

**Static electricity** is the buildup of electric charges on an object. This happens when electrons move from one object to another object and stick on the second object.

For example, when you rub a balloon on your hair, you rub electrons off your hair and onto the balloon. Your hair has lost electrons. Now it has more protons than electrons, so it has a positive charge. The balloon has gained electrons, so now it has a negative charge. The total number of electrons hasn't changed. Some have just moved from one place to another place.

If you hold the balloon near your hair, your hair will be pulled toward the balloon. Your positively charged hair is attracted to the negatively charged balloon. And you might hear a crackling sound. The "extra" electrons on the balloon jump to your hair all at once. This produces a tiny spark, the crackling sound you hear.

Lightning is a gigantic electric spark that leaps from a negatively charged cloud to a positively charged object on the ground.

## Current Electricity

When you turn on a lamp, the bulb lights up. This happens because the lamp is receiving a constant flow of electrons through a wire. The constant flow of electrons is called an **electric current.**

Some electric currents are stronger than others. Strong electric currents are produced when many electrons pass a point in a short amount of time. Weak electric currents are produced when fewer electrons pass the point in the same amount of time. Electric current is measured in a unit called the **amp.**

Electric current

Batteries and power plants "push" electrons through wires. The energy of this push gets transferred to electrons. The stronger the push, the more energy the electrons carry. The more energy the electrons carry, the more work they can do, like turning the blades in a food blender. The "push" that is given to the electrons is measured in a unit called the **volt.**

High voltage

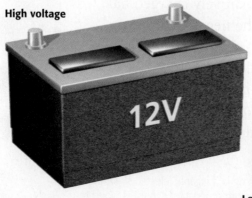

12V

1.5V

Low voltage

**Conductors and Insulators of Electricity** All materials resist, or work against, the flow of electrons. Some materials resist the flow of electrons more than other materials do. It's as if you tried to run through water and through air. You'd move more easily through air than through water. The water would resist your movement more than the air would.

Materials that allow electricity to move through them easily are called **conductors** (kun DUK turz). Conductors are used when you want electrons to move from one place to another. Copper is a very good conductor of electricity. That's why most electrical wires are made of copper.

**See Also**

Conductors and Insulators of Heat page 293

If you've ever gotten an electric shock, you know it can be unpleasant. Electric shocks can cause serious injuries and even death. Electricity must be kept from going where it is not wanted. This is done by covering wires with materials that resist the flow of electricity. Materials that resist the flow of electricity are called **insulators** (IN suh lay turz).

The electric cords in your home are made of copper wires covered with plastic or rubber, or both. Rubber and plastic resist the flow of electricity. That makes them good insulators.

Poor conductors, good insulators

Good conductors of electricity

## Electric Circuits

An **electric circuit** (SUR kit) is a pathway that electrons flow through. A flashlight is a good example of an electric circuit.

When the flashlight is turned on, electrons flow through the batteries to the bulb and then back to the other end of the batteries. The circuit is a complete loop.

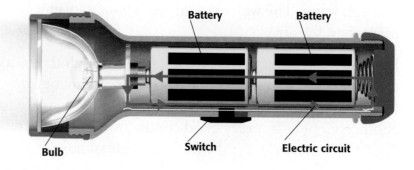

Battery      Battery

Bulb      Switch      Electric circuit

Electric circuits allow electrical energy to be changed into other forms of energy.

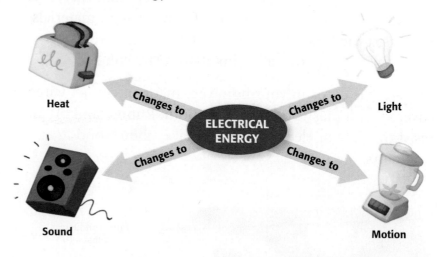

Heat     Changes to     Changes to     Light

ELECTRICAL ENERGY

Changes to     Changes to

Sound          Motion

**Parts of a Circuit** Every circuit must have a source of "push" for the electrons. That means the circuit must include a battery or an electrical outlet. It must have wires to conduct the electricity. It also has a device that it operates, such as a light bulb or a radio. And a circuit usually has one or more switches. A switch starts and stops the flow of electrons through the circuit.

# Open and Closed Circuits

When you turn on a lamp, you don't want it to stay on forever. To turn an electrical device on or off, you have to close or open a circuit.

When you close a circuit, electrons have a complete pathway to flow through. The device starts working. When you open a circuit, you put a gap in it. Electrons cannot cross the gap. The device stops working.

You use a switch to close and open a circuit. A switch is a piece of metal that you can move. To close the circuit, you move the metal so it connects the ends of two wires. To open the circuit, you move the metal so the wires aren't connected any more.

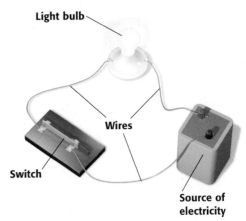

**Closed circuit**
The switch is in the ON position. Think of the switch as a drawbridge. When it is in the down position, electrons can flow across the bridge from one wire to the other wire. The bulb lights.

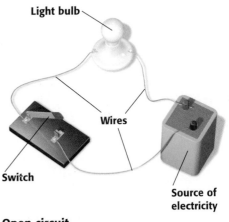

**Open circuit**
The switch is in the OFF position. Electrons can't flow from one wire to the other wire. The bulb turns off.

The switches on the electrical devices in your home aren't as simple as the switch in these pictures. But they still work the same way. They use a metal connector to open and close a circuit.

## Series and Parallel Circuits

There are two kinds of electric circuits—series circuits and parallel circuits. Both kinds of circuits have the same parts. The parts are a source of electricity, wires to conduct the electricity, devices to operate, and a switch to open and close the circuit. But series and parallel circuits connect those parts in different ways.

**Series Circuits** In a **series circuit,** the electrical devices are connected in one continuous loop. Electricity flows from the source through a switch and then through each device, one after another.

A series circuit with all devices working

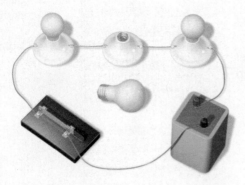

A series circuit with one device missing

If one of the devices is missing or stops working, all the other devices stop working. The missing or broken device is like a switch. It makes a gap in the circuit, and the electricity stops flowing.

**Parallel Circuits** In a **parallel** (PAR uh lel) **circuit,** each device has its own separate loop. The electric current doesn't have to flow through one device to reach the next device. If one device is missing or stops working, the other devices will keep working. That's because there are other pathways that the electricity can take as it flows through the circuit.

Your home is wired with many separate circuits. And every device that is connected to a circuit has its own "mini-circuit" with a switch. That's why when you turn on the light in your kitchen, the toaster and the blender and the microwave oven and the coffeemaker don't all go on, too!

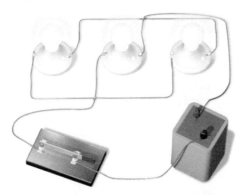

**A parallel circuit with all devices working**

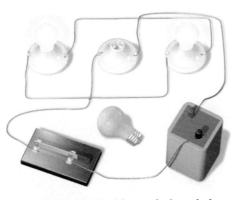

**A parallel circuit with one device missing**

# Magnetism

Magnetism is a force that pulls across a distance. If you hold an iron nail 1 centimeter away from a magnet, you can feel the pull of magnetism. If you let go of the nail, it will jump to the magnet. Magnets attract objects made of iron and a few other materials.

The areas of a magnet where the force of magnetism is strongest are called the poles. All magnets have two poles, a north pole and a south pole. Opposite poles attract, or pull on, each other. Like poles repel, or push away, each other.

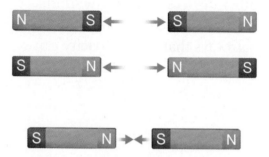

If you try to put two north poles together, you'll feel them pushing each other away. The same thing will happen if you try to put two south poles together. But if you put a north pole and a south pole together, you'll feel them pulling on each other.

## Did You Know?

Poles aren't always at the "ends" of a magnet. Even a round magnet has two poles! They're on the two flat sides of the magnet.

No matter how many pieces you cut a magnet into, each piece will still be a whole magnet with a north pole and a south pole.

## Magnetic Fields

A magnet produces a force around it. The area around a magnet where the force of magnetism can be felt is called a **magnetic field.** A magnetic field is invisible, but you can see its effects. Lay a sheet of paper over a magnet and sprinkle iron filings on the paper. The filings will form a pattern of lines. These lines are called **magnetic lines of force.**

See Also

Magnetic Force
pages 272–273

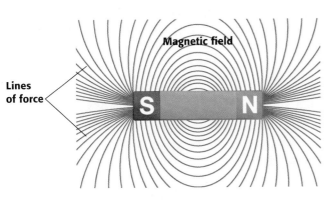

**Magnetic field**

**Lines of force**

The lines of force are bunched closer together at a magnet's poles. This shows that the magnetic field is strongest near the poles.

Some materials can be made into magnets. An iron nail is made of iron atoms. Each iron atom acts like a tiny magnet. It has a north pole and a south pole. But most of the time, the nail's atoms are not lined up with each other. Their poles point in all different directions. The whole nail doesn't act like a magnet.

Stroking the nail with a magnet makes all the iron atoms line up with each other. All their north poles point in one direction. And all their south poles point in the opposite direction. The nail has been magnetized. It is now a magnet.

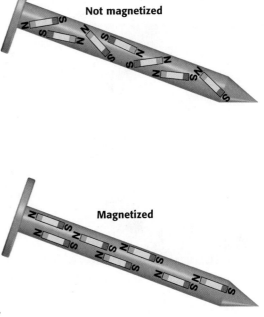

**Not magnetized**

**Magnetized**

## Electromagnetism

Electricity can produce magnetism. And magnetism can produce electricity. When you use electricity to produce magnetism, you make an **electromagnet.**

You can make an electromagnet this way: Coil a wire around an iron bar. Attach the ends of the wire to the poles of a battery. Electric current will flow through the coiled wire. The flow of electric current around the iron bar makes it a magnet.

**Electromagnet turned on**

**Electromagnet turned off**

Huge electromagnets are used in junkyards. When the magnet is turned on, it picks up metal objects. The crane moves the objects. Then the current is turned off, and the magnet drops the objects.

An electromagnet is a temporary magnet. Its magnetism can be turned on and off. When an electric current flows in the wire around the bar, the magnet is on. When the current is turned off, the magnet turns off.

You can increase the strength of an electromagnet in two ways. You can pass more current through the coil of wire. Or you can increase the number of coils around the bar. Or you can do both.

# Generators and Motors

In an electric generator, magnetism produces electricity.
In an electric motor, electricity produces magnetism.

**Generators** A **generator**
(JEN uh ray tur) changes the
energy of motion to electrical
energy. A wire loop is attached
to a rod. Steam or flowing water
turns the rod. This turns the
loop through the magnetic field
of a magnet. The magnetic field
causes electricity to flow through
the wire. As long as the wire loop
keeps turning in the magnetic
field, electricity flows through
the wire.

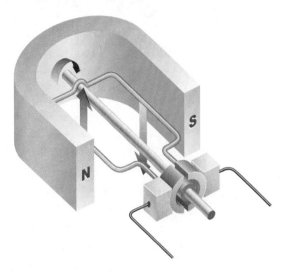

**Motors** A **motor** uses electricity to produce motion.
Electricity flows through a coil of wire wrapped around
an iron bar. The bar is in the magnetic field of a magnet.
When electricity flows through
the wire coil, the bar becomes
an electromagnet. Its poles are
repelled by the poles of the other
magnet. This makes the bar turn.
The turning bar moves other
parts of the motor.

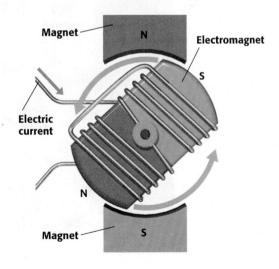

# Light and Sound

Fireworks explode in the sky. An instant later, you hear a boom. You've just witnessed two kinds of energy traveling from one place to another. The two kinds of energy are light and sound.

Your eyes detect light energy. Your ears detect sound energy. These kinds of energy are similar to each other. They both travel as waves. But they are also different from each other. Light waves and sound waves travel in different ways and at different speeds.

# Light

Light is a form of energy that travels in waves. If you toss a pebble into a pond, ripples travel outward in all directions. Like the ripples, light travels outward in all directions from a source. The source might be a candle a light bulb, a fire, the sun, or any other source. No matter what the source is, light travels in a straight line.

Light is produced when one form of energy is changed to light energy. For example, in a light bulb, electrical energy is changed to light energy. In a fire, chemical energy stored in the fuel is changed to light energy.

Light can travel through empty space where there is no air. Airless space is called a **vacuum** (VAK yoom). The space between the sun, moon, and Earth is a vacuum. In a vacuum, light travels at a speed of 300,000 kilometers per second. Light travels at slightly slower speeds through matter, such as air, water, and glass.

## Did You Know?

Light from the sun takes a little more than 8 minutes to reach Earth. Sunlight reflected by the moon takes about 1.25 seconds to reach Earth. Light from the nearest star beyond our solar system takes a little more than 4 years to reach Earth.

## Light Waves

The light you see is part of a group of waves called the **electromagnetic spectrum** (ih lek troh mag NET ik SPEK trum). The waves have different wavelengths. Some are long, and others are short.

The highest part of a wave is called the **crest.** The lowest part is called the **trough** (TRAWF). The distance between one crest and the next crest is called the **wavelength.** The wavelength can also be measured between troughs.

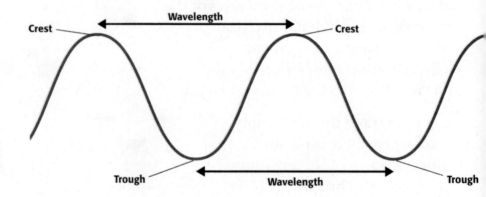

You cannot see light that travels in very long or very short wavelengths. Very short waves include gamma rays, X rays, and the ultraviolet waves that give you a sunburn. Very long waves include radio waves, microwaves, and infrared waves. Infrared waves warm your body when you are out in the sun.

The only electromagnetic waves you can see are the ones between the very long waves and the very short waves. These waves are called visible light. Visible light includes all the colors of the rainbow—red, orange, yellow, green, blue, indigo, and violet. Indigo is a dark blue-purple color. Violet is a dark purple color.

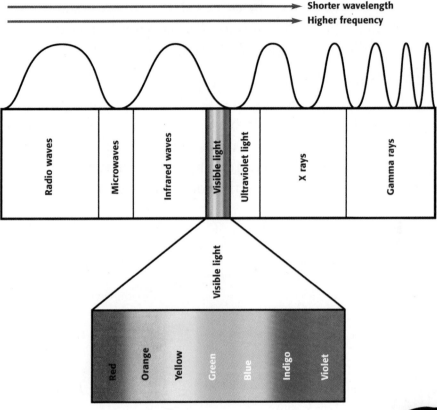

Shorter wavelength

Higher frequency

Radio waves

Microwaves

Infrared waves

Visible light

Ultraviolet light

X rays

Gamma rays

Visible light

Red

Orange

Yellow

Green

Blue

Indigo

Violet

See Also

Colors page 312

Here's an easy way to remember the colors of the rainbow from the longest waves to the shortest waves. Think of the name Roy G. Biv. The letters stand for the colors in their correct order—**R**ed, **O**range, **Y**ellow, **G**reen, **B**lue, **I**ndigo, **V**iolet.

Of all the visible light, red light has the longest wavelength and violet light has the shortest wavelength. Look at the upper-right part of the diagram at the top of this page. Notice that as waves become shorter, their frequency increases. **Frequency** (FREE kwun see) is the number of waves that move past a point in a certain amount of time. Violet light waves have a higher frequency than red light waves.

## Colors

A rain shower ends. The clouds start to break up, and the sun shines in a patch of blue sky. Suddenly a rainbow appears in the distance. What created the rainbow?

To scientists, sunlight is "white light." That means it contains all the colors of the rainbow. When rays of white light pass from one material through another material, the colors can separate. A rainbow is created when white light from the sun passes through tiny droplets of water in the air. The white light separates into the colors you see in the rainbow.

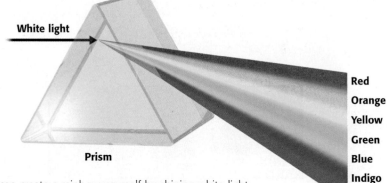

White light

Prism

Red
Orange
Yellow
Green
Blue
Indigo
Violet

You can create a rainbow yourself by shining white light through a glass bar called a prism (PRIZ um).

When light rays hit an object, they are either reflected, transmitted, or absorbed. "Reflected" means the light is bounced back by the object. "Transmitted" means the light passes through the object. "Absorbed" means the light is taken in by the object. Most objects absorb some colors of light and reflect others. Only clear objects transmit the light that hits them.

This apple looks red because it reflects red light. It absorbs the other colors, so you don't see those colors.

## Mirrors and Reflection

When you look at a mirror, you see your image. Light rays bounce off your face, hit the mirror, and bounce straight back to you. The bouncing back of light from a surface is called **reflection** (ri FLEK shun).

Light rays bounce off a mirror at the same angle they hit the mirror. If you tilt the mirror, the light from your face bounces off the mirror at an angle, not straight back to you. You don't see your face in the mirror. You see the reflection of something else.

This is like a ball bouncing off a wall. If you throw the ball straight at the wall, the ball bounces straight back to you. If you throw the ball at an angle, the ball bounces to the side at the same angle.

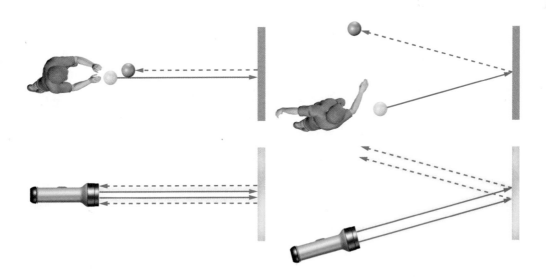

# Lenses and Refraction

When light moves through one material and into another material, the light rays can bend. The bending of light as it moves from one material into another is called **refraction** (rih FRAK shun).

A **lens** is a curved piece of clear glass or plastic that bends light rays. Lenses are used in microscopes to make objects look larger. They are used in telescopes to make distant objects look closer. Lenses in eyeglasses help people see objects more clearly.

There are two kinds of lenses used in eyeglasses. They are convex lenses and concave lenses.

A **convex lens** is thicker in the center and thinner at the edges. This shape bends light rays inward. Convex lenses are used in eyeglasses for people who are farsighted. Someone who is farsighted can see distant objects clearly, but close objects look blurry.

A **concave lens** is thinner in the center and thicker at the edges. This shape bends light outward. Concave lenses are used in eyeglasses for people who are nearsighted. Someone who is nearsighted can see close objects clearly, but distant objects look blurry.

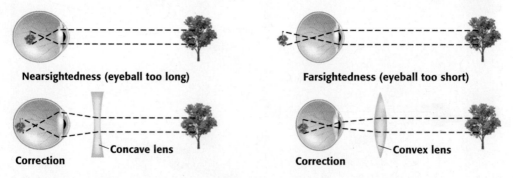

Nearsightedness (eyeball too long)

Farsightedness (eyeball too short)

Concave lens

Convex lens

Correction

Correction

For you to see an object clearly, light rays must focus on the back of your eye. If your eyeball is too short or too long, the light rays don't focus in the right place. Eyeglass lenses bend light rays so they focus correctly.

# Sound

Hold your fingers against the front of your neck and hum. You'll feel vibrations. **Sound** is a form of energy produced by vibrating objects.

When you hum, the vocal cords inside your neck vibrate. These vibrations make particles of the air around them vibrate. The vibrating air particles bump against other air particles and make them vibrate. In this way, the vibrations travel outward in all directions.

If someone is near you, vibrating air particles will hit the person's eardrums and make them vibrate. These vibrations will be passed along to nerves that lead to the person's brain, and the person will hear you humming.

The particles themselves do not move from your vocal cords to another person's ears. Only the energy of the vibrations moves. Here's how this works.

**Energy**　　　　　**Energy**

Imagine you're standing in a line with other students. You bump the students on both sides of you. Those students bump the students next to them. And they bump the students next to them. The bumping moves down the line on both sides of you. You don't move down the line, but your "bumping energy" does. Sound moves in the same way.

Sound can't move where there is no matter, such as in outer space. Sound can only move through matter. The speed of sound is different in different kinds of matter.

**Speed of Sound**

| Material | Speed (m/s) |
| --- | --- |
| Air | 340 |
| Water | 1,500 |
| Wood | 4,200 |
| Iron | 5,100 |

## Sound Waves

A canary's song is full of high notes. A lion's roar rumbles with low notes. An excited dog barks loudly. A comfortable kitten purrs softly. The different vibrations that cause these sounds are carried by sound waves with different characteristics.

As sound waves travel through air, air molecules are pressed together in some parts of the wave and are spread out in other parts of the wave. Areas where air molecules are pressed together are called **compressions** (kum PRESH unz). Areas where air molecules are spread out are called **rarefactions** (rayr uh FAK shunz). Compressions and rarefactions alternate with each other in a sound wave. The compressions might happen quickly or slowly. They might be hard or soft.

Compression  Rarefaction  Compression  Rarefaction  Compression

**Air molecules**

The **frequency** (FREE kwun see) of a sound wave is the number of compressions that move past a point in a certain amount of time.

**High and Low Sounds** In high sounds, such as a canary's song, compressions happen more often. The frequency is higher. In lower sounds, such as a lion's roar, compressions happen less often. The frequency is lower. The greater the frequency, the higher the sound. The **pitch** of a sound is how high or low the sound is.

**Loud and Quiet Sounds** Both a canary's song and a lion's rumble can be either loud or quiet. Louder sounds are created by larger vibrations of an object. The larger vibrations cause stronger movement of air molecules as the sound travels.

When you bang hard on a drum, you make a loud noise. That's because the vibrating drumhead pushes hard on the surrounding air molecules. The sound can travel a long distance.

If the first child gives a huge push to the next child, every child in line will feel a big bump. The "bumping energy" will move all the way down the line.

Quieter sounds are created by smaller vibrations of an object. The smaller vibrations cause weaker movement of air molecules.

When you tap a drum gently, you make a quiet sound. The vibrating drumhead makes the surrounding air molecules vibrate just a little. The sound might not even be heard across the room.

If the first child gives a gentle push to the next child, the other children in line will feel only small bumps. The last child in line might not even feel a bump.

# Natural Resources and the Environment

The map said there was treasure! *WHERE* is it?

The environment holds a treasure chest of materials that are useful to people. These materials are called **natural resources.** Oil, minerals, water, plants, animals, and the air you breathe are all natural resources. Unfortunately, getting and using natural resources can harm the environment. It's important for people to understand how to use natural resources wisely and keep from harming the environment we all depend on.

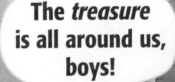

The *treasure* is all around us, boys!

# Natural Resources

All the things that keep you alive and make you comfortable come from natural resources. There are two basic kinds of natural resources. One kind is **energy resources,** such as oil and solar energy. The other kind is **material resources,** such as air, water, soil, wood, minerals, plants, and animals.

The environment holds only a certain amount of some resources. When they are used up, nature cannot replace them quickly enough to meet people's needs. These are called **nonrenewable** (nahn rih NOO uh bul) **resources.** Coal, oil, and natural gas are nonrenewable resources.

Nature can produce other resources again and again. These are called **renewable resources.** Renewable resources include trees, foods, and fresh water. If we are careful, we will not run out of these resources.

## Energy Sources

We use energy for many purposes. Trucks rumble down highways, carrying all sorts of products from one place to another. Buses, cars, trains, and ships move people. We need energy to keep all these vehicles moving.

Lights blaze in homes, factories, schools, and office buildings. We use energy to keep these lights on. We tune into television and radio programs and speak to people on telephones. Energy makes this possible. Factories use energy to run machines that make products such as cement, steel, toys, and clothing.

People use energy from many different sources. For example, for thousands of years, people have used the energy stored in wood and coal to heat their homes and cook their food. Today, we use the energy in fuels, flowing water, and wind to produce the electricity that powers our lights, furnaces, and machines.

## Fossil Fuels

Forms of Energy
page 285

Energy Changes
page 286

Sources of Heat
page 290

**Fuels** are materials that are burned to produce heat energy. The heat energy is used to run cars and trains, to warm buildings, and to produce electricity in power plants.

Most of the fuels we use today were formed from the decayed remains of ancient plants and animals. The remains of ancient plants and animals are called **fossils** (FAHS ulz), so these fuels are called **fossil fuels.** Oil, coal, and natural gas are the three major fossil fuels. Jet fuel, gasoline, and many other fuels are made from oil.

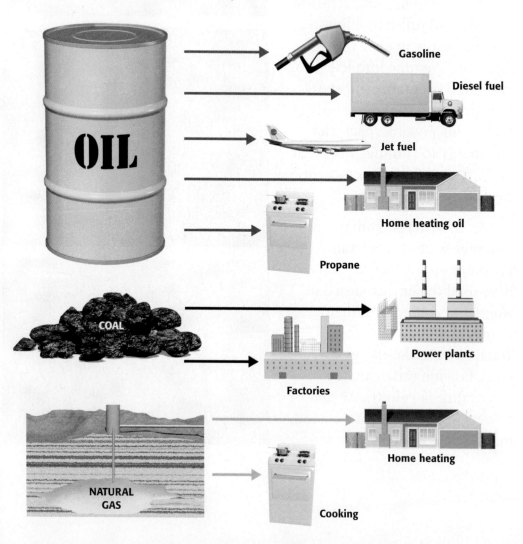

Gasoline

Diesel fuel

Jet fuel

Home heating oil

Propane

COAL

Power plants

Factories

NATURAL GAS

Home heating

Cooking

**How Fossil Fuels Are Formed**  When the ancient plants were alive, they used the energy in sunlight to make their own food. Some of that food was stored in the plants' bodies as chemical energy. Animals that ate the plants took in the chemical energy. Some of the chemical energy was stored in the animals' bodies.

Energy From the Sun page 287

When the ancient plants and animals died, their remains settled to the bottom of the swamp, lake, or ocean where they lived.

Particles of sand, soil, and mud settled on top of the remains. More decayed remains and more particles built up into layers.

Over millions of years, the particles were pressed and cemented together to form solid rock. The remains of the dead plants and animals were trapped between rock layers.

Heat and pressure gradually changed the remains into oil, coal, and natural gas.

Fossil fuels are still forming today. But because they take millions of years to form, we have to think of them as nonrenewable resources. People use fossil fuels much faster than nature can make them.

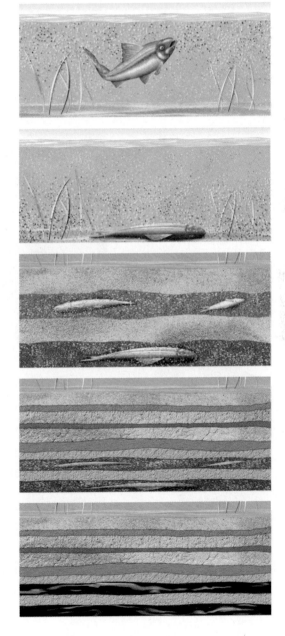

## Solar Energy

On January 3, 2004, a space probe named *Spirit* landed on Mars. Soon after landing, parts of the probe began to unfold like flower petals. The parts contained solar cells. A solar cell changes solar energy into electrical energy. The electricity from *Spirit*'s solar cells powered scientific instruments and cameras.

Here on Earth, groups of solar cells are mounted on the roofs of buildings. The cells produce electricity for lighting and heating the buildings.

Solar energy is a renewable energy source. People will never run out of sunlight!

Solar panels on the roofs of buildings also use solar energy to heat water. The heated water is then pumped through pipes to keep the buildings warm. This is called an **active solar heating system.**

In a **passive solar heating system,** sunlight passes through windows and heats stone or another material inside the building. When the air cools at night, the material gives off heat to keep the building warm.

## Energy From Water

Moving water has kinetic energy that can be used to generate electricity. Machines inside dams change the energy of moving water into electrical energy.

See Also

Energy Changes
page 286

Generators
page 307

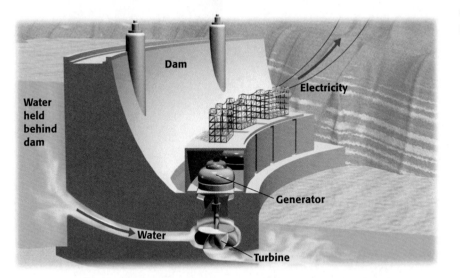

A dam is built across a river. Water flows through openings in the dam. The moving water turns the blades of a machine called a turbine. The turbine's spinning blades turn a rod that is connected to a generator. The generator produces electricity.

Damming a river changes the ecosystem. People have to decide between their need for electricity and the needs of plants and animals that depend on the river.

In some coastal areas, the moving water in ocean tides is used to generate electricity. A dam is built over a narrow bay. Rising and falling tides power turbines and generators, just like in a river dam.

See Also

Tides page 195

The water in rivers and along ocean coasts is always moving. So moving water is a renewable energy resource.

## Energy From Wind

See Also
Generators
page 307

Windmills change the energy of moving air into electrical energy. Wind turns the windmill's blades. The blades turn a rod that is connected to a generator that produces electricity.

Since wind cannot be used up, it is a renewable energy resource. But using windmills to generate electricity only works well in places where wind blows steadily.

This "wind farm" at Altamont Pass in California has thousands of windmills.

## Nuclear Energy

See Also
Parts of an Atom
page 249

All matter is made up of atoms. Each atom has a core called the nucleus. The parts inside the nucleus are very tightly held together. When they are broken apart, a tremendous amount of energy is released. This energy is called nuclear (NOO klee ur) energy because it comes from an atom's nucleus.

Some nuclear energy comes out of an atom as heat. In a nuclear power plant, this heat is used to turn liquid water into steam. The steam turns the parts of a generator to produce electricity.

This is the Rancho Seco nuclear power plant in Sacramento, California.

## Geothermal Energy

If you've ever seen a picture of an erupting volcano, you know there is hot melted rock deep below Earth's surface. This heat is called **geothermal** (jee oh THUR mul) **energy.** Geothermal energy can be used to produce electricity.

**WORD WATCH**

The word part *geo* comes from a Greek word that means "Earth." *Thermal* comes from a Greek word that means "heat."

Geothermal energy is a renewable energy resource because it is constantly produced inside Earth.

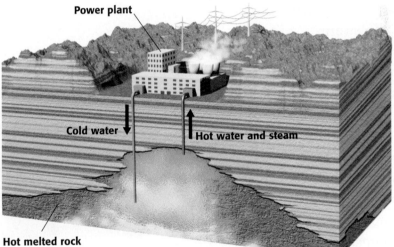

Power plant

Cold water

Hot water and steam

Hot melted rock

Hot melted rock heats water deep below ground. Hot water and steam rise up a pipe to a power plant. There, the steam is used to turn blades in a machine called a turbine. The turbine turns a rod that is connected to a generator. The generator produces electricity. The cool water is pumped back down into the ground to be heated again.

**See Also**

Generators page 307

### Did You Know?

In the country of Iceland, water heated by geothermal energy is used to heat homes, offices, schools, and other buildings. It's also used to heat greenhouses where crops can be grown year-round.

Keyword: Alternative Forms of Energy
www.scilinks.org
Code: GSS45120

## Energy From Plants and Animals

Energy From the
Sun page 287

The bodies of plants and animals contain stored chemical energy. When plant and animal products are burned, the chemical energy changes to other forms of energy. Plant and animal products are renewable energy resources.

**Wood** Wood has probably been used longer as a fuel than any other material. In many parts of the world, wood is burned to heat homes, cook food, and heat water. Wood is a renewable energy resource if new trees are planted to replace ones that were cut down.

**Peat** Peat forms when swamp plants die and decay. Dried peat is burned to produce heat for homes and to cook food. Peat is usually used where coal and other fuels are too expensive or are not available.

Peat is a major source of fuel in countries such as Ireland and Russia.

**Dung** Dung is solid animal waste. Dried dung is used as fuel in many developing countries. When American pioneers could not find wood on the prairies, they burned dried buffalo dung.

**Gasohol** Gasohol is a mixture of gasoline made from oil and alcohol made from plants. Gasohol can be used as a fuel for cars, buses, and other automobiles.

## Material Resources

People use thousands of different kinds of material resources. They use rich soil to grow crops. They mine minerals to get metals. They grow plants and raise animals to get food, wool, wood, paper, cotton, and leather. Clean air and water are material resources, too.

### Soil

**Soil** is a mixture of rock particles, minerals, and decayed plants and animals. Soil contains nutrients that plants need. But the nutrients can be used up by crops. Soil can be washed away by rainwater or blown away by wind. There are many ways to preserve soil and the nutrients that it contains.

See Also
Soil page 168

Plant roots hold soil in place. Land should never be left bare, or wind and water will carry the soil away. If trees are logged, new trees should be planted to replace them. When crops are harvested, the dead plants should be left in the field to cover and protect the soil until the next crop is planted.

In hilly areas, farmers plow fields to follow the shape of the land. This keeps rainwater from washing soil off the hills.

Some crops take the same nutrients out of the soil year after year. Farmers can change the crops they grow in a field each year. By doing this, the nutrients taken out by one crop will be replaced by the next crop.

SC*LINKS*
NSTA

Keyword: Explore Soil
www.scilinks.org
Code: GSS45065

## Water

Water Cycle
pages 188–189

Fresh Water
pages 190–191

Groundwater
page 192

Water Pollution
pages 342–343

All living things must have water to survive. Most living things need fresh water, water that is not salty. Fresh water is found in streams, rivers, ponds, lakes, and under ground.

Fresh water is a renewable resource because water is recycled by nature. But that doesn't mean we can't run out of water. In many places, people use fresh water faster than nature can replace it. People should use only as much fresh water as they need. It's also important to keep fresh water clean.

## Air

Air Pollution
pages 339–340

Acid Rain
page 341

Air is a mixture of gases. Animals need the oxygen in air. Plants need the carbon dioxide in air. Animals produce carbon dioxide, and plants produce oxygen, so these gases are renewable resources. But the air we breathe is not always clean.

Automobiles, factories, and power plants produce gases and solid particles that enter the air. Some of these materials are harmful to living things. Some materials can damage buildings and statues. It's important to keep our air clean.

## Rocks and Minerals

You may not think much about the rocks under your feet. But many kinds of rocks are valuable resources that people have used for thousands of years.

See
Also
Rocks
pages 164–167

The Lincoln Memorial in Washington, D.C., is made of marble.

**Rocks** Granite and marble are kinds of rock that are used for buildings and statues. The roofs of many houses in the United States are covered with tiles of slate, another rock. Glass is made from sand. Concrete is made of small pieces of rock cemented together.

**Minerals** Many rocks contain valuable substances called minerals. Over thousands of years, people have learned how to remove minerals from rocks. These minerals include metals such as silver, copper, and iron. Bridges, highway supports, and the frameworks of most large buildings are made of steel, which contains iron.

See
Also
Minerals
pages 160–163

The way a mineral is used depends on its properties. For example, copper is a good conductor of electricity. It also can be formed into thin strands. So copper is used to make electrical wires. Gold has a beautiful color and can easily be molded into different shapes. These properties make gold useful for jewelry.

## Plants and Animals

If you walk through a supermarket, you'll see many products that have come from living resources. Cereal boxes hold flakes made from plants such as corn, wheat, oats, and rice. Wheat is also used to make spaghetti and other kinds of pasta.

Apples, oranges, peaches, grapes, and tomatoes are the fruits of plants. Potatoes, onions, celery, broccoli, spinach, and spices come from the stems, roots, leaves, flowers, and seeds of plants.

Beef, pork, chicken, turkey, lamb, fish, milk, cheese, and eggs come from animal resources.

Foods are not the only products that come from living resources. Towels and clothing are made from the cotton produced by cotton plants. Leather shoes are made from the skin of cows and other animals. Wool is the hair of sheep. Paper and furniture are made from the wood of trees. Rubber comes from the sap of rubber trees. Plants and animals produce chemicals that are used to make paint, glue, shampoo, fertilizer, and many other products.

Many medicines contain chemicals that come from plants. And some medicines come from organisms besides plants. For example, the antibiotic penicillin originally came from a kind of fungus called a mold. You may have taken a form of penicillin to cure a strep throat. You also eat fungi. Mushrooms are fungi. So is yeast, which is used to make bread. Bacteria are used to make cheese, yogurt, and sauerkraut.

Living things are renewable resources because they reproduce to make more living things like themselves.

See Also

Fungi page 143

Bacteria page 145

# Pollution

Does the sky where you live ever look yellowish instead of clear blue? Have you seen an oily shine on the surface of ponds or marshes? Do people toss trash on the ground? Is rock salt spread on icy roads and then washed away into the soil?

If you answered Yes to any of these questions, you've seen pollution (puh LOO shun). **Pollution** is anything in the environment that can harm living things or damage natural resources.

Some pollution is caused by natural events such as forest fires and erupting volcanoes. But most pollution is caused by the activities of people.

## Garbage

People throw away all sorts of objects. They throw away uneaten food, cardboard boxes, glass bottles, plastic containers, metal cans, newspapers, worn out clothes, appliances, and furniture. These are all forms of solid waste, or **garbage.**

### Did You Know?

People in the United States throw away about 229 million tons of garbage every year. That's an average of $4\frac{1}{2}$ pounds of garbage each person each day.

Open dumps like this one are against the law in most places today.

### Litter

Some people don't take the time to get rid of garbage properly. They throw it on streets and sidewalks, into vacant lots, and on the ground in playgrounds and parks. This kind of garbage is called **litter.** Litter is ugly and often smelly. It also attracts disease-causing organisms and pests such as rats, cockroaches, and flies.

## Landfills

In the past, landfills were just big holes in the ground where garbage was dumped and left to pile up. Today, cities and towns use sanitary (SAN ih ter ee) landfills. These modern landfills are built to keep garbage from harming the environment and attracting pests.

Groundwater page 192

A sanitary landfill starts as a large hole in the ground. The hole is lined with layers of packed clay and plastic. Drains are installed. The clay, plastic, and drains keep harmful chemicals from leaking out of the landfill and into the soil. The chemicals could pollute underground water that is used for drinking and cooking. Vent pipes are installed to let methane escape. Methane is an explosive gas produced by some bacteria. Now the landfill is ready to collect garbage.

Garbage is dumped into one area in the hole. Bulldozers spread the garbage around and press it down into thin layers. Then a layer of soil is spread over the garbage and packed down. When one area in the hole is filled, workers start filling another area.

Sometimes, buildings, roads, and parks are constructed on closed landfills. The second largest shopping mall in the United States was built on a landfill in West Nyack, New York.

In time, all the areas are filled with packed garbage and soil. When that happens, the landfill is closed. A thick layer of soil is spread over the top and packed down. Small plants and trees are planted to keep the soil from washing away.

Sanitary landfills are a safe way to get rid of garbage. But there's a big problem. As cities and towns grow larger and people occupy more land, less land is available for landfills. People are running out of places to put their garbage.

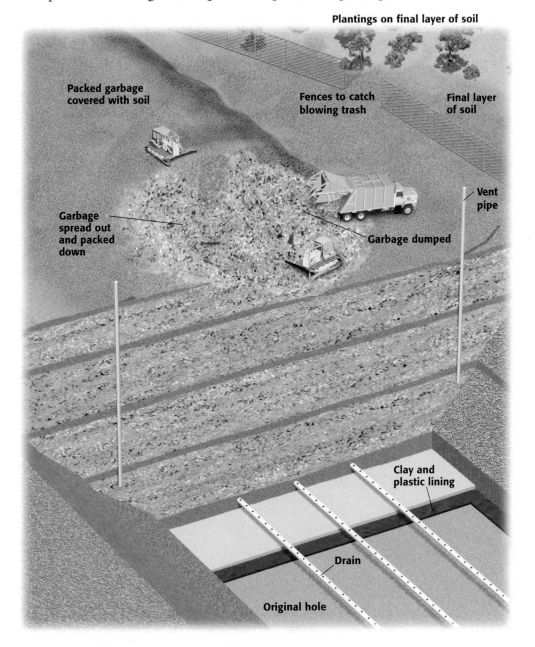

Plantings on final layer of soil

Packed garbage covered with soil

Fences to catch blowing trash

Final layer of soil

Vent pipe

Garbage spread out and packed down

Garbage dumped

Clay and plastic lining

Drain

Original hole

## Burning Trash

Landfills take up a lot of space. To reduce the need for landfills, some communities burn trash in an incinerator (in SIN uh ray tur). An **incinerator** is a kind of furnace designed for burning waste materials.

Many incinerators accept trash from several towns or cities. These incinerators are the size of a large building. They can turn a 30-gallon bag of trash into a 3-gallon bag of ash. Some incinerators use heat from the burning trash to boil water. The steam is used to heat buildings or generate electricity in a power plant.

There are drawbacks to incinerating trash. Incinerators can't burn glass or metal. These materials have to be removed from the trash before it is burned. Some kinds of trash produce harmful particles and gases when they are burned. These materials can pollute the air. To solve this problem, incinerators have parts called scrubbers. The scrubbers remove most harmful substances before they can enter the air.

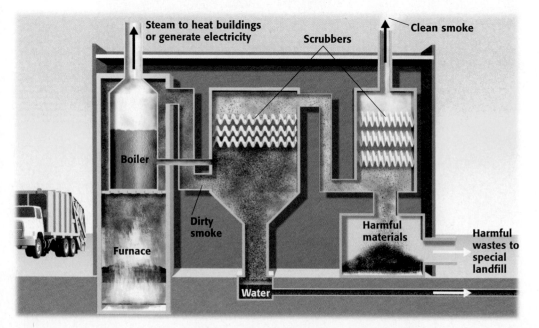

## Air Pollution

The gases in air support and protect life on Earth. Animals need the oxygen in air to release energy in food they eat. Plants take carbon dioxide from air to make their own food.

Air also contains a gas called ozone. This gas forms a protective layer high in Earth's atmosphere. It blocks some of the dangerous radiation that reaches Earth from the sun. This kind of radiation, called ultraviolet radiation, causes sunburn. It also can cause skin cancer in some people. Some kinds of air pollution can destroy ozone.

See
Also

Cell Respiration
pages 78–79

Photosynthesis
page 80

Using a sunscreen, wearing protective clothing, and shading yourself from the sun can reduce the harm caused by ultraviolet radiation from the sun.

Harmful substances that get into the air cause **air pollution.** Air pollution can make it hard for people to breathe. It can make you cough or sneeze. It can make your eyes sting. It can give you a rash.

Air pollution also harms plants. For example, trees in large cities with air pollution do not live as long as trees in the country where the air is clean. Air pollution also wears away the stone in buildings, bridges, and statues.

Some air pollution is caused by natural events. A forest fire produces soot and smoke. A volcano eruption can send harmful gases and ash high into the air. Wind spreads these materials for long distances.

Fossil Fuels
pages 322–323

Most air pollution is caused by people. The biggest source of air pollution is burning fossil fuels. These fuels are used by automobiles, factories, and power plants. When fossil fuels are burned, they release harmful gases into the air. The gases react with sunlight to form smog. Smog makes the air unhealthy to breathe.

Air pollution can be reduced. For example, many factories and power plants have installed scrubbers. These devices remove harmful substances before they can enter the air.

In some kinds of weather, smog is trapped close to the ground. The air is so unhealthy that people are warned to stay indoors.

Cars, trucks, and buses have a kind of scrubber called a catalytic (kat ul IT ik) converter. A catalytic converter is part of the automobile's exhaust system. It converts, or changes, some of the harmful gases into harmless carbon dioxide gas and water.

## Did You Know?

Los Angeles, California, has some of the worst smog in the world. The city has passed strict laws to help control air pollution.

## Acid Rain

Acids are chemicals that can wear away or dissolve materials such as metals, stone, and cement. Acids can burn your skin, your eyes, and the lining of your nose, throat, and lungs.

Rain normally contains some acids, but the amount is not enough to be harmful. But sometimes acids from air pollution form and fall to the ground in rain. Rain that contains unhealthy amounts of acid is called **acid rain.**

Acid rain forms when some gases from automobiles, factories, and power plants combine with water in the air. When the gases combine with water, they form acids. Rain carries the acids to Earth's surface.

Living things can be harmed by acid rain. Acid rain has stunted the growth of trees in the eastern United States. Acid rain has also poisoned ponds and lakes in the Northeast, killing fish and other water organisms.

Acid rain also damages buildings, bridges, monuments, statues, and even headstones in cemeteries. The acids eat away at stone, brick, and metal. Over time, the material crumbles into pieces and falls apart.

The metal of the Statue of Liberty in New York harbor was damaged by acid rain and had to be repaired.

## Water Pollution

Groundwater
page 192

Erosion and
Deposition
pages 172–173

All living things need water to survive. Water is found on Earth's surface in streams, lakes, ponds, rivers, and oceans. Water is also found below Earth's surface as groundwater. Both surface water and groundwater can be polluted.

**Pollution by Sediments** Sediments are particles of rock, soil, and sand. Sediments can be washed or blown into bodies of water. As the particles float in the water, they block sunlight from reaching down into the water. This harms plants, fish, and other organisms living in the water. As sediments build up over time, they can clog rivers and streams.

**Pollution by Sewage** Sewage is made up of human wastes, detergents, soaps, and food scraps that have been rinsed down drains. When these materials are dumped into bodies of water, they can harm living things that use or live in the water.

**Pollution by Chemicals** Chemicals dumped or washed into streams, rivers, and lakes from factories, farms, and mines can poison living things. Harmful chemicals can also soak into the soil and pollute groundwater.

**Pollution by Disease-Causing Organisms** Human wastes and animal wastes can contain bacteria and other organisms that cause disease. Sometimes these wastes are washed into bodies of water or are dumped there. The organisms then spread to people who use the water for drinking, cooking, or washing.

**Pollution by Heat** Some factories and power plants use water to cool machines. The water heats up. The hot water is then piped into a body of water. Organisms that cannot live or reproduce in warm water are harmed.

## Oil Spills

Oil spills happen when a ship carrying oil crashes or leaks or when an underwater oil well leaks. The oil spreads out over the water surface. It injures or kills sea animals. It washes up on beaches and harms plants and animals there. People cannot use the beaches.

Sea birds that are coated with oil cannot eat or fly.

*Did You Know?*

The worst oil spill in U.S. history happened in March 1989 when the oil tanker *Exxon Valdez* hit underwater rocks in Prince William Sound, Alaska. More than 10 million gallons of oil leaked into the water.

# Conserving Resources

The world doesn't have an endless supply of natural resources. We have to make our natural resources last longer. The wise use and protection of natural resources is called **conservation** (kahn sur VAY shun).

## Conserving Energy

See Also
Fossil Fuels
pages 322–323

The best way to conserve our energy resources is to reduce our use of fossil fuels. Oil and coal are used in power plants and factories to produce electrical energy and to run machines. Gasoline made from oil is used to run cars, trucks, and buses. Natural gas is used to heat buildings and cook food.

Here's how you, your family, and your community can conserve the fuels that are used to produce energy.

- Use public transportation instead of the family car. If there's no public transportation where you live, share rides with other people. And whenever you can, ride your bicycle. It doesn't use any fuel at all!

- Suggest that your family buy cars that get high mileage from a gallon of gas. Your family could also buy a car that runs partly on electricity.

- Turn down the thermostat in your house at night. During the day, wear warm clothes and keep the thermostat at the coolest temperature that is comfortable.

- Use energy-saving light bulbs, like the one shown here.

- Turn off the lights when you leave a room.

- Your family or community might be able to use some renewable energy resources. For example, pathway lights that run on solar cells don't use electricity produced with fossil fuels.

## Conserving Material Resources

Material
Resources
pages 329–333

Material resources include air, water, soil, metals, plastics, glass, plant products such as wood and paper, and animal products such as wool and leather. People need these resources to lead healthy, comfortable lives.

You and other people can conserve material resources by following the three **R**s.

Reduce the use of resources.

Reuse resources.

Recycle resources.

### Reduce

There are many ways to reduce the amount of resources you use. One important way is to buy products with the least amount of packaging. Encourage your family to do these things.

- Buy products "in bulk."
  That means buying several of the same product in one large package instead of each one in a separate package.

- Buy larger sizes of things that will last a long time, such as paper products and dry pasta.

- Look for products that don't have a lot of unnecessary packaging. Think about how much packaging will end up as trash.

 SCiLINKS

Keyword: Recycling
www.scilinks.org
Code: GSS45125

Here are some ways you and your family can reduce the amount of water you use.

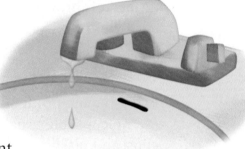

- If there's a dripping faucet in your home, fix it.
- Replace ordinary showerheads with water-saving showerheads.
- If a toilet needs to be replaced, buy one that uses the least amount of water per flush.
- Don't let the water run while you're brushing your teeth.

Here are some ways your family can conserve resources when shopping for groceries.

Remember: Paper is made from trees, and plastics are made from oil.

- Bring used grocery bags to the store. When you reuse bags, you conserve trees and oil.
- When you're buying fruit and vegetables, choose ones that are not already in packages. Put them in a used bag from home.

Here are a few more tips.

- Buy used products instead of new ones.
- Repair broken items instead of buying new ones.
- Rent or borrow tools.
- Share newspapers, magazines, paperback books, and clothing.

## Reuse

Wash glass and plastic containers and use them again instead of throwing them in the garbage. You can store small items such as screws, nails, and buttons in glass baby food jars and plastic medicine vials. You can keep baseball cards or other collections in shoe boxes.

Avoid buying products that can be used only once. For example, people usually throw away paper plates, paper cups, and plastic forks, knives, and spoons after one use. Instead, wash the plastic items and use them again. Better still, use regular dishes, glasses, and silverware.

Build a compost (KAHM post) pile with materials your family would usually throw away. **Compost** is a mixture of soil and decayed material that provides nutrients for plants. A compost pile is made of layers of soil and layers of waste materials that will decay. As they decay, they break down into substances that plants need to grow well. You can use the compost in a flower garden, a vegetable garden, or pots for houseplants.

Waste materials you can safely use in a compost pile include fruit and vegetable scraps, yard waste such as leaves and grass clippings, coffee grounds, eggshells, potato peels, and shredded newspapers. Cover each layer of waste material with a layer of soil. Keep the pile moist. Every month or so, mix the pile with a pitchfork to let air into it.

## Recycle

Don't throw away materials that can be recycled. These are the kinds of materials you can recycle.

- glass bottles and jars
- aluminum cans
- plastic containers
- newspapers (Some recycling programs accept magazines and catalogs, too.)

Find out how materials are recycled where you live. Your family's trash collector might give you a small reusable bin to put out with your garbage. Or you might have to take the materials to a recycling center.

During recycling, items are turned back into the material they were made from. Then the material is used to make new items. For example, aluminum cans are melted, and the aluminum is used to make new cans. Old newspapers are treated so they can be made into new, clean paper. Plastic items are shredded, melted, and molded into new shapes.

# Protecting Wildlife

Habitats
page 127

Human activities can harm wildlife. This is especially true when people damage or destroy an organism's habitat. An **organism** (OR guh niz um) is any living thing. A **habitat** (HAB ih tat) is the environment where an organism lives, such as a forest or stream.

When a habitat is changed, the animals that live there have to move somewhere else. But sometimes they can't move. And plants aren't able to move at all. The organisms would die out in that place. If that is the only place where they live, they would become extinct. **Extinction** (ik STINGKT shun) happens when the last member of a species dies. A **species** (SPEE sheez) is a group of organisms of the same kind.

Species page 128

Today, thousands of species are in danger of becoming extinct. Many human activities can cause extinction.

**Hunting** Animal species are harmed if too many of the animals are killed. For example, gray wolves in the western United States were killed by farmers and ranchers because some wolves were killing their sheep and cattle. The wolves were almost completely wiped out in most areas. Today, gray wolves are protected by laws. They are also being put back into some of their habitats, such as Yellowstone National Park.

**Over Fishing** Today's fishing boats can catch thousands of fish at a time. Some species of fish are caught faster than they can reproduce. Those species begin to die out. This has happened to salmon in the Northwest and cod, haddock, and flounder in the Northeast.

**Pollution** Many kinds of pollutants harm wildlife. For example, poisons are used to kill insects that feed on crops. Animals that eat the poisoned insects die, too. Rain washes the poisons off fields and into streams. There, the poisons kill frogs, fish, and other wildlife. Animals that eat the poisoned animals are also killed. Poisons move through food chains and food webs.

See Also

Food Chains
page 137

Food Webs
page 138

**Loss of Habitat** Damaging or destroying a habitat harms many species. For example, if trees are cut down in a forest, birds that depend on the trees for food and places to build nests cannot live there any more. If the birds spread the seeds of certain plants, the plants could die out. Other animals that hunted the birds for food could also die out.

Sometimes people can change a habitat back to what it used to be. For example, new trees can be planted in an area that was cleared by logging. Old dams that were built along a river can be torn down. Water can be let back into a marsh or swamp that was drained.

## Endangered Species

Many countries have passed laws to protect species from extinction. In 1973 the U.S. government passed the Endangered Species Act. This law identifies species throughout the world that might become extinct.

The law created two categories of species that need help. **Endangered species** are ones that could become extinct very soon if they are not helped. **Threatened species** are ones that could become endangered if their numbers keep decreasing.

These are just a few of the endangered animals that are found in the United States.

**Florida panther**

**Whooping crane**

**Stellar sea lion**

**Black-footed ferret**

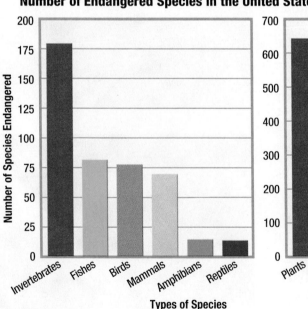

**Number of Endangered Species in the United States**

Number of Species Endangered

Types of Species: Invertebrates, Fishes, Birds, Mammals, Amphibians, Reptiles, Plants

*Source: U.S. Fish and Wildlife Service, 2012*

**Protected Areas** Many countries around the world have set aside areas where endangered and threatened species are protected. An area like this is called a **wildlife preserve, sanctuary** (SANGK choo er ee), or **refuge** (REF yooj). Farming, hunting, and most other human activities are not allowed in the protected areas.

There are more than 400 places in the United States where species are protected. This one is Yellowstone National Park in Wyoming, Idaho, and Montana.

**Captive Breeding** Some zoos, animal parks, and wildlife centers help endangered species by breeding them and raising the young. This is called **captive breeding.** An endangered bird called the California condor was saved this way.

In 1982, only 22 California condors were alive in the wild. It looked like the species would become extinct very soon. Scientists decided to capture all the wild condors. The captive birds began breeding and producing chicks. As the number of condors increased, scientists began releasing some into the wild.

In January 2004, there were 215 California condors: 82 were living in the wild, 32 were in pens waiting to be released, and 101 were being kept in zoos and wildlife centers to continue the captive breeding program.

Keyword: Endangered Species
www.scilinks.org
Code: GSS45130

# Science, Technology, and Engineering

Thanks to *technology*, I give you the Sprinkler-Tron 4000!

**T**echnology (tek NAHL uh jee) is any tool or machine designed to help people in some way. A bike helmet is a technology. It is designed to protect your head if you fall off your bike. A sprinkler system is a technology. It is designed to help farmers water their crops. Science and technology depend on each other. Technology affects the people in a society, and society affects technology.

**Thanks to *Bessie*. She's all the technology *I* need!**

# Science and Engineering

A computer, a cell phone, and a satellite are all examples of technologies. But technology includes much more than complicated machines.

One of the earliest technologies created by humans was a cutting tool made from a rock. They sharpened the rock by chipping at the sides with another rock. Then they attached the rock to a wooden handle to make an ax. How was the ax "technology"? It was a tool that people made to do a job or solve a problem.

Early humans used this ax to cut up animals for food and to make clothing from animal furs.

The development of technology depends on the work of both scientists and engineers. A **scientist** is someone who studies the natural world. An **engineer** is someone who designs technology to solve problems.

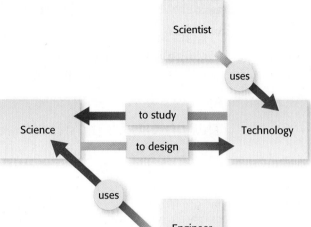

Engineers must understand science in order to design technologies. For example, understanding the properties of magnets allowed scientist and engineer Michael Faraday to invent the electric generator. A generator uses magnets to produce electricity.

**See Also**

Generators and Motors
page 307

Sometimes, ideas for new technology come from observing nature. For example, engineers in Japan studied butterfly wings to see what made them waterproof. They used their findings to create a similar kind of waterproof material in the laboratory.

## Did You Know?

Scientists and engineers aren't always different people. Many scientists throughout history have acted as engineers and invented new technologies.

# Engineering Technology

When engineers are designing a new technology, they go through a series of steps. Every technology is designed to solve a problem. So you know that the first step must be identifying a problem.

This chart shows the steps in technology design. One example is shown down the left side of the chart.

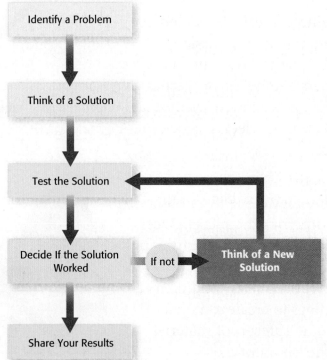

A phone booth on the side of a country road needs light so people can see when they are inside it. But there is no electric power to the phone booth.

Put a solar panel and a battery on top of the booth. The energy gathered can be used to power a light bulb in the booth at night.

Put up the solar panel. Connect wires from the panel and the battery to a light source in the booth. Also connect a sensor that will "tell" the lighting system when it is dark. See if the bulb lights at night.

The bulb stayed lit all night. It worked!

Write a report about what you found out. Share your report with other people who might have a similar problem.

**Identify a Problem**

**Think of a Solution**

**Test the Solution**

**Decide If the Solution Worked**

**If not**

**Think of a New Solution**

**Share Your Results**

There is never just one way to solve a problem. Engineers often test many different ideas before they choose the best solution.

# How Technology Helps Scientists

Scientists are always asking questions about the natural world and then trying to find the answers. Observation is an important part of that process. Technology helps scientists with their observations.

Think about a scientist observing tiny organisms with a microscope. Or a meteorologist using satellite pictures to track a hurricane. Or an astronomer using a telescope to view Mars. Scientists use technology to help them see things that they cannot see with just their eyes.

Technology helps scientists get more information about the natural world. This information might answer a question the scientists had. It might also raise some new questions. For example, astronomers examining telescope photographs of Mars saw what looked like dry riverbeds on the planet's surface. This observation led scientists to wonder whether there had been liquid water on Mars's surface in the ancient past.

Engineers have designed and built various space probes to visit Mars. Some probes have carried robot rovers to look for evidence of water and determine if Mars could be safely explored by humans.

Keyword: Robots
www.scilinks.org
Code: GSS45135

# How Technology Helps All of Us

Technology helps people live safer, healthier, and more comfortable lives than people did in the past.

**In the past**

**Today**

Years ago, there wasn't always enough food to eat. Plowing and harvesting were hard work and took a long time. Today, farm technology allows people in the United States and other developed countries to grow huge quantities of food.

In the past, garbage and other waste piled up in the streets. The wastes attracted rats and spread disease. Today, garbage collection and sewage systems remove wastes.

**In the past**

**Today**

**In the past**

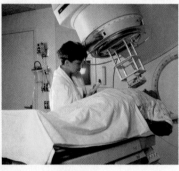

**Today**

Not very long ago, many people died of common diseases. Today's technology helps doctors find out what is wrong with a patient. Vaccines prevent serious diseases such as polio and smallpox. Many kinds of medicines are available to treat illnesses.

Modern technologies are not available to everyone in the world. Many people still struggle with hunger and disease every day.

## Science and Technology Work Together

New discoveries often give scientists ideas for new kinds of technology. Here's one example.

See Also

Bacteria page 145

Hundred of years ago, scientists did not know that bacteria existed. Then in 1683, a Dutch scientist named Anton von Leeuwenhoek (LAY vun huk) developed a new technology. He made curved lenses that magnified objects. Leeuwenhoek used the lenses to build the first microscope.

Bacteria are too small to see with just your eyes. These are the bacteria that cause strep throat.

Once scientists had microscopes, they could observe the tiny bacteria and other organisms that cause diseases in people and animals. Then they discovered that some natural substances could kill bacteria. These substances are called antibiotics (an tih by AHT iks). Scientists used technology to produce medicines from natural antibiotics. Later, they found ways to create new antibiotics in laboratories.

These pictures show Anton von Leeuwenhoek and the simple microscope he invented.

# Technology Is Always Changing

No technology is ever a final solution. Technologies can always be improved. One example is the telephone.

In 1840, the fastest way to send a message over a long distance was to use a telegraph. The telegraph is a machine that sends electrical signals through wires. The signals are short and long clicking noises.

The telegraph machine required trained telegraph operators to send and receive messages.

Early telephones had to be wound up with a hand crank before making a call. The call had to go through an operator.

Then in 1876, while he was experimenting with a telegraph machine, American inventor Alexander Graham Bell discovered how to send voice messages through telegraph wires. The first telephone was created.

In time, telephone technology improved enough that telephone operators were no longer needed. People could just pick up a phone and call anyone anywhere.

Today, cellular telephones let people make and receive phone calls wherever they happen to be. Some cell phones even send pictures and e-mail.

## No Technology Is Perfect

Technologies are developed to solve problems. But that doesn't mean they only do good. Some technologies create new problems while trying to solve others.

Antibacterial soap is a good example. Antibacterial soap contains antibiotics (an tih by AHT iks), which are substances that kill bacteria. Antibacterial soap was developed to kill harmful bacteria that might be on our hands or our dirty dishes. Since some bacteria cause diseases, killing them seemed like a good idea.

BAC-OFF
ANTIBACTERIAL
HAND SOAP
KILLS BACTERIA
ON CONTACT!

Unfortunately, not all kinds of harmful bacteria are killed by the antibiotics in soaps. Scientists say that these kinds of bacteria are "resistant" to antibiotics. Resistant bacteria survive and reproduce. Their offspring are also resistant. Over time, all those kinds of bacteria are resistant to the antibiotics.

Resistant bacteria are dangerous to public health. That's because doctors use antibiotics to cure people who are infected with harmful bacteria. But when resistant bacteria get into our bodies and make us sick, antibiotics can't kill them. These resistant bacteria then move easily from one person to another, making lots of people sick.

See
Also

Bacteria
page 145

# Science and Society

A **society** (suh SY ih tee) is a group of people who all live under the same set of rules. The society you live in includes the members of your family and all the people in your neighborhood, your town, your state, and even your country. People in a society make decisions about what activities go on in that society.

Suppose some people in your town want to use pesticides to kill caterpillars that are damaging trees in the town park. But other people are afraid that the pesticides will get into the water supply and make people sick. The people in your town have to talk about the benefits and risks of spraying pesticides. Then the people must decide what to do.

Not everyone in a society is a scientist. Not everyone can offer an expert opinion on questions of technology. But members of a society must be able to ask the right questions to get the information they need in order to make a decision.

Suppose some members of your community want to make it illegal to burn wood in fireplaces and wood stoves. They say that wood smoke is a major cause of air pollution in your town. Other members of your community don't think wood smoke causes pollution.

Members of a society often disagree about whether a certain technology should be used. A public discussion lets all sides give their opinions. This is a good way to make sure that all the benefits and risks are considered.

To help them make a decision, the members of the community could bring in a pollution expert. The expert might present data that show how smoke from wood fires causes air pollution. The members of the community would then have to consider this data when making their final decision.

## Making Decisions

How do the members of a society go about making a decision about a new technology? First, they compare the benefits and risks of the technology. A **benefit** is a good result. A **risk** is a result that might be harmful.

Imagine that a society is debating whether or not to let farmers grow a "super" tomato. This new kind of tomato was developed by scientists to be more resistant to garden pests than ordinary tomatoes. The society would have to look at the benefits and risks of the new technology.

### Benefits of SUPER Tomato

People could grow tomatoes that were less likely to be eaten by insects.

Farmers would make more money selling "super" tomatoes.

### Risks of SUPER Tomato

No one knows whether tomatoes changed by science would harm the people or animals that eat them.

A "super" tomato might take over and wipe out the other tomato plants we have today.

Some members of the society might think that the benefits of the "super" tomato outweigh the risks. Others might feel that the risks outweigh the benefits. In the end, the members of the society must make a decision about whether to allow "super" tomatoes. Not everyone will agree with the decision.

## Many Different People Contribute to Science

Scientific research has been going on for thousands of years. So has the development of new technologies. Medicines are a good example.

Since ancient times, people have used natural materials to treat infections and diseases. Several hundred years ago, people in Peru discovered that the bark of the cinchona (sing KOH nuh) tree would bring down a high fever when someone had malaria (muh LAYR ee uh), a serious tropical disease. Bark was taken to Europe, where many people were dying of malaria. The South American medicine saved many European lives.

Later, German scientists studied the bark. They found the chemical that reduced high fevers. They used what they learned to make malaria medicine in a laboratory. Since that time, scientists in other countries have developed even better drugs to treat malaria.

Bark from the cinchona tree was the first medicine used to treat malaria.

By sharing what they learn, scientists around the world help each other make scientific discoveries.

# Scientists Are Affected by Society

Not every scientific idea is immediately accepted by a society. That's because scientific ideas sometimes do not agree with the strong beliefs that a society holds. For example, consider the case of Galileo.

Galileo was an Italian astronomer who lived from 1564 to 1642. Galileo was interested in how Earth, the planets, and the sun move in space. From Earth, it looks like the sun and planets revolve around Earth. Most people in Galileo's time believed that Earth is the center of our solar system.

Planets page 228

Galileo had made careful observations and had done some experiments. His results led him to think that the sun is the center of our solar system. Galileo said that Earth and the other planets revolve around the sun.

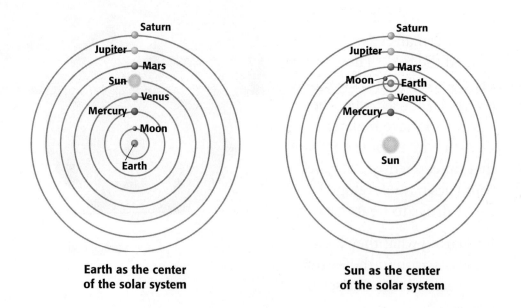

**Earth as the center
of the solar system**

**Sun as the center
of the solar system**

The planets beyond Saturn—Uranus and
Neptune—were not known in Galileo's time.

Because Galileo had collected data to support his idea, other scientists accepted it. But when Galileo presented his idea to other members of his society, they rejected it. The people had always believed that Earth is the center of the universe. Galileo's idea said that Earth is not the center. You can probably see why an idea that went against everything you believed about the world would be very frightening.

The idea that the sun is the center of the solar system was first suggested by Nicolaus Copernicus, a Polish astronomer. Galileo is the one who collected data to support the idea.

Members of Galileo's society decided to put him on trial, like a criminal. They made him announce to everyone that his idea was wrong. He was forced to spend the rest of his life imprisoned in his own home.

Scientists who came after Galileo gathered more data. The data showed that the sun, not Earth, is at the center of our solar system. In time, all members of society accepted Galileo's idea.

Even in modern times, scientists must deal with the beliefs and fears of the members of their society. For example, when vaccines were first developed, people were afraid to be vaccinated. They thought vaccines would make them sick. But over time, many scientific tests showed that vaccines help prevent disease. Society began to accept vaccination as a way to stay healthy.

# Almanac

This Almanac includes helpful information that you may need for science. Mathematics is an important tool in science, so the first two sections of the Almanac review skills related to using numbers. The Study Skills section has suggestions to help you make the best use of your time in class and on long-term projects. The information in Test-Taking Skills has study hints for both regular tests and standardized tests. At the end of the Almanac are some useful reference maps and tables.

# Numbers in Science

Numbers are very important in science. Calculators can help you work with numbers, but first you have to know what the numbers mean. Whenever you make a measurement in a science activity, you use math. Whenever you collect data and make a graph, you use math. This section gives brief reminders of some of the math skills you may need in science.

$0.25 = \frac{1}{4}$  $-15°C$  $500 \text{ cm}^3$

$365.25 \text{ days}$  $2 \text{ m/s}$

$90\%$  $\frac{4}{5}$

## Decimals

You can use decimals instead of fractions to write values less than 1. In decimals, place value shows how many tenths, hundredths, or thousandths you have. For example, one tenth is 0.1 and two hundredths is 0.02.

This table shows examples of how to read decimals.

| Hundreds | Tens | Ones | | Tenths | Hundredths | How to Read |
|----------|------|------|---|--------|------------|-------------|
| | | 0 | . | 7 | 5 | seventy-five hundredths |
| | | 0 | . | 8 | | eight tenths |
| 3 | 6 | 5 | . | 2 | 5 | three hundred sixty-five AND twenty-five hundredths (days in an Earth year) |
| 6 | 8 | 6 | . | 9 | 8 | six hundred eighty-six AND ninety-eight hundredths (Earth days in a Mars year) |

When a decimal also has a whole number, read the decimal point as "and."

For any value less than 1, write a zero before the decimal point. For example, write **0.25, not .25**. That way, no one will mistake your decimal for a whole number.

## Rounding Decimals

Here's how to round the lengths of a year on Earth and on Mars to the nearest whole day.

| To round the length of one year to full days | Earth | Mars |
|----------------------------------------------|-------|------|
| 1. Find the number of whole days in the ones place. | 365.25 | 686.98 |
| 2. Look at the digit one place to the right—the tenths place. | 365.25 | 686.98 |
| 3. If that digit is less than 5, round down. If that digit is 5 or greater, round up. | 2 is less than 5 Round down to 365. | 9 is more than 5 Round up to 687. |

*Source: NASA, National Space Science Data Center Planetary Fact Sheets (Web site)*

Earth's year is about 365 days. Mars's year is about 687 Earth days.

## Exponents

**Exponents** are a quick way to show that a number or measurement unit has been multiplied by itself a certain number of times. You use exponents when you describe area or volume.

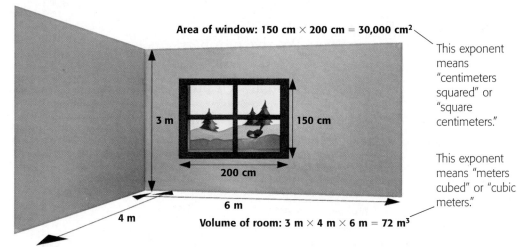

**Area of window: 150 cm × 200 cm = 30,000 cm²**

This exponent means "centimeters squared" or "square centimeters."

This exponent means "meters cubed" or "cubic meters."

3 m

150 cm

200 cm

6 m

4 m

**Volume of room: 3 m × 4 m × 6 m = 72 m³**

### Powers of Ten

Science includes some very large numbers. Using powers of 10 makes these numbers easier to compare and shorter to write. Here's an example.

On August 27, 2003, Mars was closer to Earth than it had been in thousands of years—only fifty-five million, seven hundred sixty thousand kilometers! This number can be written as

55,760,000 kilometers

You can also write this number using powers of 10. One million equals ten to the sixth power—in other words, 10 multiplied by itself 6 times.

$$1{,}000{,}000 = 10 \times 10 \times 10 \times 10 \times 10 \times 10 = 10^6$$

Fifty-five million can be written as $55 \times 10^6$. So another way to write fifty-five million, seven hundred sixty thousand kilometers is $55.76 \times 10^6$ kilometers.

## Negative Numbers

A negative number is any number less than zero. You will sometimes see negative numbers in descriptions of temperature.

Negative numbers are written with a negative sign (−). Positive numbers are much more common, so the positive sign (+) is usually left out.

Be alert whenever you have to compare or find the difference between two negative numbers.

−10°C means 10 degrees below 0

Positive: 20°C > 15°C

Negative: −17°C < −5°C

20 degrees Celsius is warmer than (greater than) 15 degrees Celsius, but *negative* 17 degrees Celsius is colder than (less than) *negative* 5 degrees Celsius.

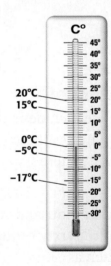

The best way to find the difference between two negative numbers or between a positive and a negative number is to draw a number line. You can think of the thermometer in the picture as a vertical number line. Count the degrees between −17°C and −5°C. The difference is 12°C. That is, −17°C is 12 degrees colder than −5°C. Or to put it another way, −5°C is 12 degrees warmer than −17°C (though it still isn't warm!). Now find the difference between −5°C and 20°C. You should get 25°C.

## Fractions

Most fractions show parts of a whole. Every fraction has a numerator and a denominator. The **numerator** (NOO muh ray tur) is the number above the line. The **denominator** (dih NAHM uh nay tur) is the number below the line.

**Examples**

| Numerator: how many equal parts | $\frac{2}{3}$ | $\frac{3}{5}$ | $\frac{7}{8}$ |
|---|---|---|---|
| Denominator: equal parts in whole | | | |

Sometimes it helps to simplify fractions so you are using smaller numbers in the numerator and denominator. For example, Eli counted trees in the woods near his house. Here are his data.

Eli divided the numerator and the denominator by 5 to reduce each fraction. He could have reduced $\frac{2}{8}$ to $\frac{1}{4}$, but then the fractions would not have the same denominator.

| Kind of Tree | Number | Fraction of total |
|---|---|---|
| Oak | 25 | $\frac{25}{40} = \frac{5}{8}$ |
| Maple | 10 | $\frac{10}{40} = \frac{2}{8}$ |
| Sassafras | 5 | $\frac{5}{40} = \frac{1}{8}$ |
| Total | 40 | |

Sometimes you need to compare, add, or subtract fractions. To do these things, the fractions need to have the same denominator. Eli's friend Cameron counted trees in the woods near his house. He found that $\frac{2}{3}$ of the trees were oak, $\frac{1}{3}$ were maple, and none were sassafras. Which boy's woods has a larger fraction of trees that are oaks?

Rename the fractions so they have the same denominator In this example, it's 24.

Eli's $\dfrac{5 \times 3}{8 \times 3} = \dfrac{15}{24}$        Cameron's $\dfrac{2 \times 8}{3 \times 8} = \dfrac{16}{24}$

See Also

Decimals
page 371

Now you can compare the two fractions: $\frac{16}{24}$ is more than $\frac{15}{24}$. Cameron's woods has a greater fraction of oak trees.

# Rates, Ratios, and Percents

Rates, ratios, and percents are ways of showing how much of something there is compared with something else.

## Rates

A **rate** describes how much of something there is compared with something else when the two things are not measured with the same units. When a rate is written as a fraction, read the fraction bar as "per."

> I feed the mice 4 scoops per day. That's a rate of $\frac{4 \text{ scoops}}{1 \text{ day}}$.

> I can make the wheel turn 60 times per minute! That's a rate of $\frac{60 \text{ turns}}{1 \text{ minute}}$.

## Ratios

A **ratio** compares the amounts of two things that are measured with the same units. A ratio can be given as a fraction or as a proportion. A proportion is written with two dots called a colon. Read the colon as "to."

> The ratio of plain mice to spotted mice is 1:2.

> The ratio of spotted mice to plain mice is $\frac{2}{1}$ or 2:1 (two TO one).

## Percents

A **percent** is a comparison that describes parts of a whole when the whole is 100. A percent is shown with the percent sign (%).

**WORD WATCH**

*Percent* means "per hundred."

The table shows the number of players for each instrument in a school band of 50 players.

What percent of the band plays clarinet?

Write the fraction of band members who play clarinet.

$$\frac{10}{50} = \frac{?}{100}$$

Find an equivalent fraction.

$$\frac{10 \times 2}{50 \times 2} = \frac{20}{100}$$

Write the percent as a fraction with the numerator blank.

$$\frac{20}{100} = 20\%$$

So, 20% of the band plays clarinet.

|  | Number of players |
|---|---|
| Clarinet | 10 |
| Drums | 5 |
| Flute | 12 |
| Trombone | 8 |
| Trumpet | 13 |
| Other | 2 |
| **Total** | **50** |

What if 90 percent of the band members can attend a rally? How many is that?

Ninety percent means "90 out of 100." Write the percent as a fraction.

$$\frac{90}{100} = \frac{?}{50}$$

Then write a second fraction using the actual number of players (50) for the denominator.

$$\frac{90 \div 2}{100 \div 2} = \frac{45}{50}$$

Find the numerator that makes this fraction equal $\frac{90}{100}$.

So, 45 players can attend the rally.

## Averages

One way to make sure that data are accurate is to repeat measurements. But repeating measurements can give you a *lot* of data! Finding averages in your data gives you a way to describe what's generally true.

Karen investigated how many water drops stayed on pennies before the water spilled off. She did 10 trials using a different penny each time. Here are the 10 measurements she made.

| Penny | 1 | 2 | 3 | 4 | 5 | 6 | 7 | 8 | 9 | 10 |
|---|---|---|---|---|---|---|---|---|---|---|
| Drops of water | 17 | 18 | 17 | 17 | 13 | 20 | 30 | 16 | 14 | 18 |

**Mean** The mean is one kind of average. The **mean** is the average found by adding together all measurements, then dividing the sum by the number of measurements.

$$17 + 18 + 17 + 17 + 13 + 20 + 30 + 16 + 14 + 18 = 180$$

18 —— Mean number of drops

Number of measurements —— 10)180 —— Sum of all measurements

The mean is 18 drops.

**Median** The **median** is the value that falls in the middle of a set of data. To find the median, first arrange all the data in order.

13    14    16    17    17    17    18    18    20    30

There is an even number of measurements (10), so no number is exactly in the middle. But the numbers on either side of the middle are both 17. So 17 is the median number of water drops. If the two numbers in the middle are different, then the median equals the mean of the two numbers in the middle.

**Mode** The **mode** is the measurement that appears most often in a data set. In the water drop data set, the number 17 appears three times—more than any other measurement. So the mode for that data set is 17 drops.

**Frequency** **Frequency** is the number of times each measurement appears. These are the frequencies for the water drop data set.

13 once, 14 once, 16 once, 17 three times,
18 twice, 20 once, 30 once

**Range** The **range** is the difference between the lowest and highest values in a data set. To find the range, subtract the smallest measurement from the largest. For the water drop data, the range is 17 drops.

30 drops − 13 drops = 17 drops

Look closely at any value that is very different from the other values in a data set. In the water-drop data, the lowest number (13) is 1 less than the next higher number (14). But the highest number (30) is *10* more than the next lower number (20). That's a big difference! The girl who did the investigation went back to look. Penny 7, with 30 drops, had many deep scratches. The other pennies did not have deep scratches. This suggests a new investigation to answer this question: *How do scratches affect the number of water drops that a penny's surface can hold?*

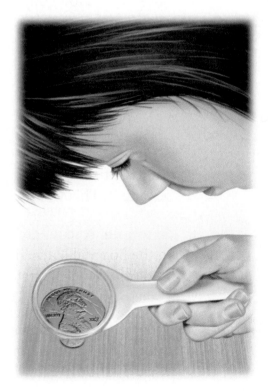

# Solving Math Problems in Science

Math is an important tool for answering many science questions. "How much longer is a rubber band when it is stretched?" "How fast did the toy car move?" "What is the area of the field we're observing?" Often, these questions can be answered by solving math problems. This section gives you help doing that.

## Understanding the Problem

Take the time to understand a problem before you start solving it. This will save you time in the long run.

**Example** A scout group is making gift bags for 32 children in the hospital. Each gift bag has 1 card, 2 snacks, 1 book, 1 coloring book, 8 crayons, and 1 toy. It takes 5 minutes to make each bag. How long will it take to make 32 bags?

**What is the problem asking?** This problem gives more information than you need. Don't let it confuse you. Focus on what it's asking, "How long will it take to make 32 gift bags?"

See Also

Problem Solving
Steps
pages 382–383

**What do you already know?** Look for information about the task and time. The problem tells you the group is making 32 gift bags, and each bag takes 5 minutes.

**Draw a picture.** Your picture doesn't have to look like a real math problem. It just has to help you imagine what you have to do.

1 bag

32 bags = ? min.

**Think about problems you've already done.** Have you ever figured out how much money you need to buy several of the same item? How did you figure it out?

Other ways to understand a problem include acting it out, using small objects, making a list or table, and looking for patterns.

**Estimate!** Before you begin, it helps to have some idea of what your answer should be. Each bag takes 5 minutes. There are about 30 bags. In your head, multiply 30 × 5. Your estimate is about 150 minutes.

# Problem Solving Steps

Once you understand a problem, follow these steps to solve it.

1. Choose the operation.
2. Write and solve a number sentence.
3. Check the units.
4. Check your work.

**Example** A scout group is making gift bags for 32 children in the hospital. It takes 5 minutes to make each bag. How long will it take to make 32 bags?

First make sure you understand the problem. An example of how to do this is shown on pages 380–381.

**Choose the Operation** Decide which math operation to use—addition, subtraction, multiplication, or division. In the example, each bag takes 5 minutes, and there are 32 bags. You could use addition, but multiplication will be faster.

**Write and Solve the Number Sentence** Use the operation you chose and values from the problem. Remember to include the units.

5 minutes per bag × 32 bags = ? minutes total

Set up the number sentence so it's easier to solve.

32 bags
× 5 minutes per bag
160 minutes

**Check the Units** When you solve a problem, you come up with a number. You also need a unit. A **unit** tells what that number stands for. In the example, you found out how much time something would take. So first check that your answer has a unit of time. Yes, the unit is minutes. Is this the best unit for this answer? Sixty minutes equals one hour. For more than 60 minutes, the usual unit is hours or hours and minutes. Here is how to change the units.

$$\begin{array}{r} 2 \text{ R } 40 \\ 60\overline{)160 \text{ minutes}} \\ \underline{120} \\ 40 \end{array}$$

It will take 2 hours and 40 minutes to make all 32 bags.

> Pay attention to the units *before* you start calculating the answer. You can't add apples and oranges unless you think of them as fruit. The same is true with measurements. You can't add 1 foot plus 14 inches and get either 15 feet or 15 inches for your answer! First you have to change 1 foot to 12 inches *or* change 14 inches to 1 foot 2 inches. The answer would be 26 inches or 2 feet 2 inches.

**Check Your Work** Two simple ways to check your work are to check your arithmetic and work the problem backward. You also can compare your answer with an estimate. The answer is 160 minutes. The estimate (from page 381) is 150 minutes. So this is about right.

## Using Calculators

Calculators are useful tools, but they only do what you tell them to do. They always give you an answer, but not always the right answer! Here's how to get the answer you need.

- Calculators are all different. Ask for help if you do not know how to use a certain calculator.

- Some calculators show only whole numbers and decimals. If you need fractions or remainders, use a calculator that shows those, or do the work on paper.

- All calculators work well for solving problems with metric system units. English units are trickier. If you need an answer in feet and inches or in pounds and ounces, it might be easier to do the work by hand.

- Calculators often show more digits than you need. Round off to the tenths or hundredths place.

## Useful Equations

An **equation** is a number sentence that shows how different numbers or measurements are related. Here are some useful science equations.

| | |
|---|---|
| **Speed** is the distance an object moves per unit of time. Rates such as meters per second (m/s) are used to describe speed. | A toy car moves 300 centimeters in 5 seconds. What is its speed?<br><br>**speed = distance ÷ time**<br>speed = 300 cm ÷ 5 s<br>speed = 60 cm/s |
| **speed = distance ÷ time** | The car's speed is 60 centimeters per second. |

The **distance** something travels equals its speed multiplied by the time it travels.

**distance = speed × time**

A bus traveled for 2 hours (h) at 40 miles per hour (mph). How far did the bus travel?

distance = speed × time
distance = 40 mph × 2 h
distance = 80 miles

The bus traveled 80 miles.

**Area** is the size of a surface. Its units are squares of length units, such as square meters ($m^2$).

area of a rectangle:
**area = length × width**

A vegetable garden is 10 meters long and 5 meters wide. What is its area?

5 m

10 m

area = length × width
area = 10 m × 5 m
area = 50 $m^2$

The garden has an area of 50 square meters.

**Volume** is the size of a three-dimensional space. Its units are cubes of length units, such as cubic centimeters ($cm^3$).

**volume of a block-shaped object:
volume = length × width × height**

A shoe box is 20 cm long, 10 cm wide, and 5 cm deep. What is the volume of the box?

volume = length × width × height
volume = 20 cm × 10 cm × 5 cm
volume = 1,000 $cm^3$

The shoe box has a volume of 1,000 cubic centimeters.

**Density** is the amount of mass (grams) something has per unit of volume (cubic centimeters)

**density = mass ÷ volume**

A section of karate mat has a mass of 500 grams and a volume of 10,000 $cm^3$. What is its density?

density = mass ÷ volume
density = 500 g ÷ 10,000 $cm^3$
density = 0.05 g/$cm^3$

The density of the mat is 0.05 grams per cubic centimeter.

Exponents
page 373

# Study Skills

"How can I possibly get this done on time?" "Where on Earth can I find *that* out?" "Is this story for real, or is it just one of those Internet legends?" In this section, you will find information to help you answer these and other questions that you might have when you are doing your science work. Managing Your Time gives tips for making the most of your time in school. You'll also find suggestions for completing long-term projects on time. Finding Information has helpful ideas for research reports, including how to find the best books, magazines, and Web sites for your needs.

## Managing Your Time

Maybe you have trouble finishing things on time. Or maybe you forget part of what you have to do. If so, you might envy people who seem to get things done on time without even trying. They can tell you that it does take effort. But it isn't hard once you know what to do.

### Classroom Time

Here are some hints for completing class work during a science lesson.

- **Listen and pay attention.** Any time your teacher starts giving directions, listen and think about what he or she is saying. Ask questions if you do not understand something.

- **Plan your time.** Imagine yourself doing the work. Think about how much time you have to do it. Then think about how long it should take to do each part. If you are doing an activity, plan time to clean up.

- **Stay on track.** Get started right away. Check the time while you are working. If half the time is gone, you should be halfway done.

- **Ignore distractions.** Your friend talks. The pencil sharpener grinds. A ball bounces off the window. *Ignore these things.* They slow you down.

You can safely ignore unimportant sounds, but *do not ignore a fire alarm!*

## Long-Term Projects

There is no need to lose sleep to complete a long-term project. These tips will help you get it done on time.

**Plan Ahead** Suppose you have two months to plan and complete a Science Fair project. The project will include an investigation, a report, and a poster. Before you do anything else, write a schedule.

**Week 1:** Choose project topic, get teacher's OK.

**Week 2:** Read about the topic (library).

**Week 3:** Plan investigation, get teacher's OK.

**Weeks 4–6:** Do investigation, collect data.

**Week 7:** Analyze data, write draft of report, sketch poster.

**Week 8:** Do final report and poster.

**Week 9:** Science Fair!!!

**Gather Materials** Gather materials *before* you need them. In the example, gather library materials in week 1 so you'll have them for week 2. Get your teacher's OK early in week 3 so you can gather materials for the investigation in week 4.

If you need to go to a store, tell the adults at home a couple of days *before* you need the materials.

**Keep on Schedule** Oops! Week 2 went by and you didn't get to the library. Don't panic, but do catch up. Read about your topic *and* plan your investigation during week 3.

## Finding Information

Sometimes you need to find information on certain topics. Good places to look are books, magazines, and the Internet (or World Wide Web). Look for information that is right for your grade level, right for your topic, correct in its facts, and up to date.

See Also

Evaluating Sources page 392

### Finding Books and Magazines

A library is the best place to find books and magazines. Your school library has materials for the grades in your school. Your local library may have a children's room. In these two places, you can be sure you'll find information that's right for your grade level. If you need help finding something, ask the librarian.

Many libraries have a computer database that lists their books and magazines. Some libraries have a card catalog. Both let you search for materials in three different ways.

- by **title**
- by **author**
- by **subject**

For science information, search by subject. If you can't find what you need, look under another heading. For example, if you don't find anything under *Tornadoes,* look under *Weather* or *Storms.*

## Searching the Web

An on-line search can link you to millions of Web sites in less than a second. Some sites are created by experts. Others are written by students like you. Some are in languages you cannot read. So how do you find information that is most useful to you?

Your best tool for searching the Web is a search engine. A **search engine** is a Web site that lets you look for other Web sites by typing in a topic, also called a **keyword.** Some search engines are just for students. Using sites like these can save you hours of time. Many student search engines take you to sites that librarians or teachers have already chosen for you. Some search engines include an index. Here's what you might see if you click on the *Science* topic of an index.

```
═══════════════════ @Browse ═══════════════════
◁ ▷ ⊗ ⟳ ⬤ ✉
┌──────────────────────────────────────────────┐
│ http://www.browse.com                         │
└──────────────────────────────────────────────┘

                    Browse! ▶
               Best Browser Ever For Kids!
                 Search: [            ]

    Science

    Animals (amphibians, birds, endangered mammals,
             pets, reptiles...more)

    Air (airplanes, balloons, clouds, gases, pollution...more)

    Chemistry (activities, kitchen, matter...more)
```

**See Also**

Listing Sources
page 393

Clicking on any one of the links will take you to a list of Web sites that have information on the topic.

When you use information *from* a Web site, write down information *about* the Web site. Put that information in the bibliography of your report.

## On-Line Guidelines

Searching on line is a great way to find information. Make sure you do it safely. Imagine you are in the world's biggest public library. Use the same common sense you'd use in any big, crowded public building.

- Follow your school's and your parents' rules.
- Do not give your name, address, or phone number on line. Use only your first name, or make up a name. Use the school's address.
- Protect your password. Keep it to yourself.
- Avoid computer viruses. Do not open or answer messages from people you do not know.
- Be polite! Use words that you'd be happy to have your parents and teachers hear.
- Report to an adult anything that's out of the ordinary.

Some Web sites invite students to e-mail questions to scientists. Before you do this, make sure your question is one that the scientist can answer. For example, don't ask an animal scientist about stars. Also check to see if the answer is already posted somewhere on the Web site. Look for a link to FAQs—Frequently Asked Questions.

## Evaluating Sources

Books, magazines, and Web sites exist for lots of reasons. Some are for education. Some are for entertainment. Some are written by experts, and others are written by people with a hobby. Here are ways to make sure that the sources you use have the right information for your project or report.

**Who wrote this?** What organization publishes the source? Information usually is correct when it comes from museums, government groups such as NASA or the EPA, nonfiction publishers, and colleges and universities.

**When was this written?** Even the best science information gets out of date. Look for the copyright date on a book or Web site. Also look for the *last update* on a Web site.

**Can I understand this source?** Read a little bit of it to see if it's right for you. If not, look for another source.

**Why was this written?** Find information that was written to educate. A funny book about living with a pet monkey may be true, but it was written to entertain. Avoid information that advertises something or that wants you to agree with someone's opinion.

## Listing Sources

Write down information about each source you use.
List the source information in a bibliography with your
report or project. For every source, give the following
information.

- the author's name
- the title of the source
- where it was published
  (city or Web site)
- the name of the publisher
- when it was published

*Chris Pellant*
*"Rocks and Minerals"*
*New York, NY*
*DK Publishing, Inc.*
*1992*

## Using Your Own Words

When you write a report, you are telling people what *you*
understand about a topic. It's important to use *your* words.
Explaining an idea in your own words helps you
understand and remember it better. Besides,
copying someone else's words
and pretending they are
your own is a form of
stealing! If you want to
*borrow* a few of someone
else's words, that's called a
quote. Put it in quotation
marks and name the
source. Otherwise, use
your own words.

*"Bats have been moving into*
*abandoned mines for about as*
*long as miners have been packing*
*up their picks and shovels to go in*
*search of more promising diggings."*
*(M. Brock Fenton, Bats magazine,*
*Fall 2003)*

# Test-Taking Skills

You probably take tests and quizzes that your teacher gives. Many states also have standardized tests. These tests are given to almost every student at a certain grade level in the whole state. Both kinds of tests find out how much you have learned about a subject. This section gives tips that will help you do as well as you can on tests.

## Getting Ready for a Test

The first step is keeping up with your work.

- Pay attention in class. Ask questions about things you don't understand.

- Read actively. Ask yourself questions about what you are reading. Look for the answers.

- Do your homework on time. Look it over when you get it back. Was there anything that you did not understand? Where could you do better next time?

## Ways to Study

Another part of getting ready for a test is studying. Try more than one method for best results.

**Review.** Look over your notes, journal, handouts, homework, and reading assignments. Do you understand the main ideas? Do you know what each vocabulary term means?

**Study with other students.** Ask each other questions about the topic. Is there something you don't agree on? Is there something you are confused about? Can you explain things to the other students?

**Ask questions.** If there is anything you do not understand, ask your teacher. He or she will be glad to explain, as long as you do not ask in the middle of the test!

Study ahead of time so you can ask questions in class the day *before* the test.

**Use memory tricks.** Make up a silly saying to help yourself remember. For example, suppose you want to remember the order of the planets outward from the sun—Mercury, Venus, Earth, Mars, Jupiter, Saturn, Uranus, Neptune, and Pluto. You could use the silly saying "**M**y **V**ery **E**ager **M**other **J**ust **S**erved **U**s **N**ine **P**izzas."

**Diagram ideas.** Make a web or concept map to show how ideas fit together.

See Also

Concept Maps
page 396

## Concept Maps

A concept is an idea. A concept map is a way to show what you understand about ideas. Making a concept map can help you see how ideas are connected to each other.

### Making a Concept Map

1.  List words that describe the concept.

2.  From the list, choose the one word that best describes the main concept. Put that word at the top. Circle it.

3.  Choose words that help support the main concept. Write those below the main concept. Circle them.

4.  Draw lines to connect the main concept to the ones below it. Near the lines, write how the concepts are related.

5.  Continue until you've used all your words.

Concept maps can show what you still need to learn. This map made a student wonder if all three kinds of rocks were made of minerals. He looked it up before the test.

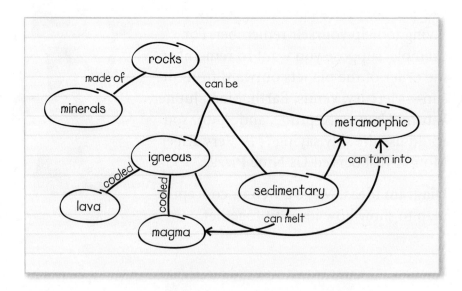

## Taking a Test

Follow these tips for great test results. The tips work for tests your teacher gives you and for standardized tests.

**Before the test…**

- Gather everything you need. Have more than one pencil. Sharpen them. Get an eraser. Clear your desk.
- Ask about the rules. Is there a time limit? Do you write out the answer or fill in a bubble?
- Relax. A calm, positive attitude will help you succeed.

**During the test…**

- Before you start, look through the test. Make sure you have every page. Ask for anything you are missing.
- Plan your test time. Give yourself less time for questions with short answers. Give yourself more time for open-ended questions.
- Answer shorter items first, then longer ones.
- Skip items you are unsure of. Go back to them later.
- Check your work before you hand it in. Have you answered every question completely? Is your name on your paper? Is your handwriting clear?

## Tips for Multiple-Choice Questions

A multiple-choice test gives you a choice of answers. You do not have to remember the right answer, but you do have to recognize it. Read every choice. Some choices are false. Some are true but do not answer the question. Sometimes you can figure out the answer if you use what you already know about the subject.

**Example** Gravity is stronger on Jupiter than on Earth because Jupiter _____.

A. is smaller than Earth

You remember that Jupiter is the biggest planet. So this is wrong.

B. is an outer planet

You're not sure what an outer planet is. Skip for now.

C. has more mass than Earth

If Jupiter is bigger, it might have more mass.

D. has storms that move through its gassy surface

This might be true, but is it the answer? Earth has storms. Storms do not change gravity. So this isn't the answer.

Pay attention to words such as *not, all, most, least, always, never, alike,* and *different.* These words change the meaning of a question.

You've ruled out choices A and D. Compare B and C with the test item. The item tells you that Jupiter has stronger gravity. Choice B says Jupiter is an *outer planet.* Choice C says Jupiter has *more mass.* The meaning of *stronger* is closer to the meaning of *more* than *outer.* Your best guess is C.

## Tips for True-False Questions

True-false questions can be answered quickly, but they can be tricky. Here's how to give the answer you intend to give.

- Write the whole word *true* or *false*, not just *T* or *F*. That way, your *T* won't be confused with an *F*.

- Read the directions. Some tests ask you to write just *true* or *false*. Others ask you to change an underlined word to make a false statement true.

  <u>false</u>  5. In a pond food chain, fish are ~~producers.~~ <u>consumers</u>

- Read carefully. Watch for these words: *not, all, none, never, always, sometimes, could, must.* In this example, one item is true, the other is false.

  <u>true</u>  6. The first organism in any food chain is always a producer.

  <u>false</u>  7. The first organism in any food chain is never a producer.

## Tips for Short-Answer Items

Short-answer items ask you for a word or phrase. Sometimes the word or phrase answers a question or gives information.

11. What is the primary source of energy for nearly all living things?

    <u>the sun</u>

12. Name three main processes in the water cycle.

    <u>evaporation, condensation,</u>

    <u>precipitation</u>

Other times, the word completes a statement.

3. The north pole of one magnet <u>repels</u> the north pole of another magnet.

## Tips for Questions With Diagrams

Often, a diagram is key to understanding a science concept. That's why science tests include diagrams.

- **Understand the diagram.** Does it show something you could see, such as the parts of a plant? Or does it explain a process, such as the water cycle?
- **Read the labels.** Notice what they are for.
- **Compare the question and diagram.** What does the diagram show that can help answer the question?

**Example** Look at the pictures below. Then list the items in order of least mass to greatest mass.

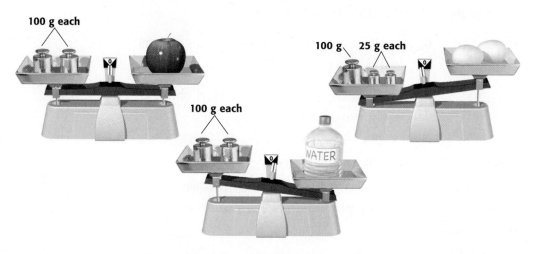

**Understand the diagram.** If both pans have the same mass, they balance. If not, the lower pan has more mass.

**Read the labels.** The labels tell you how much mass is in the left pan of each balance.

**Compare the question to the diagram.** The question says to list items from least to greatest mass. The diagram shows that the apple is 200 grams. The water is more than 200 grams. The eggs are less than 150 grams. The correct answer is *eggs, apple, water bottle.*

## Open-Ended Questions

Some questions have more than one correct answer. These questions ask you to think about a situation, then write a short paragraph. Do your thinking *before* you start writing the paragraph. Jot down ideas. Use common sense as well as science knowledge. Make sure you answer the question completely. Give evidence to support your thinking.

**Example**  Town A and Town B are on the coast. They are separated by a long, narrow inlet of water. The only way to get from one town to the other by car is to drive on the highway for two hours. Residents have decided that they need a way to shorten this travel time.

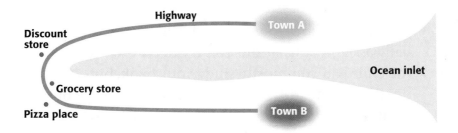

- Describe **two** possible ways to shorten the travel time between the two towns.

- Choose **one** of these ways, and describe **two** new problems that might result.

*Source: Adapted from the Massachusetts Comprehensive Assessment System (MCAS): Science and Technology/Engineering, Grade 5, Spring 2002*

A bridge is one way to shorten the travel time, but you need two. A ferry boat? A tunnel? A helicopter? Okay, you have two ways. Think about the second part. A bridge might get in the way of ships. It might hurt animals. Traffic would be heavier. Okay, you have enough problems. Now you can start writing your paragraph.

# When You Get a Test Back

Going over your test results can help you to do better on the next test.

- Read any notes from your teacher. They are there to help you. If you don't understand them, ask.

- Questions you missed may come up on later tests. Find out the right answers now.

- Look over the kinds of questions you got wrong. Are you losing points on easy items? Then maybe you made careless mistakes. On harder items? Then spend more time preparing for that type of question. The important thing is to learn from your mistakes so you will do better next time.

- Think about how you prepared. Did you keep up with daily assignments, or did you try to do everything at the end? Did you mostly study your book, but some questions came from your journal notes? Figure out what worked, and plan to do it again when you study for the next test. Figure out what didn't work, and make a better plan for preparing next time.

# Maps

A **map** is a picture of all or part of Earth's surface. Maps are used in science to show landforms, bodies of water, weather, climate, resources, and other things.

## Understanding Maps

Different kinds of maps are used for different purposes. But most maps have certain things in common.

### Longitude and Latitude

Places on maps are located using an imaginary grid of lines on Earth's surface. Lines of **longitude** (LAHN jih tood) run through the North and South Poles. Longitude is measured east and west of a longitude line called the prime meridian. Lines of **latitude** (LAT ih tood) circle Earth in an east-west direction. Latitude is measured north and south of the equator. Every point on Earth is described by its longitude and latitude.

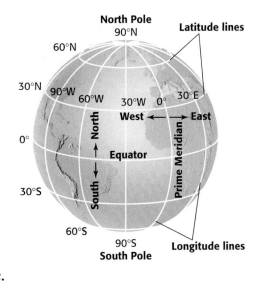

## Parts of a Map

A map **legend,** also called a map **key,** is a box or space near one edge of the map. It has symbols and information that explain marks on the map.

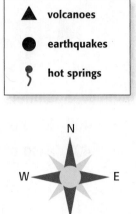

volcanoes

earthquakes

hot springs

A **compass rose** shows north, south, east, and west for the map. The compass rose may be at the top or bottom of the map. If there isn't one, assume that north is at the top.

N

W ← → E

S

Ratios page 376

A **map scale** tells you the real distances shown on the map. Some map scales look like little rulers. Other map scales are given as a ratio. Another type of map scale uses an equation showing how a unit of length on the map relates to a unit of length on Earth. All three of the scales below are for the same map.

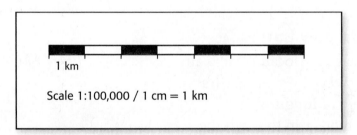

1 km

Scale 1:100,000 / 1 cm = 1 km

## Shapes of Maps

A **map projection** is a way to show a picture of a round Earth on a flat map. Every map projection has something it does well and something it does poorly. Mapmakers choose the projection that works best for the job the map needs to do. Often, the type of projection is written somewhere on the map.

A **Mercator projection** shows shapes well, but it makes areas near the North and South Poles look much larger than they really are.

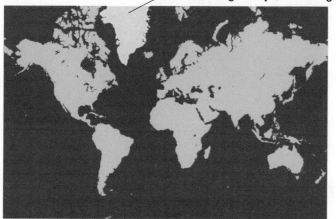

Greenland: right shape, but wrong size

An **equal-area projection** shows the land and oceans close to the right sizes, but some shapes are squeezed and squashed out of shape.

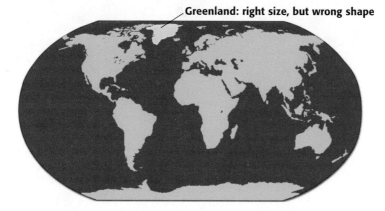

Greenland: right size, but wrong shape

# Map of North America

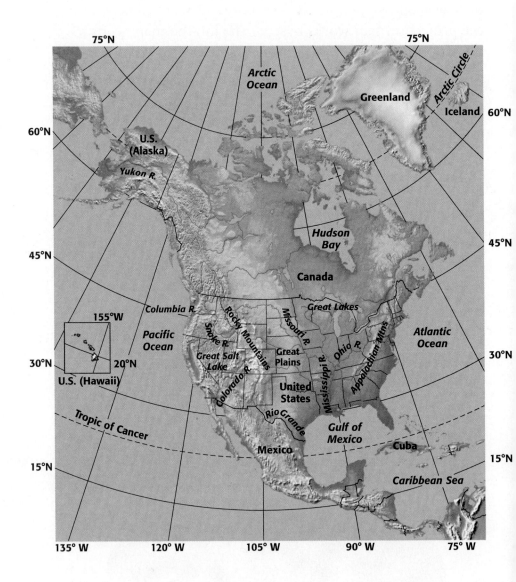

# Map of the World

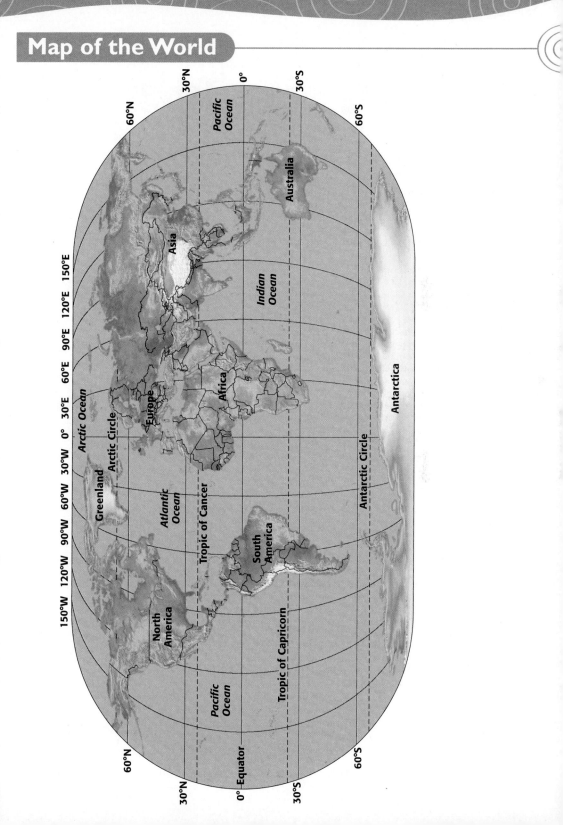

# Measurement Tables

## Metric Units and Equivalents

Use these tables when you need to know how different units equate with each other.

| Linear Measure (length, distance) | |
|---|---|
| 1 centimeter | 0.01 meter |
| 1 decimeter | 0.1 meter |
| 1 meter | 100 centimeters |
| 1,000 meters | 1 kilometer |

| Capacity Measure | |
|---|---|
| 1 milliliter | 0.001 liter |
| 1 liter | 1,000 milliliters |
| 1,000 liters | 1 kiloliter |

| Volume / Capacity Equivalents | |
|---|---|
| 1 cubic centimeter ($cm^3$) | 1 milliliter (mL) |
| 1 cubic decimeter ($dm^3$) | 1 liter (L) |

| Mass | |
|---|---|
| 1 milligram | 0.001 gram |
| 1 gram | 1,000 milligrams |
| 1,000 grams | 1 kilogram |
| 1,000,000 grams | 1 metric ton |

# English Units and Equivalents

## Linear Measure (length, distance)

| | |
|---|---|
| 1 inch | |
| 1 foot | 12 inches |
| 1 yard | 3 feet |
| 1 mile | 5,280 feet |
| 1 mile | 1,760 yards |

## Liquid Measure

| | | |
|---|---|---|
| 1 cup | | 8 fluid ounces |
| 1 pint | 2 cups | 16 fluid ounces |
| 1 quart | 2 pints | 32 fluid ounces |
| 1 gallon | 4 quarts | 128 fluid ounces |

## Weight

| | |
|---|---|
| 1 ounce | |
| 1 pound | 16 ounces |
| 1 ton | 2,000 pounds |

## Time

| | |
|---|---|
| 60 seconds | 1 minute |
| 60 minutes | 1 hour |
| 24 hours | 1 day |
| 7 days | 1 week |
| 52 weeks | 1 year |
| 365.25 days | 1 year |
| 12 months | 1 year |

# Common Abbreviations

| | | | |
|---|---|---|---|
| c | cup | lb | pound |
| °C | degrees Celsius | m | meter |
| cm | centimeter | mg | milligram |
| $cm^2$ | square centimeter | mi | mile |
| $cm^3$, cc | cubic centimeter | min | minute |
| dm | decimeter | mL | milliliter |
| °F | degrees Fahrenheit | mm | millimeter |
| fl oz | fluid ounce | oz | ounce |
| ft | foot | qt | quart |
| gal | gallon | s | second |
| g | gram | tsp | teaspoon |
| h | hour | T | tablespoon |
| in. | inch | yd | yard |
| kg | kilogram | y | year |
| L | liter | | |

# Changing Units

| to change | multiply by | to change | multiply by |
|---|---|---|---|
| cm to in. | 0.40 | in. to cm | 2.54 |
| m to yd | 1.09 | yd to m | 0.91 |
| km to mi | 0.62 | mi to km | 1.61 |
| mL to fl oz | 0.03 | fl oz to mL | 29.57 |
| L to gal | 0.26 | gal to L | 3.79 |
| g to oz | 0.04 | oz to g | 28.35 |
| kg to lb | 2.21 | lb to kg | 0.45 |

# Yellow Pages

# History of Science

This *History of Science* section includes a time line of science events and short biographies of some famous scientists and inventors. A **time line** lists important events in the order they took place. A **biography** (by AHG ruh fee) is the story of someone's life.

This section doesn't include every event and person in science, of course. It's impossible to tell the whole story of science discoveries and inventions in just a few pages. *History of Science* gives you a brief look at some of the better-known science events, scientists, and inventors of the past 550 years.

Notice that important events in U.S. history are listed below the blue bar in the time line. This should help you understand when science events happened.

# Science Time Line 1450-1600

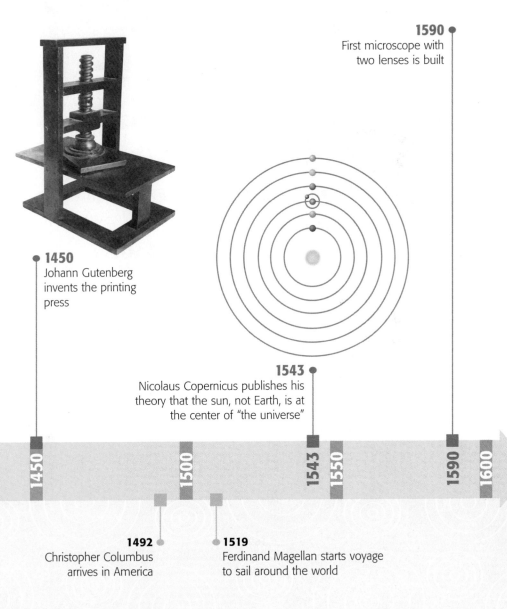

**1590** ●
First microscope with
two lenses is built

● **1450**
Johann Gutenberg
invents the printing
press

**1543** ●
Nicolaus Copernicus publishes his
theory that the sun, not Earth, is at
the center of "the universe"

1450

1500

1543

1550

1590

1600

**1492** ●
Christopher Columbus
arrives in America

● **1519**
Ferdinand Magellan starts voyage
to sail around the world

**American History**

# Science Time Line 1600-1700

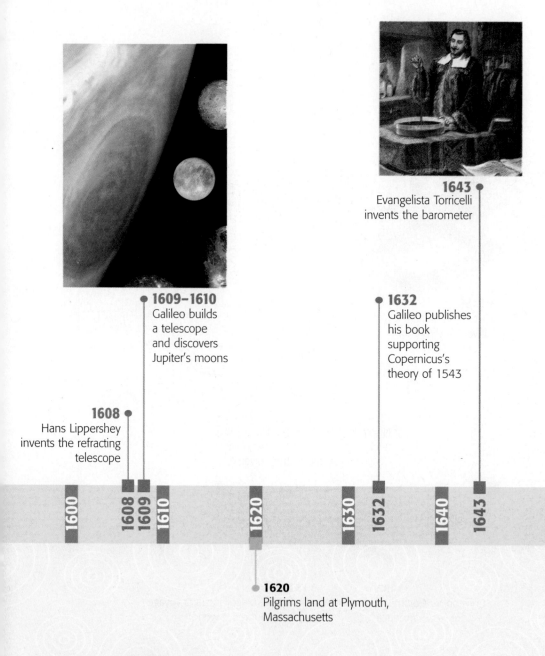

**1643** ●
Evangelista Torricelli
invents the barometer

● **1609–1610**
Galileo builds
a telescope
and discovers
Jupiter's moons

● **1632**
Galileo publishes
his book
supporting
Copernicus's
theory of 1543

**1608** ●
Hans Lippershey
invents the refracting
telescope

| 1600 | 1608 | 1609 | 1610 | 1620 | 1630 | 1632 | 1640 | 1643 |

● **1620**
Pilgrims land at Plymouth,
Massachusetts

*American History*

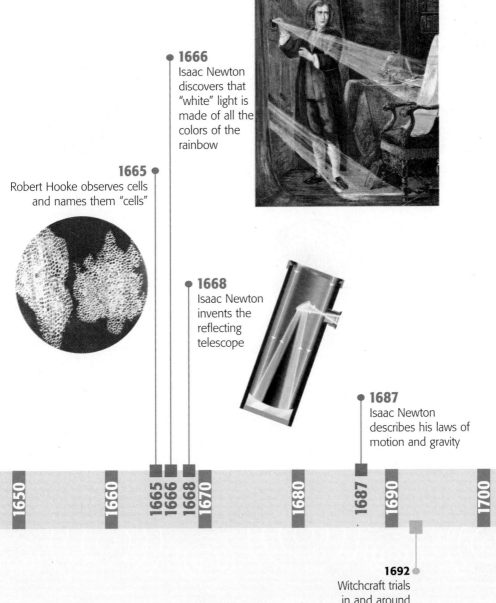

**1666**
Isaac Newton discovers that "white" light is made of all the colors of the rainbow

**1665**
Robert Hooke observes cells and names them "cells"

**1668**
Isaac Newton invents the reflecting telescope

**1687**
Isaac Newton describes his laws of motion and gravity

1650  1660  1665 1666  1668 1670  1680  1687 1690  1700

**1692**
Witchcraft trials in and around Salem, Massachusetts

# Science Time Line 1700-1800

**1705**
Edmund Halley predicts that a certain comet will return in 1758; it does and is named Halley's comet

**1742**
Anders Celsius invents his temperature scale

**1735**
Carolus Linnaeus publishes the first modern method of classifying living things

**1714**
Gabriel Fahrenheit invents the mercury thermometer and a temperature scale

1700 | 1705 | 1710 | 1714 | 1720 | 1730 | 1735 | 1740 | 1742

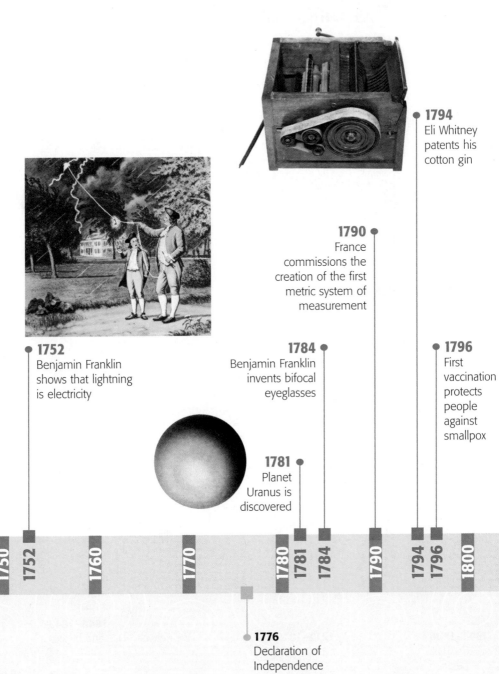

**1794**
Eli Whitney patents his cotton gin

**1790**
France commissions the creation of the first metric system of measurement

**1752**
Benjamin Franklin shows that lightning is electricity

**1784**
Benjamin Franklin invents bifocal eyeglasses

**1796**
First vaccination protects people against smallpox

**1781**
Planet Uranus is discovered

1750  1752  1760  1770  1780 1781 1784  1790  1794 1796  1800

**1776**
Declaration of Independence is signed

# Science Time Line 1800-1900

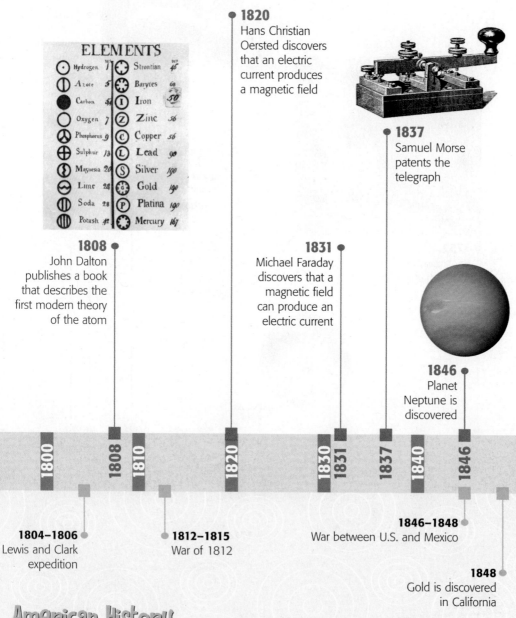

**1820**
Hans Christian Oersted discovers that an electric current produces a magnetic field

**1837**
Samuel Morse patents the telegraph

**1808**
John Dalton publishes a book that describes the first modern theory of the atom

**1831**
Michael Faraday discovers that a magnetic field can produce an electric current

**1846**
Planet Neptune is discovered

1800  1808  1810  1820  1830  1831  1837  1840  1846

**1804–1806**
Lewis and Clark expedition

**1812–1815**
War of 1812

**1846–1848**
War between U.S. and Mexico

**1848**
Gold is discovered in California

American History

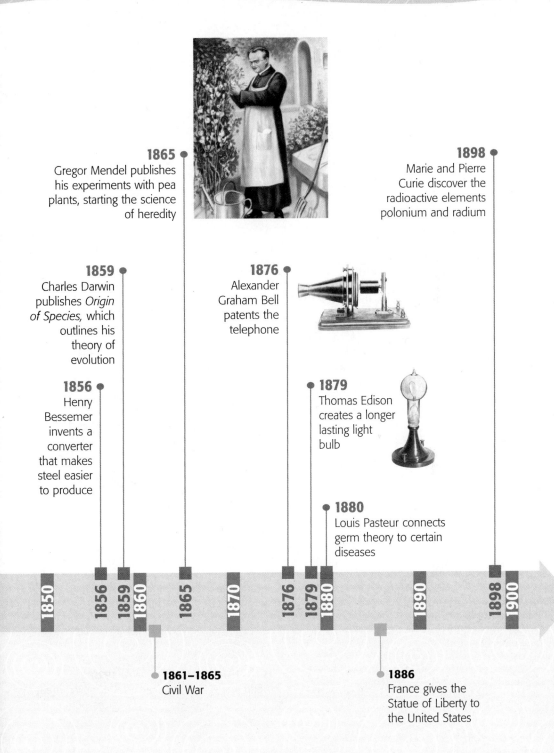

**1865**
Gregor Mendel publishes his experiments with pea plants, starting the science of heredity

**1898**
Marie and Pierre Curie discover the radioactive elements polonium and radium

**1859**
Charles Darwin publishes *Origin of Species,* which outlines his theory of evolution

**1876**
Alexander Graham Bell patents the telephone

**1856**
Henry Bessemer invents a converter that makes steel easier to produce

**1879**
Thomas Edison creates a longer lasting light bulb

**1880**
Louis Pasteur connects germ theory to certain diseases

1850  1856  1859  1860  1865  1870  1876  1879  1880  1890  1898  1900

**1861–1865**
Civil War

**1886**
France gives the Statue of Liberty to the United States

# Science Time Line 1900-1950

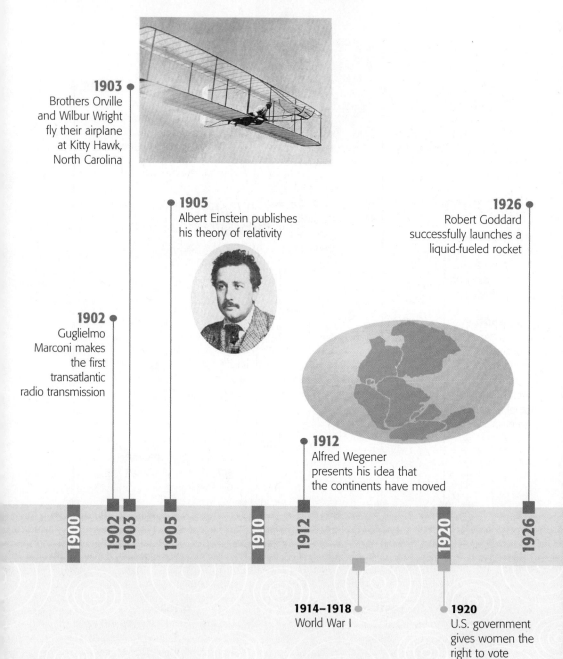

**1903**
Brothers Orville and Wilbur Wright fly their airplane at Kitty Hawk, North Carolina

**1905**
Albert Einstein publishes his theory of relativity

**1926**
Robert Goddard successfully launches a liquid-fueled rocket

**1902**
Guglielmo Marconi makes the first transatlantic radio transmission

**1912**
Alfred Wegener presents his idea that the continents have moved

1900 · 1902 · 1903 · 1905 · 1910 · 1912 · 1920 · 1926

**1914–1918**
World War I

**1920**
U.S. government gives women the right to vote

American History

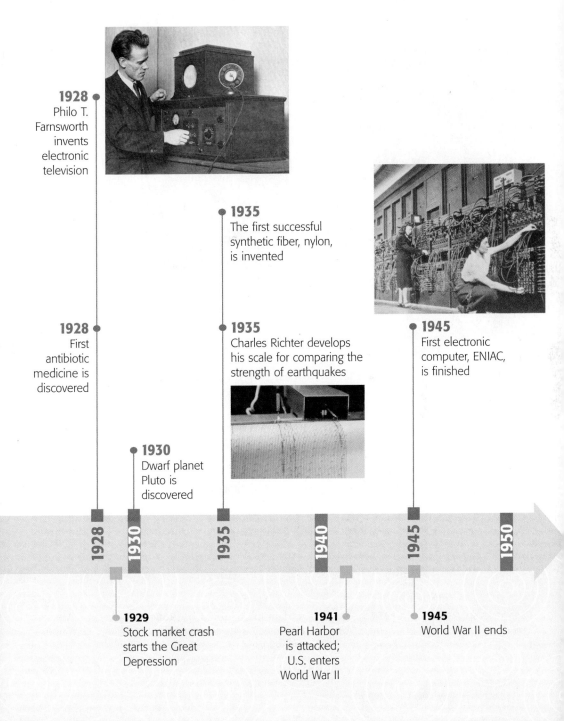

**1928**
Philo T.
Farnsworth
invents
electronic
television

**1935**
The first successful
synthetic fiber, nylon,
is invented

**1928**
First
antibiotic
medicine is
discovered

**1935**
Charles Richter develops
his scale for comparing the
strength of earthquakes

**1945**
First electronic
computer, ENIAC,
is finished

**1930**
Dwarf planet
Pluto is
discovered

1928

1930

1935

1940

1945

1950

**1929**
Stock market crash
starts the Great
Depression

**1941**
Pearl Harbor
is attacked;
U.S. enters
World War II

**1945**
World War II ends

# Science Time Line 1950-2000

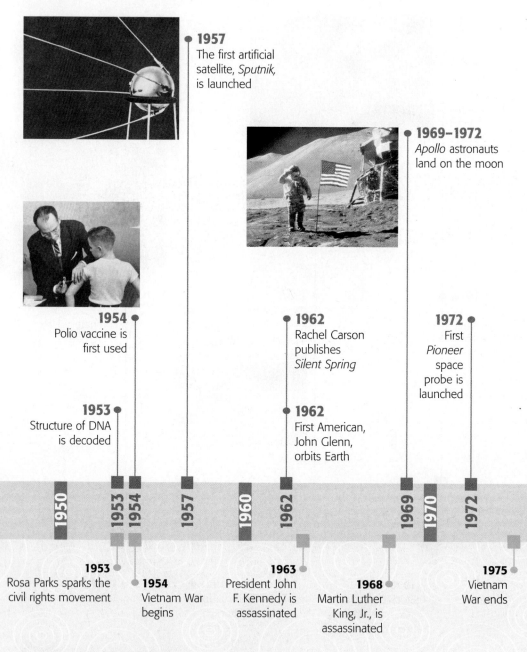

**1957**
The first artificial satellite, *Sputnik,* is launched

**1969–1972**
*Apollo* astronauts land on the moon

**1954**
Polio vaccine is first used

**1962**
Rachel Carson publishes *Silent Spring*

**1972**
First *Pioneer* space probe is launched

**1953**
Structure of DNA is decoded

**1962**
First American, John Glenn, orbits Earth

**1950** **1953** **1954** **1957** **1960** **1962** **1969** **1970** **1972**

**1953**
Rosa Parks sparks the civil rights movement

**1954**
Vietnam War begins

**1963**
President John F. Kennedy is assassinated

**1968**
Martin Luther King, Jr., is assassinated

**1975**
Vietnam War ends

## American History

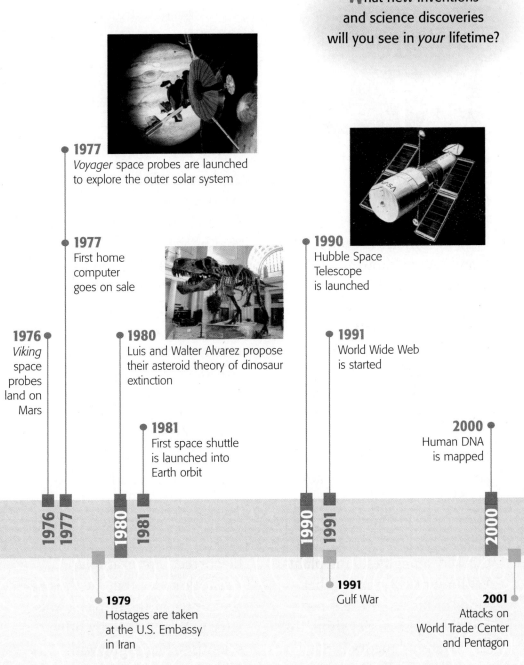

**W**hat new inventions and science discoveries will you see in *your* lifetime?

**1977**
*Voyager* space probes are launched to explore the outer solar system

**1977**
First home computer goes on sale

**1990**
Hubble Space Telescope is launched

**1976**
*Viking* space probes land on Mars

**1980**
Luis and Walter Alvarez propose their asteroid theory of dinosaur extinction

**1991**
World Wide Web is started

**1981**
First space shuttle is launched into Earth orbit

**2000**
Human DNA is mapped

1976
1977
1980
1981
1990
1991
2000

**1979**
Hostages are taken at the U.S. Embassy in Iran

**1991**
Gulf War

**2001**
Attacks on World Trade Center and Pentagon

# Famous Scientists and Inventors

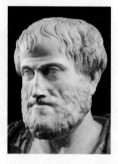

**Luis Alvarez (1911–1988)**
**Walter Alvarez**
**(1940–present)**
Luis Alvarez won the Nobel
Prize for physics in 1968. But
many people know him better
for his work with his son,
Walter Alvarez, a geologist. The
two men discovered a special
layer of rock in many places on
Earth. The rock contains a lot
of the element iridium. Iridium
is rare on Earth but is common
in space objects. Tests showed
that the rock layer formed at
about the time the dinosaurs
became extinct. The Alvarezes
thought that a giant asteroid hit
Earth. Dust from the asteroid
blocked sunlight, killing plants.
Without plants, many other
kinds of life became extinct.
Most scientists today think that
the Alvarezes' theory is the
most likely explanation for
dinosaur extinction.

**Aristotle (384–322 B.C.E.)**
Aristotle lived in ancient
Greece. Today we would say
that he was both a philosopher
and a scientist. When he was
alive, there was no difference
between the two. Aristotle
made many careful
observations of the natural
world. He came up with the
first system for classifying
living things. He figured out
the water cycle. Aristotle's
ideas and observations were
the best science information
that many people had for
many centuries. But not all
of his ideas turned out to
be correct. For example,
Aristotle's idea that Earth is at
the center of the universe was
later proven wrong by other
scientists, beginning with
Nicolaus Copernicus.

**Alexander Graham Bell (1847–1922)**

Alexander Graham Bell grew up in Scotland and later lived in the United States and Canada. He is best known for inventing the telephone. His family was always interested in sound, especially the sound of the human voice. His mother was deaf, and young Alexander liked to think up new ways to communicate with her. His father encouraged his inventions. As a young man, Bell worked as a teacher of the deaf. The telephone is the most famous of his many important inventions. But his main goal in life was to improve communication between deaf and hearing people.

**Rachel Carson (1907–1964)**

Rachel Carson was a scientist and writer who lived and worked in the United States. As a girl, she spent many hours exploring the outdoors. As an adult, she made her living by combining her interests in science and writing. She wrote many books and magazine articles about science for both adults and children. Her most famous book, *Silent Spring,* warned about the dangers of using pesticides. These chemicals are meant to kill insects, but they were also killing birds and other animals. Her bestselling book launched what is now called the environmental movement.

**George Washington Carver (1864?–1943)**

George Washington Carver was an American chemist and inventor. He was born into slavery near the end of the U.S. Civil War. As a boy, he showed an early interest in plants. He earned two degrees in science at Iowa State University. His most important work was done during his many years at Tuskegee Institute in Alabama. His lifelong work was to teach farmers how to manage their land. Part of his work included finding new uses for crops that improve the land, such as peanuts. Peanut butter is his best-known invention, but he created hundreds of others.

**Nicolaus Copernicus (1473–1543)**

Nicolaus Copernicus was born in Poland and lived there most of his life. He is best known for his theory that Earth and the other planets move around the sun. Before that time, most people thought the sun, stars, and planets move around Earth. Copernicus's new idea was very controversial. He self-published his ideas secretly in a small book when he was a young man. Then he started working on a book that explained his theory in detail. This book was published many years later, within a few days of his death. His theory was accepted only after many more years of controversy and new evidence.

**Marie Curie (1867–1934)**
Marie Curie was born in
Poland but lived most of her
adult life in France. She
studied radioactive elements,
which are elements that give
off energy from inside their
atoms. She was the first
scientist to win two Nobel
Prizes. The first she shared
with her husband, Pierre, and
another scientist. The second
was awarded to her alone.
Because she was one of the
first people to work with
radioactive elements, she
did not know that they can
cause illness. She died of an
illness that was caused by
the radioactive elements
she studied.

**Charles Darwin (1809–1882)**
Charles Darwin was born in
England and lived there except
when he traveled. His
observations of animal species
in South America influenced
his ideas about natural
selection. Natural selection
describes how new kinds of
species develop from kinds
that already exist. This
happens because differences in
organisms make them more
likely to survive than
organisms that do not have
those differences. Darwin's
theory of evolution through
natural selection was not
accepted by many scientists
when Darwin first published it.

**Thomas Edison (1847–1931)**
Thomas Edison is one of the most famous inventors in history. He lived in the United States his entire life. As a boy, he was mostly schooled at home. He even set up his own chemistry lab in the basement. He started working when he was a teenager and used his earnings to fund his inventions. As an adult, he built large laboratories and hired many skilled and talented people to work with him. Over 1,000 patents were given to him for inventions such as the light bulb, the phonograph (an early way to record sound), the motion picture camera and projector (which made movies possible), and storage batteries.

**Albert Einstein (1879–1955)**
Albert Einstein was born in Germany. He lived in Germany, Switzerland, and the United States and traveled throughout the world. Einstein is best known for his theory of relativity. This theory includes the famous equation $E = mc^2$. The equation describes the fact that a small amount of mass can be turned into a very large amount of energy. Einstein's work went beyond the laws of physics that Isaac Newton had described. Einstein's theory of relativity also paved the way for a better understanding of nuclear energy. But he was unhappy when nuclear weapons were invented, and he argued against using them.

## Michael Faraday (1791–1867)

Michael Faraday lived in England his whole life. His family was poor, so when he was 12 years old, he left school to work for a bookbinder. He read all the science books that came through the shop! Later, he wrote to a famous scientist asking for a job—and he got one. That job got him started as a scientist. Faraday is best known for a discovery about electricity and magnetism: Moving a wire through a magnetic field makes an electric current flow in the wire. That discovery made it possible for others to figure out how to produce and use electricity.

## Alexander Fleming (1881–1955)

In science, it is important to keep experiments neat and organized. But if Alexander Fleming had kept his lab neater, he might not have discovered penicillin! Fleming was born in Scotland and lived there and in England. One day in 1928, he was cleaning up his very messy lab. Many of the dishes from his old experiments were moldy. But in one of the dishes, bacteria did not grow near the mold. Fleming wondered if something in the mold was killing the bacteria. He was right, and his discovery led to new, life-saving medicines called antibiotics.

**Benjamin Franklin (1706–1790)**

Benjamin Franklin was born in Boston and lived in both the United States and England. He is best known for his important role in the American Revolution. But he also created many important inventions and made many scientific discoveries. Through his famous experiment with a kite, he demonstrated that lightning is a form of electricity. He invented the Franklin wood stove, which uses less wood and is safer than a fireplace. And his need for two different pairs of eyeglasses led him to invent bifocals.

**Galileo Galilei (1564–1642)**

Galileo lived in Italy. He had a good education and learned to think for himself. He did many experiments on how things move and how they fall. Later, Galileo's work helped Newton figure out the laws of motion. Galileo did not invent the telescope, but as soon as he heard about it, he built his own. When he used one to look at the sky, he made amazing discoveries: mountains on the moon, stars in the Milky Way, and four moons orbiting Jupiter! Jupiter's moons helped support Nicolaus Copernicus's theory that the sun, not Earth, is at the center of the universe.

**Jane Goodall (1934–present)**
Jane Goodall says she has been interested in animals for longer than she can remember. She was born in England. She still has a home there, but she travels all over the world. Her important work as a scientist was done in East Africa. There, she spent years observing chimpanzees in their natural habitat. Her work completely changed people's ideas about chimpanzees. She discovered that they make tools, eat meat, and live together in groups with a social structure. Her way of working was controversial when she started. But now it is an accepted way to study primates.

**Robert Hooke (1635–1703)**
Robert Hooke was born and lived in England. As a boy, he was often sick and couldn't go to school. But he worked very hard to learn about everything around him through reading, observing, and experimenting. Most of his life, Hooke had the job of experimentalist. He did several new experiments every week and reported his work to other scientists. Today, he is best-known for the experiments he did with a microscope that he built. His most famous discovery was that living things are made of cells. In fact, he gave them the name "cells."

**Johannes Kepler (1571–1630)**
Johannes Kepler lived in what is now Germany. He is best known for figuring out the three laws of planetary motion that are named for him. The laws explain that planet orbits are ellipses (ovals), not circles. The laws also explain how the planets move in these orbits. Kepler's work supported Copernicus' theory that planets orbit the sun, not Earth. Kepler also designed his own telescope, explained how a pinhole camera works, and figured out that the eye receives images upside down.

**Lewis Latimer (1848–1928)**
Lewis Latimer was a great inventor in the great age of inventors. His parents escaped slavery by fleeing to Boston before he was born. His family was poor, so he left school while he was still young and took a job. But he taught himself many subjects, including drafting (technical drawing), which led to his career as an inventor. He helped Alexander Graham Bell by drawing the diagrams for Bell's telephone patent. Latimer is best known for his work with Thomas Edison. He was one of the original Edison Pioneers and designed major improvements to the light bulb.

## Anton von Leeuwenhoek (1632–1723)

Anton von Leeuwenhoek was unusual for scientists of his day. He did not have a science education, and he did experiments in his spare time while running his own business. But his work was so important that he was made a member of a famous group of scientists, the Royal Society of London. Leeuwenhoek spent years carefully describing things that he observed through lenses. He made most of the lenses himself. With his lenses, he discovered microscopic pond life, bacteria, tiny fossils, and hundreds of other things no one had ever seen before.

## Isaac Newton (1643–1727)

Isaac Newton lived in England. He is best known for three major contributions to science. His law of universal gravitation describes how the force of gravity works. His three laws of motion describe the forces that control the motions of objects. And he was the first to discover that "white" light is made up of all the colors of the rainbow. He is a giant in the history of science, yet he wrote to Robert Hooke, "If I have seen further than others, it is by standing on the shoulders of giants." By this he meant that his work built on the work of other scientists.

**Louis Pasteur (1822–1895)**
When Louis Pasteur was a boy in his native France, he thought he might be an artist. Luckily for all of us, he went into science! Pasteur's experiments proved that many diseases are caused by microscopic germs. He also showed how to prevent these diseases by avoiding germs and by using vaccinations. One way to avoid germs is to heat food to kill germs before eating it. Most milk and many juices are now "pasteurized" to keep people safe. Pasteur also made important discoveries about chemicals, but he is best known for his work on diseases.

**Ptolemy (85?–165?)**
Ptolemy lived in Egypt and was a citizen of the Roman Empire. He is best known for his model explaining how the planets move in the sky. But he thought that the planets move around Earth. That is what Aristotle had written a few hundred years earlier. Ptolemy's model was wrong, but it did explain almost all observations about planets. His model was also very good at predicting planet movement. Ptolemy's model lasted nearly a thousand years, until Nicolaus Copernicus suggested a new idea.

## James Watt (1736–1819)

James Watt lived in Scotland most of his life. When he was a young man, someone gave him a steam engine that needed to be fixed. He didn't just fix it, he figured out how to make new steam engines that worked much better. His engines were so good that many factories soon switched to using steam engines instead of horses. He described the power of his engines in units of "horsepower"—the number of horses it would take to do the work of one engine. Today, the metric system's unit of power is the watt, which was named in his honor.

## Orville Wright (1871–1948)
## Wilbur Wright (1867–1912)

The Wright brothers were born in Ohio and lived there most of their lives. As children, they liked to invent things, and their parents encouraged them. When they grew up, they built and sold bicycles, but they became very interested in flying machines. Many people were working on flying machines at that time. The Wright brothers built their own gliders and airplanes and tested them in secret on a soft, sandy beach in North Carolina. There, in 1903, they flew the first airplane that used its own power.

# Science Word Parts

Many parts of science words come from words in other languages. This table lists a few of those word parts. Some parts are prefixes at the beginning of a science word. Others are suffixes at the end of a word. And some, called *word roots*, can come at the beginning, the end, or in the middle. Knowing the meaning of word parts can help you understand science words.

| Word Roots | Meaning | Examples |
| --- | --- | --- |
| dict | say | predict, prediction |
| flect | bend back | reflect, reflection |
| fract | break | refract, fraction |
| lev | raise | elevation |
| lith | stone | lithosphere |
| morph | shape, form | metamorphic |
| syn | put together | photosynthesis |
| trop | turning | geotropism |
| vor | eat | carnivore |

| Prefixes | Meaning | Examples |
| --- | --- | --- |
| alt-, alto- | high | altitude |
| amphi- | both | amphibian |
| arthr-, arthro- | joint | arthropod |
| astr-, astro- | star | astronomy |
| bar-, baro- | pressure, weight | barometer |
| bio- | life | biology |
| carn-, carni- | meat | carnivore |
| chlor, chloro- | green | chlorophyll |
| circ- | around | circuit |
| curr- | run | current |

| Prefixes continued | Meaning | Examples |
|---|---|---|
| de- | opposite of | decomposer |
| end-, endo- | inside | endoskeleton |
| ep-, epi- | over, above | epicenter |
| equ-, equi- | equal | equator |
| exo- | outside | exoskeleton |
| geo- | earth | geology |
| gravi- | heavy | gravity |
| hemi- | half | hemisphere |
| herb-, herbi- | plant | herbivore |
| hydro- | water | hydroelectric |
| ign- | fire | igneous |
| in- | not | inactive |
| luna- | moon | lunar eclipse |
| meta- | change | metamorphic |
| micro- | small | microscope |
| non- | not | nonrenewable |
| omni- | all | omnivore |
| photo- | light | photosynthesis |
| pre-, pro- | before | predict |
| re- | again | recycle |
| sed- | settle, sit | sedimentary |
| sol- | sun | solar |
| strat- | sheet, layer | stratus |
| tele- | distant | telescope |
| therm- | heat | thermometer |

| Suffixes | Meaning | Examples |
|---|---|---|
| -graph | write, draw, record | telegraph |
| -logy | study | biology |
| -meter | measuring tool | thermometer |
| -saur | lizard | dinosaur |
| -scope | tool for observing | telescope |
| -sphere | ball, globe | hydrosphere |

# Glossary of Science Terms

**absolute age:** the actual age of a rock, rock layer, or fossil

**absolute magnitude:** the actual brightness of a star

**abyssal plain:** a large, flat surface on the ocean floor (**196**)

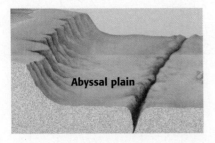

Abyssal plain

**acceleration:** a change in an object's speed or direction (**277**)

**acid rain:** rain that contains unhealthy amounts of acid (**341**)

**active solar heating system:** a system that uses the sun's energy to heat water, then pumps the heated water through pipes to warm a building (**324**)

**adaptation:** a structure or behavior that helps an organism survive in its surroundings (**77**)

**Gills are an adaptation for living in water.**

**air:** a mixture of gases that surrounds Earth (**198**)

**air mass:** a large "bubble" of air that has about the same temperature and humidity throughout it (**208**)

**air pollution:** the presence of harmful substances in the air (**339**)

**air pressure:** the weight of air pushing on everything around it (**199, 203**)

**alloy:** a solution of two different metals

**altitude:** height above sea level; also called *elevation*

**alveoli:** tiny sacs in the lungs where oxygen enters the blood and carbon dioxide leaves the blood

**amp:** the unit used to measure electric current (**298**)

**amphibian:** an animal that has a backbone and lives in water when it is young and on land when it is an adult (**85, 154**)

**amplitude:** a measure of how hard air molecules push on other molecules next to them as a sound wave passes through the air

**anemometer:** a weather instrument that measures wind speed (**202**)

**animal:** an organism that is made of many cells, breathes oxygen, eats other organisms, and can move on its own (**141**)

**antibiotic:** a substance that kills bacteria (**361, 363**)

**anus:** the opening where solid wastes leave the body (**117**)

**apparent magnitude:** how bright a star appears to be in the night sky

**area:** the size of a surface (**385**)

**artery:** a blood vessel that carries blood away from the heart (**123**)

**arthropod:** an animal that has a hard outer skeleton and legs with joints (**148**)

**asteroid:** a large space rock that orbits the sun (**226, 230**)

**atmosphere:** the air that surrounds Earth (**64, 158, 198**)

**atom:** the smallest particle of a substance that has all the properties of that substance (**248**)

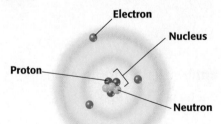

**atomic number:** the number of protons in the nucleus of one atom of an element (**250**)

**auditory nerve:** the nerve that carries messages about sound from the ear to the brain

**axis (of Earth):** an imaginary line that passes from the North Pole to the South Pole through Earth's center (**218**)

**axis (on a graph):** the up-and-down line at the left side of a graph or the side-to-side line at the bottom of a graph (**66, 72**) *Also see* **horizontal axis, vertical axis**

**B**

**bacteria:** organisms that are made of one cell with no nucleus; also called *monerans* (**145**)

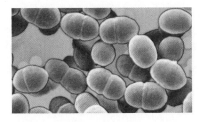

**balanced forces:** forces that act against each other and do not cause a change in motion

**bar graph:** a graph that shows the same kind of data for different things (**66**)

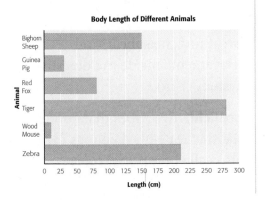

Body Length of Different Animals

**barometer:** a weather instrument that measures air pressure (**203**)

**bay:** an area of water that is partly surrounded by land

**behavior:** something an organism does (**77, 92**)

**benefit:** a good result of using a technology (**366**)

**big bang theory:** a theory that describes the beginning of the universe as a huge explosion

**bile:** a digestive juice that is made by the liver and stored in the gall bladder until it is needed for digestion in the small intestine (**117**)

**biodiversity:** the variety of different species in an area

**biomass:** fuel that comes from plants and animals

**biome:** a very large area of land with a certain kind of climate and certain kinds of organisms living there

**bird:** an animal that has a backbone, feathers, wings, and lightweight bones, breathes air, and lays eggs with a hard shell (**152**)

**black hole:** an object in space with gravity so strong that it pulls everything into it, even light

**blizzard:** a snowstorm with high winds and low temperatures (**215**)

**blood:** a tissue made of blood cells floating in a liquid; carries materials throughout an animal's body (**105, 123**)

**boiling point:** the temperature at which a substance changes from a liquid to a gas (**265**)

**brain:** the organ in the nervous system that is the control center of the body (**124**)

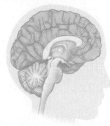

**brain stem:** the part of the brain that controls automatic body activities such as breathing, heartbeat, and movements inside the digestive system (**125**)

**bronchi:** two tubes that connect the trachea with the lungs (**121**); also called *bronchial tubes*

**buoyancy:** see *buoyant force*

**buoyant force:** the upward push of a liquid or gas on an object (272)

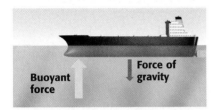

**butte:** a steep hill that stands alone in a flat area (172)

**camouflage:** the shape, color, or pattern of an animal that helps it blend in with its surroundings

**capillary:** a narrow blood vessel that connects an artery to a vein (123)

**captive breeding:** a way of helping endangered animals by keeping them in a zoo, animal park, or wildlife center, breeding them, and raising their young (353)

Captive breeding has saved the California condor from extinction.

**carbon dioxide:** a gas made of carbon and oxygen atoms that plants need for photosynthesis (255)

**carbon dioxide and oxygen cycle:** the movement of carbon dioxide and oxygen between organisms and the air (132)

**cardiac:** having to do with the heart

**carnivore:** an animal that eats other animals (**134**)

**cartilage:** tissue in the skeletal system that is strong but more flexible than bone (**112**)

**cast:** a fossil that formed when a space left by an organism was filled with minerals or grains of rock that turned into solid rock (**186**)

**catalytic converter:** a part in an automobile's exhaust system that changes harmful gases into a harmless gas and water (**340**)

**cell:** the smallest living part of an organism (**99**)

**cell membrane:** a soft, flexible structure that surrounds a cell and controls the movement of substances into and out of the cell (**100, 103**)

**cell respiration:** the process of releasing energy from nutrients (**78**); also called *cellular respiration*

**cell wall:** the rigid outer covering of a plant cell (**102**)

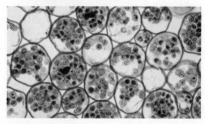

**Plant root cells**

**cementing:** the gluing together of rock particles to form sedimentary rock

**cerebellum:** the part of the brain that coordinates the movement of muscles and helps you keep your balance (**125**)

**cerebrum:** the part of the brain that controls conscious body movements, learning, thinking, memory, and imagination and receives information from sense organs (**125**)

**charge:** a property of matter; charge can be positive or negative; also called *electric charge*

**chemical bond:** a connection between atoms that joins them together to form molecules

**chemical change:** a change that produces a new substance (**260, 266**)

Rusting is a chemical change.

**chemical formula:** a set of symbols that describe the number and kind of elements in a compound (for example, $CO_2$ for carbon dioxide)

**chemical property:** the ability of a substance to change into a new substance with different properties (**246**)

**chemical reaction:** the changes that happen to substances during a chemical change (**266**)

When baking soda and vinegar react, they form carbon dioxide.

**chemical symbol:** a one- or two-letter abbreviation for an element's name (**250**)

**chlorophyll:** a green substance in plant leaves that captures the energy in sunlight (**80, 103**)

**chloroplast:** a tiny green structure that contains chlorophyll, found in leaf cells (**80, 103**)

**circle graph:** a round graph that shows parts of a whole (**64**); also called a *pie chart*

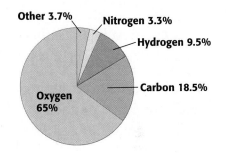

Other 3.7%   Nitrogen 3.3%
Hydrogen 9.5%
Carbon 18.5%
Oxygen 65%

**circuit:** a complete path of conductors that an electric current can flow through (**300**)

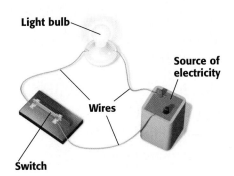

Light bulb
Source of electricity
Wires
Switch

**circuit breaker:** a switch that automatically opens a circuit when too much electricity flows through it

**circulatory system:** the group of organs that work together to move blood throughout the body (**108, 122**)

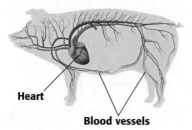

Heart

Blood vessels

**cirrus cloud:** a high, feathery cloud made of ice crystals (**206**)

**classification:** the grouping of organisms based on their similarities and differences (**139**)

**cleavage:** the breaking of a mineral along a smooth, flat surface (**161**)

**climate:** the general weather of an area over a long period of time (**216**)

**cloud:** a mass of water droplets or ice crystals that have clumped together in the atmosphere (**206**)

**cold front:** the leading edge of a moving mass of cooler air (**209**)

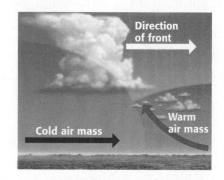

Direction of front

Cold air mass

Warm air mass

**comet:** a mountain-size chunk of ice and dust that orbits the sun (**233**)

**commensalism:** a relationship between two different kinds of organisms in which one organism is helped and the other is not harmed

**community:** populations of different kinds of organisms that live in the same place at the same time (**129**)

**compass:** a tool that uses a magnetized pointer to show magnetic north

**compass rose:** a map symbol that shows north, south, east, and west (**404**)

**competition:** the struggle of organisms against each other to get the same resource

**compost:** a mixture of soil and decayed material that provides nutrients for plants (**348**)

**compound:** a substance whose molecules contain atoms of different elements (**254, 256**)

**compound machine:** a machine made of two or more simple machines (**283**)

**compression:** an area in a sound wave where air molecules are pressed together (**316**)

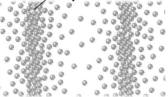
Compression

**concave lens:** a lens that is thinner in the center and thicker at the edges, a shape that bends light outward (**314**)

**concept map:** a diagram that shows connections between ideas (**396**)

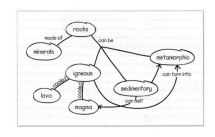

**conclusion:** a statement that tells what an investigation showed, based on observations and data (**18**)

**concrete:** a mixture of sand and minerals that is used in buildings, roads, and sidewalks (**331**)

**condensation:** the process of changing from a gas to a liquid (**189**)

**condensation point:** the temperature at which a substance changes from a gas to a liquid (**265**)

**condense:** to change from a gas to a liquid as the temperature decreases

**conduction:** the movement of heat between objects that touch each other (**292**)

Heat energy

**conductor:** a material that allows heat energy or electricity to pass through it easily (**293, 299**)

**conifer:** a plant that produces seeds in cones

**conservation:** the wise use and protection of natural resources (**344**)

**constellation:** a group of stars that ancient people thought formed a picture in the sky (**236**)

**consumer:** an organism that gets energy by eating other organisms (**134**)

**continental drift:** an early theory that described the movement of continents, later replaced by the plate tectonic theory

**continental shelf:** the gently sloping underwater part of a continent (**196**)

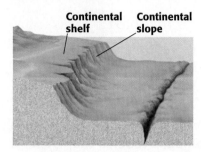

Continental shelf    Continental slope

**continental slope:** the sharp drop at the edge of the underwater part of a continent (**196**)

**contract:** to get shorter, like a muscle when it contracts (**104**)

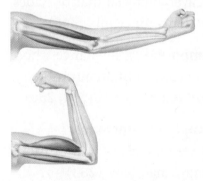

**control:** to keep all the variables in an experiment the same except the one variable being tested (**8**)

**convection:** the movement of heat energy through liquids and gases in currents (**294**)

**convex lens:** a lens that is thicker in the center and thinner at the edges, a shape that bends light inward (**314**)

**core:** the center of Earth, made of solid metals; also called *inner core*

**crater:** a bowl-shaped structure at the top of a volcano or on a planet or moon

**Meteor Crater in Arizona**

**crest:** the highest part of a wave (**311**)

**crust:** Earth's outer layer, made of solid rock (**159**)

**crystal:** a solid material found in nature that has straight edges and flat sides or that breaks into pieces with straight edges and flat sides (**160**)

**cumulonimbus cloud:** a huge vertical cloud that can produce a thunderstorm (**207**); also called a *thunderhead*

**cumulus cloud:** a puffy, white cloud with a flat bottom (**207**); also called a *fair-weather cloud*

**current (in an electric circuit):** a constant flow of electrons through a conductor (**298**)

**current (in an ocean):** a river of water that moves through an ocean (**194**)

**cytoplasm:** a jellylike liquid that fills most of a cell (**101, 103**)

**data:** the pieces of information collected in an investigation (**10**); singular *datum*

**data table:** a chart made of columns and rows for recording information (**60**)

| Hourly Temperature, May 10, 2004 ||
| Time | Temperature (°F) |
| --- | --- |
| 8:00 A.M. | 58 |
| 9:00 A.M. | 60 |
| 10:00 A.M. | 62 |
| 11:00 A.M. | 63 |
| 12:00 noon | 65 |
| 1:00 P.M. | 65 |
| 2:00 P.M. | 66 |
| 3:00 P.M. | 64 |

**decibel:** the unit used to measure the loudness of sound

**decomposer:** an organism that gets energy by feeding on dead materials and wastes (**136**)

**delta:** a large flat area of land at the mouth of a river (**172**)

**denominator:** the number below the line in a fraction (**375**)

**density:** the amount of mass in a known volume of an object or substance (**245, 385**)

**deposition:** the process in which materials eroded by water, wind, or ice are dropped in a new place (**172**)

**desalination:** the process of removing salts from sea water to produce fresh water

**desert:** a biome that has very little rain and few plants

**diaphragm:** a sheet of muscle below the lungs that helps them expand and contract

**digestive system:** the group of organs that work together to break food down into nutrients that the body can use (**108, 116**)

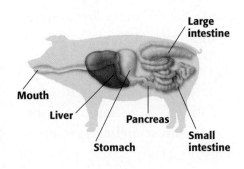

Large intestine
Mouth
Liver
Pancreas
Stomach
Small intestine

**dissolve:** to form a solution with another substance (**259**)

**dry cell:** a device that uses chemicals to produce electricity; also called a *battery*

**dune:** a hill of sand that is deposited by the wind

**earth science:** the study of planet Earth and objects in space (**157**)

**earthquake:** a shaking of Earth's crust caused by rock slabs moving against each other deep below Earth's crust (**180**)

**eclipse:** one object in space casting its shadow on another object in space (**224**)

**eclipse of the moon:** Earth casting a shadow on the moon (**224**)

**eclipse of the sun:** the moon casting a shadow on Earth (**224**)

**ecology:** the study of how living and nonliving things interact (**126**)

**ecosystem:** all the living and nonliving things that interact with each other in an environment (**130**)

**efficiency:** how much work a machine does compared with how much energy is put into it

**egg:** the first stage in the life cycle of many organisms

**Frog eggs**

**egg cell:** a female cell that joins with a male cell to produce a new organism **(87)**

**El Niño:** a temporary change in climate caused by temperature shifts in the Pacific Ocean

**electric charge:** a property of matter; charge can be positive or negative

**Like charges repel each other.**

**Unlike charges attract each other.**

**electric circuit:** a complete pathway of conductors that electrons flow through **(300)**

**electric current:** a constant flow of electrons through a conductor **(298)**

**electric discharge:** a sudden movement of electric charges

**electric forces:** the attraction or repulsion of electric charges

**electricity:** a form of energy that is produced when electrons move from one place to another place **(296)**

**electromagnet:** a temporary magnet created by a flow of electric current around an iron bar **(306)**

**electromagnetic radiation:** energy that can travel through space; also called *electromagnetic spectrum*

**electromagnetic spectrum:** a group of waves, including visible light, that can travel through space **(310)**

**electron:** a particle that is in the space around the nucleus of an atom and has a negative charge **(249)**

**element:** a pure substance made of only one kind of atom **(250)**

**elevation:** the land's height above sea level **(217)**; also called *altitude*

**ellipse:** a flattened circle (220, 228)

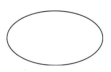

**embryo:** a plant or animal in the earliest stage of development

**emergency:** anything that seriously threatens a person's life or health (**36**)

**endangered species:** a species that could become extinct very soon if it is not helped by people (**352**)

Whooping crane

**endoskeleton:** an internal skeleton made of bones and cartilage (**149**)

**energy:** the ability to do work (**284**)

**energy pyramid:** a diagram that shows the amount of energy passed on at each level of a food chain

**energy resources:** materials in the environment that people can use as sources of energy (**320**)

**engineer:** someone who designs technology to solve problems (**357**)

**environment:** the surroundings that an organism lives in

**epicenter:** the point on Earth's surface directly above the focus of an earthquake (**180**)

**equal-area projection:** a map projection that shows sizes well but changes the shapes of areas near the North and South Poles (**405**)

Greenland: right size, but wrong shape

**equation:** a number sentence that shows how different numbers or measurements are related (**384**)

**equator:** an imaginary line that circles Earth halfway between the North and South Poles

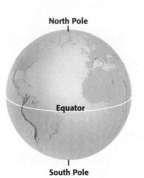

North Pole

Equator

South Pole

**equinox:** a day when the hours of darkness and light are about equal, either the first day of spring or the first day of fall

**erosion:** the movement of weathered materials by water, wind, or ice (**172**)

**esophagus:** the tube in the digestive system that connects the mouth to the stomach (**117**)

**estuary:** a place where fresh water from a river empties into the ocean and mixes with it

**evaporate:** to change from a liquid to a gas

**evaporation:** the process of changing from a liquid to a gas (**188**)

**excretory system:** the group of organs that work together to get rid of wastes that cells produce (**118**)

**exoskeleton:** a hard outer covering that protects an animal's soft body parts inside (**148**)

**exosphere:** the highest layer of air in Earth's atmosphere (**199**)

**exotic species:** a species that does not usually live in an area but is brought there on purpose or by accident

**experiment:** a scientific investigation that tests a hypothesis (**4**)

**exponent:** a small, raised number used to show that a number or measurement unit has been multiplied by itself a certain number of times (for example, $10^3$) (**373**)

**extinction:** the dying out of a species (**350**)

**fault:** a crack in Earth's crust (**175, 180**)

**fault-block mountains:** mountains that formed when blocks of rock slid upward or downward along a fault (**175**)

**fern:** a kind of plant that has roots, stems, and leaflike fronds and reproduces with spores (**86**)

**fertile:** describes soil that can support plant life

**fertilization:** the joining of an egg cell and a sperm cell (**87**)

**filament:** a thin wire that glows in some kinds of light bulbs

**filter:** a device used to separate the parts of a mixture by passing the mixture through it

**fish:** an animal that has a backbone, scales or rough skin, and fins, lives in water, and breathes with gills (**155**)

**flash flood:** a sudden rush of water that overflows a stream after a heavy rain

**flower:** the part where seeds are made in many kinds of plants (**87**)

**focal point:** the point where light rays come together after passing through a lens

**focus:** the point deep below Earth's surface where an earthquake starts (**180**)

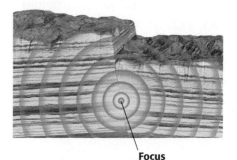

Focus

**fog:** a layered cloud that forms close to the ground (**207**)

**folded mountains:** mountains that formed when land was squeezed together (174)

**food chain:** the path of food energy from one organism to another in an ecosystem (137)

**food web:** overlapping food chains with different pathways for the flow of food energy in an ecosystem (138)

**force:** a push or pull (268)

**fossil:** the remains or traces of an organism that lived long ago (185, 322)

Insect fossilized in amber

**fossil fuel:** a fuel that formed from the decayed remains of ancient plants and animals (322)

**fracture:** the breaking of a mineral along a rough or jagged surface (161)

**freeze:** to change from a liquid to a solid when temperature drops (264)

**freezing point:** the temperature at which a substance changes from a liquid to a solid (264)

**frequency (in a data set):** the number of times each measurement appears (379)

**frequency (of waves):** the number of waves that move past a point in a certain amount of time (311, 316)

**friction:** a force between two surfaces rubbing against each other; friction works against motion (274)

**front:** a place where one air mass meets and pushes aside another air mass (208)

**fruit:** a structure that grows from a flower and contains seeds

**fuel:** a material that is burned to produce heat energy (322)

**fulcrum:** the support that a lever turns around (**282**)

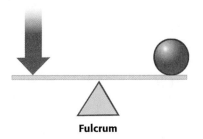

Fulcrum

**function:** the "job" that a body part does in an organism (**77, 98**)

**fungus:** an organism that feeds on dead organisms or their wastes, cannot move on its own, and reproduces with spores (**143**); plural *fungi*

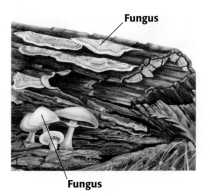

Fungus

Fungus

**fuse:** a device that prevents fires by melting when too much electricity flows through a circuit

G

**galaxy:** a group of millions of stars (**235**)

**gall bladder:** an organ in the digestive system that stores bile until it is needed for digestion in the small intestine (**117**)

**garbage:** solid waste that people throw away (**335**); also called *trash*

**gas:** a state of matter in which the substance takes both the shape and the volume of its container (**262**)

**gasohol:** a mixture of gasoline and alcohol, used as fuel for automobiles (**328**)

**generator:** a device that uses magnets to change the energy of motion to electrical energy (**307**)

**geocentric model:** the idea that Earth is at the center of the universe

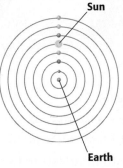

**geothermal energy:** heat from melted rock deep below Earth's surface, used to heat buildings and produce electricity (**327**)

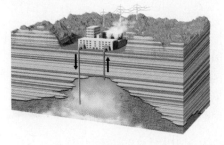

**geotropism:** the downward growth of a plant's roots and upward growth of its stem in response to gravity (**97**)

**germination:** the sprouting of a plant from a seed

**gills:** structures in an organism that remove oxygen from water (**154**)

**glacier:** a large body of moving ice that stays frozen all year (**173, 190**)

**global warming:** a rise in Earth's average worldwide temperature

**glucose:** a kind of sugar that is made by plants and broken down in cells to release energy (**78, 80, 103**)

**graph:** a drawing that shows the relationships between sets of data

**gravity:** the force that pulls objects toward each other (**227, 270**)

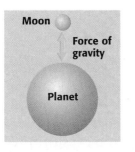

**greenhouse effect:** the process of Earth's atmosphere trapping heat near Earth's surface

**groundwater:** water that collects underground in cracks and spaces in rock (**192**)

**habitat:** the environment where an organism lives (**127, 350**)

**hardness:** the ability of a mineral to resist being scratched (**162**)

**hazardous waste:** waste from factories or power plants that can be harmful to people or the environment

**headland:** a piece of land that sticks out into an ocean or large lake

**heart:** the organ in the circulatory system that pumps blood throughout the body (**106, 123**)

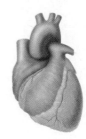

**heart muscle:** the kind of muscle tissue that makes the heart beat and pump blood throughout the body (**115**); also called *cardiac muscle*

**heart rate:** the number of times a heart beats in one minute **(12)**

**heat energy:** the energy of moving particles in a substance **(289)**; also called *thermal energy*

**heliocentric model:** the idea that the sun is at the center of the solar system

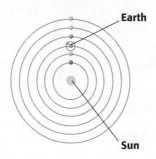

**herbivore:** an animal that eats only plants or plant products **(134)**

**hertz:** the unit used to measure wave frequency

**hibernation:** a deep sleeplike state when an animal's body processes slow down **(93)**

**high:** on a weather map, an area where the air pressure is higher than it is in surrounding areas

**horizontal axis:** the side-to-side line at the bottom of a graph **(66, 68, 72)**

**humidity:** water vapor in the air **(204)**

**humus:** decaying plant and animal material in soil **(168)**

**hurricane:** a very large and violent tropical storm **(214)**

**hydroelectric energy:** electricity that is produced using the energy of water moving through a dam

**hydrosphere:** all the liquid water and ice on Earth's surface, liquid water in the ground, and water vapor in the atmosphere **(157)**

**hydrotropism:** the growth of a plant's roots toward moisture in the soil **(97)**

**hygrometer:** a weather instrument that measures relative humidity **(204)**

**hypothesis:** an idea that can be tested by an experiment or an observation **(6)**

**ice age:** a time in Earth's history when year-round ice covered more land than it does now

**icecaps:** sheets of ice that cover areas around the North and South Poles (**190**)

**igneous rock:** rock that formed from cooled magma or lava (**164**)

Granite is an igneous rock.

**incinerator:** a furnace designed for burning waste materials (**338**)

**inclined plane:** a simple machine made of a flat, sloping surface (**280**)

**index fossil:** a fossil of a known age that is used to figure out the age of the rock around it

**inertia:** the tendency of an object to resist a change in motion (**277**)

**inference:** an explanation that you can figure out without observing something directly (**18**)

**infrared waves:** a kind of invisible energy from the sun that transfers heat

**inherited trait:** a characteristic that is passed from parents to their offspring (**82**)

**inner core:** the center of Earth, made of solid metals (**159**)

**instinctive behavior:** a behavior that an animal inherits from its parents (**93**); also called *instinct*

**insulator:** a material that does not let heat energy or electricity pass through it easily (**293, 299**)

**intertidal zone:** the part of the land that is covered and uncovered by tides every day (**196**)

**intestine:** see *large intestine, small intestine*

**invertebrate:** an animal that does not have a backbone (**146**)

**jet stream:** a steady worldwide wind that blows from west to east high above Earth (**211**)

**joint:** a place where two or more bones meet (**113**)

**joule:** a unit used to measure energy or work

**key:** an explanation of symbols used on a map (**404**); also called a *legend*

**keyword:** a word used to search for Web sites about a certain topic (**390**)

**kidneys:** the two organs in the urinary system that filter wastes from the blood (**118**)

**kinetic energy:** the energy of motion (**285**)

**kingdom:** the largest grouping of organisms in scientific classification

**lake:** a large body of still water **(191)**

**landfill:** a place where garbage is dumped **(336)**

**landform:** a natural structure on Earth's surface

**landslide:** the sudden downhill movement of a huge mass of rock, soil, and mud **(182)**

**large intestine:** the organ in the digestive system that removes water from undigested wastes before they leave the body **(117)**

**larva:** the small, wormlike stage in the life cycle of some insects **(84)**

**larynx:** a structure in the throat that contains vocal cords for making sound; also called the *voice box*

**latitude:** the distance north or south of the equator **(217, 403)**

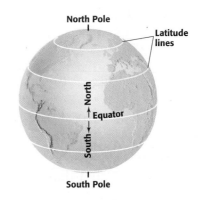

**lava:** melted rock that flows out of the ground onto Earth's surface **(164, 178)**

**leaf:** the plant organ where photosynthesis occurs to make food for the plant **(107)**

**learned behavior:** a behavior that an animal develops by observing other animals or by being taught (**93**)

**legend:** an explanation of symbols used on a map (**404**); also called a *key*

**lens:** a curved piece of clear glass or plastic that bends light rays (**314**)

**lever:** a simple machine made of a long bar or board that turns around a support that does not move (**282**)

**life cycle:** the stages of growth and development that an organism goes through in its lifetime (**84**)

**life science:** the study of plants, animals, and all other living things (**75**); also called *biology*

**ligament:** an organ in the muscular system that holds bones together at a joint

**light:** a form of energy that travels in waves and can move through empty space where there is no air (**309**)

**light telescope:** a telescope that uses one or more lenses, sometimes in combination with mirrors, to capture light from distant objects (**238**); also see *refracting telescope, reflecting telescope*

**light-year:** a unit of measurement equal to the distance that light travels in one year; used to measure huge distances between objects in space

**line graph:** a graph that shows how data changed as time passed (**70**)

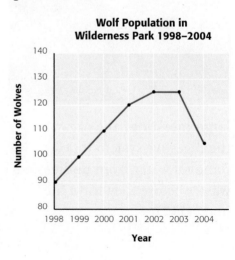

**Wolf Population in Wilderness Park 1998–2004**

**line plot:** a number line marked to show how data are grouped (**65**)

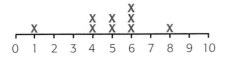

**liquid:** a state of matter in which the substance has a definite volume but takes the shape of its container (**263**)

**lithosphere:** Earth's rocky surface (**158**)

**litter:** garbage that people throw on the ground in public places (**335**)

**liver:** the organ in the digestive system that produces bile, stores extra glucose, and removes harmful substances from the blood (**116**)

**longitude:** the distance east or west of the prime meridian (**403**)

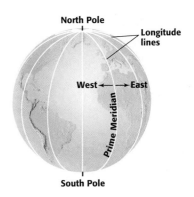

**low:** on a weather map, an area where the air pressure is lower than it is in surrounding areas

**lungs:** the two organs in the respiratory system that take in oxygen from the air and release waste gases into the air (**106, 121**)

**luster:** the way that a mineral's surface reflects light (**161**)

**Graphite has a metallic luster.**

**machine:** a tool that makes work easier, usually by letting you use less force

**magma:** melted rock below Earth's surface (**164, 178**)

**magnet:** an object that attracts iron and a few other magnetic materials (**272**)

**magnetic field:** the area around a magnet where the force of magnetism can be felt (**273, 305**)

**Magnetic field**

**Lines of force**

S N

**magnetic lines of force:** a pattern of lines formed by iron filings sprinkled on paper laid over a magnet (**305**)

**magnetism:** a force that pulls magnetic materials across a distance (**304**)

**magnifier:** a tool with a lens that makes things look larger so you can see them more clearly (**51**)

**magnitude:** the size of something, such as the brightness of a star or the strength of an earthquake

**malaria:** a serious tropical disease caused by a germ that is carried by mosquitoes (**20, 367**)

**mammal:** an animal that has a backbone and hair or fur, breathes with lungs, gives birth to live young, and feeds milk to its young (**151**)

**mantle:** the Earth layer below the crust, made of melted rock (**159**)

**map:** a picture of all or part of Earth's surface (**403**)

**map projection:** a way to show a picture of a round Earth on a flat map (**405**)

**map scale:** a marked line or a set of numbers that shows how far the distance is on land for each unit of distance on a map (**404**)

1 km

Scale 1:100,000 / 1 cm = 1 km

**marrow:** a tissue inside bones that makes certain kinds of blood cells

**marsh:** a shallow body of still or slow-moving water that has plants growing in it (**191**); also called a *swamp*

**mass:** the amount of matter in an object or substance (**39, 41, 244, 271**)

The mass of this brick is 2,000 g (2 kg).

**mass movement:** a sudden downhill movement of rock or soil, such as a landslide

**material resources:** living things and nonliving materials in the environment that are useful to people (**320**)

**matter:** the material, or "stuff," that everything is made of (**242**)

**mean:** the average found by adding together all measurements, then dividing the sum by the number of measurements (**378**)

**median:** the value that falls in the middle of a set of data (**378**)

**melting point:** the temperature at which a substance changes from a solid to a liquid (**264**)

**Mercator projection:** a map projection that shows shapes well but makes areas near the North and South Poles look much larger than they really are (**405**)

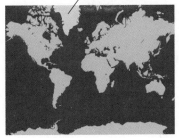

Greenland: right shape, but wrong size

**mesosphere:** the middle layer of air in Earth's atmosphere (**199**)

**metamorphic rock:** rock that formed when another kind of rock was squeezed and heated deep inside Earth's crust (**164**)

Marble is a metamorphic rock made from limestone.

**metamorphosis:** the changes in form that some insects go through during their life cycle (**84**)

**meteor:** a streak of light made by a burning meteoroid in Earth's atmosphere (**233**)

**meteorite:** a meteoroid that strikes Earth's surface (**233**)

**meteoroid:** a small space rock that orbits the sun (**226, 233**)

**metric system:** the system of measurement used in all scientific investigations, based on multiples of 10 (**38**)

**microclimate:** a small area that has temperatures, humidity, or other conditions that are different from the larger area surrounding it

**microorganism:** a living thing so tiny that it can only be seen with a microscope

**microscope:** a science tool that uses lenses to make tiny things look larger so they can be observed (**51**)

**mid-ocean ridge:** an underwater mountain chain that runs down the middle of an ocean floor (**197**)

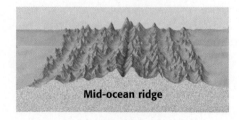

Mid-ocean ridge

**migration:** the seasonal movement of animals from one place to another **(94)**

**Milky Way Galaxy:** the galaxy that our solar system is part of **(235)**

**mimicry:** one organism's looking like another kind of organism in its environment so it can escape predators or catch prey

**mineral:** a solid natural material that has a crystal form and its own set of properties **(160)**

Sulfur

**mitochondria:** the structures in a cell that release energy from the nutrients in food **(101, 103)**

**mixture:** a combination of two or more substances that do not form a new substance **(258)**

**mode:** the measurement that appears most often in a data set **(379)**

**model:** a picture, idea, or object that represents an object or process

**mold:** a fossil that formed when an organism pressed into mud, leaving a shape that hardened in rock **(186)**

**molecule:** a particle of matter made of two or more atoms joined tightly together **(254)**

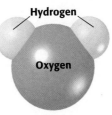

A molecule of water is made of one oxygen atom and two hydrogen atoms.

**molt:** to shed skin, scales, feathers, or an exoskeleton, usually at a particular time of year or stage of growth and development

**monerans:** organisms that are made of one cell with no nucleus; also called *bacteria*

**moon:** a natural object that orbits a planet

**moraine:** a ridge of rocks left by a glacier (**173**)

**moss:** a kind of plant that does not have true roots, stems, or leaves and that reproduces with spores (**86**)

**motion:** a change in the position of an object (**275**)

**motor:** a device that uses electricity to produce motion (**307**)

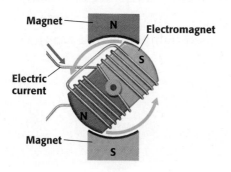

**muscle:** an organ in the muscular system that contracts and relaxes to produce movement (**115**); also see *heart muscle, skeletal muscle, smooth muscle*

**muscular system:** the group of organs that cause movement of body parts (**114**)

**mutualism:** a relationship between two different kinds of organisms in which both organisms benefit

**natural gas:** a burnable gas found under ground and used as fuel

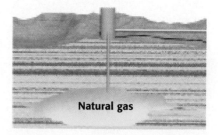

Natural gas

**natural resources:** materials in the environment that are useful to people (**319**)

**nebula:** a cloud of dust and gas in space

**negative number:** any number less than zero (**374**)

**nephrons:** tubes in the kidneys that remove wastes from the blood

**nerve:** an organ in the nervous system that carries messages to and from the spinal cord and brain (**124**)

**nervous system:** the group of organs that control all body activities (**124**)

**neuron:** a nerve cell

**neutron:** a particle that is in the nucleus of an atom and does not have a charge (**249**)

**newton:** the unit of force in the metric system (**269**)

**niche:** the role that an organism plays in its habitat (**127**)

**nimbostratus cloud:** a low, gray cloud that produces rain or snow (**206**)

**nitrogen cycle:** the movement of nitrogen between organisms and their surroundings

**noise pollution:** sound that is so loud or high-pitched that it annoys people

**nonrenewable resources:** resources that nature cannot replace quickly enough to meet people's needs (**320**)

**normal fault:** a crack in Earth's crust where a block of rock dropped downward (**175**)

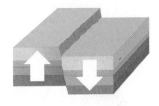

**Northern Hemisphere:** the half of Earth that is north of the equator

**North Pole (on Earth):** the northern end of the imaginary line that Earth rotates around

**north pole (of a magnet):** the end or side of a magnet that attracts the south pole of another magnet (**304**)

**nuclear energy:** energy given off when the nucleus of an atom breaks apart (**326**)

**nucleus (of an atom):** the center of an atom, made of protons and neutrons (**249**)

**nucleus (of a cell):** the structure in a cell that controls everything the cell does (**101, 103**)

**numerator:** the number above the line in a fraction (**375**)

**nutrient:** a substance that an organism needs in order to survive and grow (**76, 116**)

**offspring:** new organisms that come from parent organisms (**82**)

**oil gland:** a structure in the skin that produces oil to keep the skin soft and helps protect against germs (**119**)

**omnivore:** an animal that eats both plants and animals (**135**)

**orbit:** the path that one object in space takes around another object in space (**220, 227**)

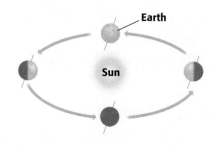
Earth

Sun

**ore:** a mineral that contains a metal or other substance that is valuable to people

**organ:** a group of different tissues that work together to perform a certain function in an organism (**106**)

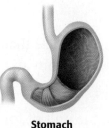
Stomach

**organ system:** a group of organs that work together to perform a certain function in an organism (**108**)

**organism:** a living thing (**76, 98, 126, 139, 350**)

**outer core:** the Earth layer below the mantle, made of liquid metals (**159**)

**ovary:** a plant or animal structure in which egg cells develop (**87**)

Ovary

**oxygen and carbon dioxide cycle:** the movement of carbon dioxide and oxygen between organisms and the air (**132**)

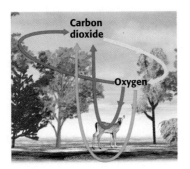

Carbon dioxide

Oxygen

**ozone:** a gas high in Earth's atmosphere that blocks some of the harmful radiation from the sun (**339**)

**pancreas:** an organ in the digestive system that produces digestive juices (**117**)

**Pangaea:** a continent that existed millions of years ago and was made of all of today's separate continents joined together

**parallel circuit:** an electric circuit in which each device has its own separate loop (**303**)

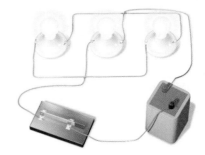

**parasitism:** a relationship between two different kinds of organisms in which one organism is helped and the other is harmed

**passive solar heating system:** a system that uses the sun's energy to heat a material inside a building to keep it warm (**324**)

**percent:** a comparison that describes parts of a whole when the whole is 100 (**377**)

**periodic table of the elements:** a chart that shows all the elements arranged by atomic number and by properties (**251**)

**peristalsis:** muscle contractions that move food through the digestive system

**petals:** colorful, sweet-smelling parts of a flower that attract insects (**87**)

**petrified fossil:** a fossil that formed when the hard parts of an organism were replaced by minerals (**186**)

**petroleum:** a liquid fossil fuel; also called *crude oil*

**phases of the moon:** the regular changes in the way the moon looks from Earth (**222**)

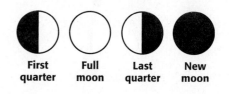

First quarter     Full moon     Last quarter     New moon

**phloem:** tubes in plant stems that carry food from the leaves to other parts of the plant (**81**)

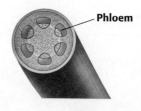

Phloem

**photosynthesis:** the process of using the energy in sunlight to make food from water and carbon dioxide (**80**)

**phototropism:** the turning of a plant's leaves toward light (**96**)

**physical change:** a change from one form to another form without turning into a new substance (**260**)

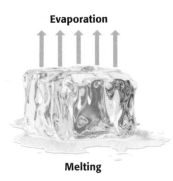

Evaporation

Melting

**physical property:** a property that can be observed, measured, or changed without changing the substance itself (**246**)

**physical science:** the study of matter, forces, motion, and energy (**241**)

**pistil:** a long tube that grows up from the ovary in a flower (**87**)

— Pistil

**pitch:** how high or low a sound is (**317**)

**planet:** a large object that orbits a star (**228**)

**plant:** an organism that is made of many cells with a cell wall, makes its own food through photosynthesis, and lives on land (**142**)

**plasma:** the liquid part of blood (**123**)

**plate:** a huge piece of Earth's crust that moves very slowly (**176**)

**plate tectonic theory:** a theory that explains how parts of Earth's crust have moved over time

**platelets:** structures in the blood that plug holes in injured blood vessels (**123**)

**polar climate:** a cold, dry climate located in bands around the North and South Poles (**216**)

**pollen:** a powdery material in flowers that contains sperm cells (**87**)

**pollination:** the transfer of pollen from the stamens to the pistil of a flower (**87**)

**pollution:** anything in the environment that can harm living things or damage natural resources (**334**)

**pond:** a small body of still water (**191**)

**population:** all the organisms of the same species that live in the same place at the same time (**129**)

**potential energy:** energy that is stored in an object (**285**)

**power:** the amount of work done in a certain amount of time

**precipitation:** water that falls to Earth's surface as rain, snow, sleet, or hail (**189, 205**)

**predator:** an animal that hunts, catches, and eats another animal

**prediction:** an idea about what will happen in the future (**19**)

**prevailing wind:** a wind that blows in the same direction across a large part of Earth

**prey:** an animal that is hunted, caught, and eaten by another animal

**prime meridian:** the imaginary line on Earth's surface used to describe distances east and west (**403**)

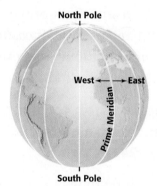

**prism:** a glass bar that separates white light into the colors of the rainbow

**producer:** an organism that makes its own food (**133**)

**property:** a characteristic of a substance (**244**)

**protist:** a small organism, usually made of one cell, that has some of the characteristics of a plant or an animal (**144**)

Euglena

**proton:** a particle that is in the nucleus of an atom and has a positive charge (**249**)

**pulley:** a simple machine made of a wheel with a rope or chain wrapped around it (**283**)

**pulse:** the heartbeats you can feel on the side of your neck or on the inside of your wrist (**12**)

**pupa:** the stage in the life cycle of some insects when the organism changes from a larva to an adult (**84**)

**quarry:** a place where rocks are taken from Earth to be used for building

**radiation:** the movement of energy through space as waves (**294**)

**radioactive:** describes an element that gives off tiny particles and energy from inside its atoms

**radio telescope:** a dish-shaped telescope that collects radio waves from outer space (**239**)

**rain gauge:** a weather instrument that measures rainfall (**205**)

**range:** the difference between the lowest and highest values in a data set (**379**)

**rarefaction:** an area in a sound wave where air molecules are spread out (**316**)

**rate:** a comparison of two values that are measured in different units (**376**)

**ratio:** a comparison of two values that are measured in the same unit (**376**)

**reclamation:** returning a damaged area to its original condition

**rectum:** the organ in the digestive system that stores solid wastes until they leave the body (**117**)

**recycling:** processing waste items so the materials they are made of can be used to make new items (**349**)

**red blood cells:** cells in the blood that carry oxygen to all parts of the body (**123**)

**reflecting telescope:** a telescope with two mirrors and one lens (**238**)

**reflection:** the bouncing back of light rays from a surface (**313**)

**refracting telescope:** a telescope with two lenses (**238**)

**refraction:** the bending of light rays as they move from one material into another material (**314**)

**relative age:** the age of an object or rock layer compared with the age of nearby rock layers

**relative humidity:** the amount of water vapor that the air is holding compared with the amount that it could hold at that temperature (**204**)

**renewable resources:** resources that nature produces again and again (**320**)

**reproduce:** to make more organisms of the same kind (**84**)

**reproduction:** the process of making more organisms of the same kind (**82**)

**reptile:** an animal that has a backbone and dry, leathery skin or scales, breathes air with lungs, and lays eggs with leathery shells or gives birth to live young (**153**)

Nile crocodile

**resistor:** a device in a circuit that slows the electric current but does not stop it

**respiration:** the process of breathing in air to get oxygen and breathing out waste gases (**120**)

**respiratory system:** the group of organs that work together to take in oxygen and release waste gases (**120**)

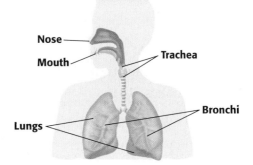

Nose — Mouth — Trachea — Bronchi — Lungs

**response:** something an organism does when it senses a stimulus (**92**)

**retina:** the tissue at the back of the eye that senses light and color

**reverse fault:** a crack in Earth's crust where a block of rock was pushed up (**175**)

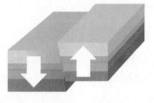

**revolution:** one complete trip of a planet around the sun (**220, 228**)

**Richter scale:** a way of comparing the strengths of earthquakes (**181**)

**rift valley:** a deep valley that runs down the middle of a mid-ocean ridge (**197**)

**risk:** a possibly harmful result of using a technology (**366**)

**river:** a wide body of slowly moving water (**191**)

**river system:** a river and all the smaller rivers and streams that flow into it

**rock:** a solid mixture of minerals that was formed in Earth's crust

**rock cycle:** the process of rocks changing into other kinds of rock (**165**)

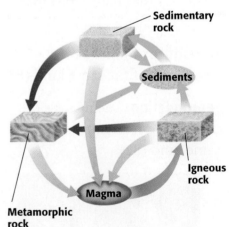

**roots:** plant structures that hold a plant in place and take in water and nutrients from the soil (**81, 107**)

**rotation:** the spinning of a planet or moon on its axis (**218**)

**salinity:** a measure of the amount of salt in sea water

**saliva:** a liquid in the mouth containing digestive juices that start breaking down some materials in food (**117**)

**sanitary landfill:** a place where garbage is buried, packed down, and covered with soil and that is built to keep harmful chemicals and gases from leaking out (**336**)

**satellite:** an object that orbits a planet (**239**)

**savanna:** a kind of grassland biome

**science journal:** a place to record what you have done in science over a long period of time (**14**)

**scientist:** someone who studies the natural world (**357**)

**screw:** a simple machine made of a flat, sloping surface wrapped around a small rod (**281**)

**search engine:** a Web site that lets you look for other Web sites about a certain topic (**390**)

**sedimentary rock:** rock that formed when sediments were pressed and cemented together (**164**)

Limestone is a sedimentary rock.

**sediments:** bits of rocks, soil, sand, shells, and the remains of organisms (**164**)

**seed:** a structure produced by a plant that contains a tiny undeveloped plant and a supply of food for the plant (**86**)

**seismograph:** a science tool that measures the strength of earthquakes

**semicircular canals:** three structures in the inner ear that sense your body position and help you keep your balance

**sense organ:** a body structure that takes in information from the environment and sends the information to the brain (**90, 125**)

**series circuit:** an electric circuit in which the devices are connected in one continuous loop (**302**)

**sewage:** human wastes, detergents, soaps, and food scraps that have been rinsed down drains (**342**)

**shoreline:** the area where the ocean meets the land (**196**)

**simple machine:** a tool that makes it easier to move an object (**280**)

**skeletal muscle:** the kind of muscle tissue that moves bones (**115**)

**skeletal system:** the group of bones, cartilage, and other tissues and organs that work together to hold the body up, give it shape, protect inner organs, make blood cells, and produce movement when muscles pull on bones (**112**)

**skin:** the organ that covers the body to protect other organs and tissues, releases some wastes, and senses pressure, pain, cold, and heat (**119**)

**small intestine:** the organ in the digestive system that finishes breaking down food with digestive juices and absorbs the nutrients (**117**)

**smog:** a kind of air pollution that forms when harmful gases in the air react with sunlight

**smooth muscle:** the kind of muscle that works automatically to carry out certain functions, such as moving food through the digestive system (**115**)

**society:** a group of people who all live under the same set of rules (**364**)

**soil:** a material made of tiny pieces of rock, minerals, and decayed plant and animal matter (**168**)

**solar cell:** a device that changes solar energy to electric energy (**324**); also called a *photovoltaic cell*

**solar energy:** energy from sunlight (**324**)

**solar flare:** an eruption on the sun's surface

**solar system:** a sun and all the objects that move around it (**226**)

**solar wind:** a stream of charged particles from the sun

**solid:** a state of matter in which the substance has a definite shape and a definite volume (**262**)

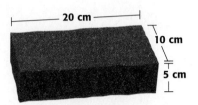

The volume of this brick is 1,000 cm³.

**solstice:** a day with the most hours of daylight or darkness, either the first day of summer or the first day of winter

**solubility:** a measure of how much of one substance will dissolve in another substance (**247**)

**solution:** a mixture with one substance spread out so evenly in another substance that you cannot tell the two substances apart (**259**)

**sonar:** the use of sound waves to measure ocean depth

**sound:** a form of energy produced by vibrating objects (**315**)

**Southern Hemisphere:** the half of Earth that is south of the equator

**South Pole (of Earth):** the southern end of the imaginary line that Earth rotates around

**south pole (of a magnet):** the end or side of a magnet that attracts the north pole of another magnet (**304**)

**species:** a group of organisms of the same kind that can mate and produce offspring like themselves (**128, 350**)

**speed:** the distance an object moves per unit of time, such as miles per hour (**276, 384**)

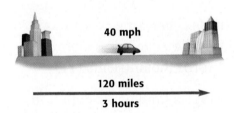

**sperm cell:** a male cell that joins with a female cell to produce a new organism (**87**)

**spinal cord:** the bundle of nerves inside the backbone that carries messages to and from the brain (**124**)

**spore:** a seedlike structure that produces a new plant (**86**)

**stamen:** the male part that produces pollen in a flower (**87**)

**standard unit:** a measurement unit that many people agree to use, such as the inch and the centimeter

**star:** an object in space that produces its own heat and light (**234**)

**Our sun is a star.**

**state of matter:** a form that matter can take—solid, liquid, or gas (**261**)

Solid    Liquid    Gas

**static electricity:** the buildup of electric charges on an object (**297**)

**stem:** the part of a plant that holds the leaves up to sunlight and moves water, nutrients and food through the plant (**107**)

**stimulus:** something that makes an organism act in a certain way (**92**)

**stomach:** the organ in the digestive system that churns food and mixes it with digestive juices (**117**)

**stratosphere:** the second-lowest layer of air in Earth's atmosphere (**199**)

**stratus cloud:** a flat, gray, layered cloud that covers the sky (**206**)

**streak:** the color of the mark that a mineral makes when it is scraped on a white tile (**161**)

**stream:** a narrow body of flowing water (**190**)

**strike-slip fault:** a crack in Earth's crust where blocks of rock move sideways past each other (**175**)

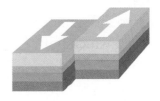

**structure:** a body part that does a certain "job" for an organism (**77, 98**)

**sunspot:** a cool spot on the sun's surface that occurs for a short time

**swamp:** a shallow body of still or slow-moving water that has plants growing in it (**191**); also called a *marsh*

**sweat gland:** a structure in the skin that makes perspiration and releases it to the skin's surface to cool the body and get rid of wastes (**119**)

**switch:** a device that opens and closes an electric circuit to stop and start the flow of electrons (**300**)

**symbiosis:** a relationship between two different kinds of organisms in which both organisms are helped

**symmetry:** having matching parts around a point or on both sides of a line through the middle

**taiga:** a biome with cool temperatures and many conifers

**tally chart:** a data table for keeping track of things that are being counted (**63**)

Bird Sightings May 9–15, 2004

| Bird | Tally | Number of Birds |
| --- | --- | --- |
| Robin | JHT JHT II | 12 |
| Crow | JHT JHT IIII | 14 |
| Chickadee | JHT II | 7 |
| Mourning dove | II | 2 |
| Blue jay | JHT | 5 |
| House sparrow | JHT JHT II | 12 |
| Cardinal | IIII | 4 |

**technology:** any tool or machine designed to help people in some way (**355**)

**tektite:** a glassy pebble made when something big from outer space hits Earth (**2**)

**telescope:** a tool for observing distant objects; also see **light telescope, refracting telescope, reflecting telescope, radio telescope**

**temperate climate:** a climate with temperatures that change with the seasons and precipitation that varies from place to place and season to season; located in bands between the polar and tropical climates (**216**)

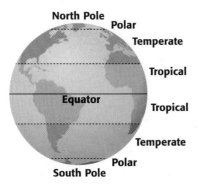

**temperature:** the average speed of the particles in a substance (**291**)

**tendon:** an organ in the muscular system that connects a muscle to a bone

**theory:** an idea that explains many observations about the natural world and predicts other observations

**thermal energy:** the energy of moving particles in a substance (**289**); also called *heat energy*

**thermometer:** a tool that measures temperature (**49**)

**thermosphere:** the second-highest layer of air in Earth's atmosphere (**199**)

**thigmotropism:** the growth of a plant in response to touch (**97**)

**threatened species:** a species that could become endangered if its numbers keep decreasing (**352**)

**thunderstorm:** a storm with lightning, thunder, rain, and sometimes hail (**212**)

**tide:** changes in water level at the shoreline that are caused by the pull of gravity between Earth and its moon (**195**)

**tissue:** a group of cells that work together to perform a certain function in an organism (**104**)

**Muscle tissue**

**tornado:** a dark funnel of strong winds that spiral upward (**213**)

**trace fossil:** a footprint, track, or burrow made by an organism and preserved in rock (**186**)

**trachea:** the tube in the respiratory system that connects the mouth and nose with the bronchi (**121**)

**trait:** a characteristic of an organism (**82**)

**transpiration:** the release of water vapor into the air from a plant's leaves

**trench:** a steep crack in the ocean floor (**196**)

**trial:** a repeat of a test or an observation (**12**)

Roxanne's Heart Rate

| Trial | Heart Rate (beats per minute) |
|-------|-------------------------------|
| 1 | 92 |
| 2 | 89 |
| 3 | 92 |
| 4 | 90 |
| 5 | 93 |
| 6 | 90 |

**tributary:** a stream or smaller river that flows into a larger river

**tropical climate:** a warm climate located in a wide band around the equator (**216**)

**tropical rain forest:** a biome with heavy rainfall and warm temperatures year-round

**tropism:** a plant's response to a stimulus such as light, water, or gravity (**96**)

**troposphere:** the layer of air in Earth's atmosphere where weather takes place, just above Earth's surface (**199**)

Troposphere

**trough:** the lowest part of a wave (**311**)

**tsunami:** a giant ocean wave caused by an undersea earthquake or landslide (**182**)

**tundra:** a biome with cold temperatures and not much rain

**ultraviolet radiation:** a kind of invisible energy from the sun that can burn the skin and cause skin cancer in some people (**339**)

**unbalanced forces:** forces that are unequal in size or direction and that change an object's motion

**unit:** a word or symbol that tells what a number stands for (**383**)

**ureters:** two tubes in the urinary system that carry urine from the kidneys to the urinary bladder (**118**)

**urethra:** the tube in the urinary system that carries urine to the outside of the body (**118**)

**urinary bladder:** the organ in the urinary system that collects and stores urine until it leaves the body (**118**)

**urinary system:** the group of organs that remove wastes from the blood and release them from the body in urine (**118**)

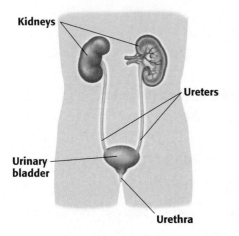

Kidneys

Ureters

Urinary bladder

Urethra

**urine:** a liquid formed in the kidneys that contains wastes

**vacuoles:** spaces in a cell that store water and nutrients until the cell needs them or store wastes until the cell can get rid of them (**101, 103**)

**vacuum:** airless space (**309**)

**variable:** anything that can change in an experiment (**8**)

**vein:** a blood vessel that carries blood toward the heart (**123**)

**velocity:** the speed and direction an object is moving

**vent:** an opening in a volcano that magma, gases, and other materials come out of

**vertebra:** one of the bones that form an animal's backbone (**146**)

**vertebrate:** an animal that has a backbone (**146**)

**vertical axis:** the up-and-down line at the left side of a graph (**66, 68, 72**)

**vibration:** a rapid back-and-forth movement that produces sound (**315**)

**villi:** tiny fingerlike structures that line the small intestine and absorb nutrients into the bloodstream

**visible light:** electromagnetic waves that you can see; includes all colors of the rainbow (**311**)

**volcanic island chain:** a group of islands made of volcanoes that built up from the ocean floor (**197**)

Volcanic island chain

**volcano:** a mountain built up from hardened lava, rocks, and ash that erupted out of Earth (**178**)

**volt:** the unit used to measure the "push" on electrons in a circuit (**298**)

**voltage:** the "push" that makes electric current move through a circuit

**volume:** the amount of space that an object or substance takes up (**44, 245, 385**)

**warm front:** the leading edge of a moving mass of warmer air (**209**)

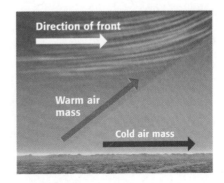

Direction of front

Warm air mass

Cold air mass

**water cycle:** the change of water from one state to another as it moves between Earth's surface and the atmosphere (**188**)

**water pressure:** the weight of water pressing on an object that is under water (**371**)

**water vapor:** the gas state of water (**189**)

**wave:** a repeating up-and-down or back-and-forth movement of matter

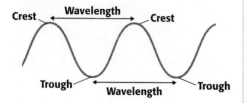

**wavelength:** the distance between one wave crest and the next crest or between one wave trough and the next trough (**311**)

**weather:** the condition of the atmosphere at a place for a short period of time (**200**)

**weather forecaster:** a person who predicts what the weather will be, based on weather data

**weather system:** an area in the lower atmosphere where the air is moving around a high or low (**208**)

**weathering:** the breaking down and wearing away of rock (**168, 171**)

**wedge:** a simple machine made of a flat, sloping surface that moves (**281**)

**weight:** a measure of the pull of gravity on an object (**46, 271**)

**wetland:** a biome where water and land meet, such as a marsh, swamp, or seasonal pond

**wheel and axle:** a simple machine made of a round object (the wheel) that turns around a rod (the axle) (**282**)

Wheel

Axle

**white blood cells:** cells in the blood that fight germs (**123**)

**wildlife preserve:** an area where endangered and threatened species are protected (**353**); also called a *wildlife refuge* or *wildlife sanctuary*

**Yellowstone National Park**

**wind:** moving air (**202**)

**wind sock:** a cloth bag, open at one end, that shows wind direction

**wind vane:** a weather instrument that shows the direction the wind is coming from (**202**)

**work:** done when a force moves an object through a distance (**280**)

X, Y, Z

**xylem:** tubes in plant stems that carry water from the roots to the leaves (**81**)

**year:** the time it takes for a planet to make one trip around the sun (**228**)

# Index

**M**

**N**

## O

## P

**Q**

# Credits

## COVER PHOTOGRAPY

### Front Cover
Comet: © StockTrek/Photodisc/Getty Images
Earth: © StockTrek/Photodisc/Getty Images
Male ion with cub: © R. Linke/Blickwinkel/
age fotostock
Boy on skateboard: © Joe McBride/Photographer's
Choice/Getty Images
Moon: NASA
Volcano: © Datacraft/sozaijiten/age fotostock
Circuit board: © Kazu Studio Ltd./Taxi/
Getty Images
Fiddlehead ferns: © Kelly Kalhoefer/Getty Images
Alder leaf: © Jeff Vanuga/Corbis
Emperor penguin: © Kevin Schafer/Stone/
Getty Images

### Back Cover
Hot air balloon: © Ron Crabtree/Photographer's
Choice RF/Getty Images
Rainbow: © Brenda Anderson/Flickr/
Getty Images
Astronaut Mae C. Jemison: NASA
Peridot gemstone: © Charles D. Winters/
Photo Researchers/Getty Images
Emperor penguins: © Kevin Schafer/Stone/
Getty Images

## PHOTOGRAPHY

### Doing Science
2 © Tom McHugh/Photo Researchers, Inc.
27(cr) © Lawrence Migdale/Photo
Researchers, Inc.
35(t) © Houghton Mifflin Harcourt
35(tc) © George Ostertag/age fotostock
35(bc) © Organica/Alamy Images
35(b) © Scott Camazine/Alamy Images
60 © George D. Lepp/Corbis

### Life Science
89(c) © Tom McHugh/Photo Researchers, Inc.
89(br) © Jeff Rotman/Photo Researchers, Inc.
89(tl) © John Shaw/NHPA/Superstock
89(tc) © Ed Reschke/Oxford Scientific/
Getty Images
89(tr) © Bach/Corbis
90(tl) © George McCarthy/Corbis

90(bl) © Digital Vision/Getty Images
90(br) © Joel Sartore/National Geographic
Image Collection/Alamy Images
90(tr) © Universal Stopping Point Photography/
Flickr/Getty Images
93 © J. L. Klein & M. L. Hubert/Photo
Researchers, Inc.
95(b) © Luis M. Alvarez/AP Images
99(bcr) © Lester V. Bergman/Corbis
99(bl) © Ed Reschke/Peter Arnold/Getty Images
99(bc) © Lester V. Bergman/Corbis
99(br) © Ed Reschke/Peter Arnold/Getty Images
99(t) © G. Wanner/ScienceFoto/Getty Images
99(tc) © A. Dowsett/Health Protection Agency/
Science Photo Library/Photo
Researchers, Inc.
134(t) © Gavin Wright/Alamy Images
134(b) © Alessandro Zocchi/YAY Micro/
age fotostock
135(t) © Nico Tondini/Robert Harding World
Imagery/Getty Images
135(b) © Digital Vision/Alamy Images
145(l) © SciMAT/Photo Researchers, Inc.
145(r) © SciMAT/Photo Researchers, Inc.
145(c) © Scimat Scimat/Photo Researchers/
Getty Images
146(cl) © Anthony Bannister/Gallo Images/
Corbis
146(bl) © Mark Webster/Lonely Planet Images/
age fotostock
146(br) © Melba Photo Agency/Alamy Images
147(tr) © Juniors Bildarchiv/Alamy Images
148(bl) © Anthony Bannister/Photo
Researchers, Inc.
148(br) © Dr. Paul Zahl/Photo Researchers, Inc.
151(l) © Daniel Heuclin/naturepl.com
152 © Nigel Pavitt/AWL Images/Getty Images
152(tr) © Frank Leung/Vetta/Getty Images
153(tl) © Kenneth Jones/Alamy Images
53(tr) © Guenter Fischer/Imagebroker RF/
age fotostock
153(b) © Brandon Borgelt/age fotostock
154(l) © Rod Planck/Photo Researchers, Inc.
154(r) © Radius Images/Corbis
155(br) © Tom McHugh/Photo Researchers, Inc.
155(tl) © Gerard Lacz/age fotostock
155(tr) © Ralph Clevenger/Corbis

## Earth Science

160(br) © Kevin Schafer/Peter Arnold/
  Getty Images
160(t) © Houghton Mifflin Harcourt
160(bl) © Digitalpress/Kalium/age fotostock
161(tl) © Houghton Mifflin Harcourt
161(tr) © Houghton Mifflin Harcourt
161(b) © Houghton Mifflin Harcourt
162 © Houghton Mifflin Harcourt
162 © Pascal Goetgheluck/Photo
  Researchers, Inc.
164(t) © Houghton Mifflin Harcourt
164(c) © Houghton Mifflin Harcourt
164(br) © Houghton Mifflin Harcourt
164(bl) © Houghton Mifflin Harcourt
164 © Houghton Mifflin Harcourt
164 © Houghton Mifflin Harcourt
166(l) © Houghton Mifflin Harcourt
166(r) © Houghton Mifflin Harcourt
170 © Digital Vision/Getty Images
171 © Adam Woolfitt/CORBIS
172(b) © RIGOULET Gilles/hemis.fr/
  Getty Images
172(t) © Tetra Images/Alamy Images
173(t) © Saudi Desert Photos by TARIQ-M/
  Getty Images
173(b) © Bill Brooks/Alamy Images
174(l) © Michele Falzone/JAI/Corbis
175(tr) © Byron Moore/Alamy Images
178 © Soames Summerhays/Photo
  Researchers, Inc.
182(b) © Anatoly Maltsev/epa/Corbis
183 © Mark Lyons/AP Images
184 © George Ostertag/age fotostock
186(b) © Bernhard Edmaier/Photo
  Researchers, Inc.
186(tl) © Maciej Figiel/Alamy Images
186(tr) © Pixtal/Superstock
186(c) © Maurice Nimmo/Frank Lane Picture
  Agency/Corbis
187(bg) © Corbis
190(b) © "photos by Crow" Carol Rukliss,
  Photographer/Flickr/Getty Images
191(t) © James Marshall/Corbis
191(c) © L. Clarke/Spirit/Corbis
191(b) © Imagebroker/Alamy Images
213 © OAR/ERL/National Severe Storms
  Laboratory(NSSL)/National Weather
  Service(NOAA)
215 © David Pollack/Corbis
225 © Corbis
227 NASA
229(b) © Bettmann/Corbis
234(bg) © Otto Rogge/Corbis

235(c) R. Kennicutt/Jet Propulsion
  Laboratory(JPL)/NASA
239(t) © Stephanie Maze/Corbis

## Physical Science

284(r) © Sylvain Grandadam/Getty Images
284(tl) © rolfo/Flickr Open/Getty Images
284(bl) © Tony Shi Photography/Flickr/
  Getty Images
297(b) © John Lund/Stone/Getty Images
308 © Gino's Premium Images/Alamy Images

## Natural Resources and the Environment

320 © Royalty-Free/Corbis
321(t) © Benjamin Rondel/Corbis
321(c) © Owaki-Kulla/Corbis
321(b) © Heinrich van den Berg/Gallo Images/
  Getty Images
324(t) © Chinch Gryniewicz/Ecoscene/Corbis
326(t) © Owaki-Kulla/Corbis
326(b) © William Zhang/Industry/Alamy Images
328 © Michael St. Maur Sheil/Corbis
329 © Wolfgang Hoffmann/AgStock Images/Corbis
330 © Bill Stormont/Corbis
334 © Ashley Cooper/Corbis
335 © J. A. Giordano/Corbis SABA
339(b) © Matt Cardy/Getty Images
340 © Joel Addams/Aurora/Getty Images
341 © Andy Levin/Photo Researchers, Inc.
342 © Robert Brook/Photo Researchers, Inc.
343 © Korean Federation for Environmental
  Movement/AP Images
344 © Pavel Losevsky/Fotolia
350 © Thorsten Milse/Robert Harding World
  Imagery/Corbis
351(b) © Warren Uzzle/Photo Researchers, Inc.
351(t) © JosÃ© Enrique Molina/age fotostock/
  Getty Images
352(tr) © D. Robert & Lorri Franz/Corbis
352(bcr) © George D. Lepp/Corbis
352(t) © Thomas Kitchin & Victoria Hurst/
  All Canada Photos/Corbis
352(tc) © Danita Delimont/Gallo Images/
  Getty Images
352(b) © Roberta Olenick/All Canada Photos/
  Getty Images
353(t) © Jeff Vanuga/Corbis
353(b) © Tom McHugh/Photo Researchers/
  Getty Images

## Science, Technology, and Society

357(b) © Carlos's Pemium Images/Alamy Images
359 JPL-Caltech/NASA
360(tl) © Scheufler Collection/Corbis
360(tr) © Chris Ochsner/Topeka Capital-Journal/
  AP Images

452(r) © Alex Bartel/Photo Researchers, Inc.
453(cl) © Danita Delimont/Gallo Images/ Getty Images
454(r) © Dr. Paul Zahl/Photo Researchers, Inc.
456(bl) © Maciej Figiel/Alamy Images
457(br) © J. A. Giordano/Corbis SABA
458(br) © Bill Brooks/Alamy Images
459(tr) © Robert Brook/Photo Researchers, Inc.
460(bl) © Gavin Wright/Alamy Images
461(cl) © Houghton Mifflin Harcourt
461 © Houghton Mifflin Harcourt
462(tl) © Juniors Bildarchiv/Alamy Images
463(bl) © Anatoly Maltsev/epa/Corbis
465(bl) © Ashley Cooper/Corbis
465(br) © Houghton Mifflin Harcourt
466(br) © Thorsten Milse/Robert Harding World Imagery/Corbis
468(l) © Houghton Mifflin Harcourt
469(bl) © Houghton Mifflin Harcourt
469(tr) © Maurice Nimmo/Frank Lane Picture Agency/Corbis
471(l) © Ed Reschke/Peter Arnold/Getty Images
474(l) © Chinch Gryniewicz/Ecoscene/Corbis
476(bl) © Nico Tondini/Robert Harding World Imagery/Getty Images
478(tl) © Stephanie Maze/Corbis
478(tr) © Warren Uzzle/Photo Researchers, Inc.
479(tr) © Guenter Fischer/Imagebroker RF/ age fotostock
479(bl) © J. L. Klein & M. L. Hubert/ Photo Researchers, Inc.
481(br) © Houghton Mifflin Harcourt
481 © Houghton Mifflin Harcourt
486(l) © Imagebroker/Alamy Images
487(tl) © Tom McHugh/Photo Researchers, Inc.
488(cl) © OAR/ERL/National Severe Storms Laboratory(NSSL)/National Weather Service(NOAA)
488(bl) © Pixtal/Superstock
490(r) © Radius Images/Corbis
491(bl) © Soames Summerhays/Photo Researchers, Inc.
493(bl) © Jeff Vanuga/Corbis

## ILLUSTRATION

All art that appears on the Title page and Table of Contents was created by Barry Gott.
All charts, graphs, and tables were created by AARTPACK, Inc.

### Doing Science
Stephen Durke: 3, 8(b), 34, 37(t), 38, 41(tl, cl, cr, b), 45(t, b) 46, 47, 48, 49, 52, 53(t, c, b)
Barry Gott: xii–1, 4, 5(t, bl, br), 6(b), 7(t, bl, br), 9(t, c, bl), 10(b), 11(t, b), 12(t), 14, 15(tl, tr, bl, br), 17(t, b), 18, 20(cl, cc, cr), 21, 26(c), 29, 30, 31(t, c, b), 37(c), 39, 40, 41(tr), 42, 43(t, c, b), 50, 51(b), 54, 56, 58(t, c, b), 59(t, c, b), 63, 71
John Ward: 32, 33, 44, 55

### Life Science
Stephen Durke: 81, 82(b), 87, 96, 97(t, b), 100, 102, 104(t, b), 105(t, c, b), 107, 115, 123(bl, bc, br), 142(t, c, b), 144(t, b)
Barry Gott: 74–75, 76(t, b), 78(t), 80(t), 83(tl, tr, bl, br), 86(b), 91, 92, 98, 101, 103, 110, 127, 128, 129(t, b), 133, 137, 138, 139, 143(t, c, b), 146, 148(tl, tr, c)
Precision Graphics: 78(b), 80(b), 94, 106(t, b), 108(t, b), 109, 112, 114, 116, 118, 119, 120, 122, 123, 124, 125, 132, 149
Patrice Rossi Caulkin: 77, 79(t, cl, cr, b), 82(cl, cc, cr), 84, 85, 86(t), 88, 95(t), 126, 130–131, 136, 141 (t, bl, br), 147(c, b), 152(b)

### Earth Science
Stephen Durke: 174(tr), 175(tl), 180(t), 199, 202(bl, br), 203(t, b), 204, 205(bl), 207, 209(l, r), 212, 228(b), 236, 238(t, b)
Barry Gott: 156–157, 158, 182(t), 189(t, b), 190(t), 205(br), 206, 221(b), 234(b)
Precision Graphics: 159, 165, 169, 175(b), 176(t, b), 177, 193, 194, 195, 200, 201(l, r), 202(tl, tr), 208, 210, 211(t, c, b), 216, 217 (tl, tr, bl, br), 218, 219, 220, 221(t), 222, 223(l, r), 224(t, b), 228(t), 233(b)
Preface, Inc.: 237(t, b)
Patrice Rossi Caulkin: 168, 185, 188, 192, 196–197

### Physical Science
Stephen Durke: 244, 245(t, b), 246(t, b), 248(b), 249, 252(t, b), 253(t, b), 254(l, r), 255(t), 258, 262, 263(b), 264, 265, 266, 267(t, b), 271(t, b), 272, 280, 281(t, b), 282(tl, tc, tr, bl, br), 283(tl, tc, tr, b), 286(tl, tr, cl, cr, bl, br), 288, 289, 290(cl, cr, bl, br), 291(l, r), 294, 296, 298(b), 299, 300(t), 301(t, br), 302(t, b), 303(tl, b), 304(t, b), 305(t, c, b), 306(tl, tr), 307(t, b), 310, 311(b), 312(t), 313(t, c, b), 314, 316(b)
Barry Gott: 240–241, 242, 243, 248(t), 250(l), 255(b), 256, 257, 259(t, bl, br), 260(l, r), 261, 263(t), 269(tl, tr, bl, br), 274, 275(b), 276, 277, 278(l, r), 279(t, b), 290(t), 292 (t, b), 293(t, b), 295, 297(tl, tr), 298(t), 300(cl, cr, bl, br), 301(bl), 303(tr), 309, 311(t), 312(b), 315, 316(tl, tr, cl, cr), 317(tl, tr, bl, br)

Precision Graphics: 270, 273
Patrice Rossi Caulkin: 275(t), 287
John Ward: 268(l, r)

### Natural Resources and the Environment

Stephen Durke: 322, 323, 325(t), 327, 337, 338, 345(b), 348
Barry Gott: 318–319, 324(b), 325(b), 332, 333(t, b), 336, 339(t), 345(t), 347(t, b), 349
Patrice Rossi Caulkin: 352(bl)`

### Science, Technology, and Society

Stephen Durke: 356
Barry Gott: 354–355, 363, 364, 365(t, b), 369(t)
Precision Graphics: 368(l, r)

### Almanac

Stephen Durke: 374(t, b), 379, 400
John Edwards, Inc.: 405(t, b)
Barry Gott: 371, 373, 376(t, b), 377, 381(t, b), 383, 384(b), 385, 386, 387, 388(b), 389, 391, 392, 394, 395, 397, 398, 402
Precision Graphics: 390, 403, 406, 407

### Yellow Pages

Stephen Durke: 415(br)
Precision Graphics: 413(r), 420(br)
Patrice Rossi Caulkin: 416(b)

### Glossary

All letter mascots were created by Barry Gott.
Stephen Durke: 438(r), 439(tr), 440(tr), 441(tr), 442(tr), 443(tl), 445(tl, bl, br), 446(tr), 447(bl), 448(br), 451(tr, cr), 452(l), 455(bl, r), 456(tl), 457(tl), 458(bl), 461(bl), 464(l), 465(cl), 466(l, tr), 467(bl), 468(tr), 469(br), 470(l, br), 471(br), 473(tl, br), 474(br), 475(tl, bl), 476(br), 477(tl, bl), 478(bl, br), 481(tr), 482(tl, bl), 483(br), 484(l), 485(bl), 487(r), 488(tl), 489(tl, bl), 491(br), 492(cl, bl, r), 493(tl, tr)
John Edwards, Inc.: 453(r), 467(r)
Barry Gott: 440(tl), 446(br), 448(l), 476(tl), 480(tl), 484(r)
Precision Graphics: 440(br), 442(br), 446(l), 450(r), 453(bl), 454(l), 458(tl), 459(tl, br), 460(tl), 462(bl), 463(br), 465(tr), 469(tl), 471(tr), 472(tr, br), 473(bl, cr), 476(tr), 479(br), 480(bl, r), 481(tl), 482(r), 483(l), 485(r), 487(bl), 490(tl)
Patrice Rossi Caulkin: 438(bl), 439(bl), 440(cl), 448(tr), 451(br), 457(bl), 458(tr), 463(tr), 468(br), 483(tr), 491(tl), 492(tl)